# TOWARD A FEMINIST
# EPISTEMOLOGY

**New Feminist Perspectives Series**

*General Editor: Rosemarie Tong, Davidson College*

Beyond Domination: New Perspectives on Women and Philosophy
  *Edited by Carol C. Gould, Stevens Institute of Technology*

Claiming Reality: Phenomenology and Women's Experience
  *by Louise Levesque-Lopman, Regis College*

Dehumanizing Women: Treating Persons as Sex Objects
  *by Linda LeMoncheck*

Evidence on Her Own Behalf: Women's Narrative as Theological Voice
  *by Elizabeth A. Say, California State University, Northridge*

Gendercide: The Implications of Sex Selection
  *by Mary Anne Warren, San Francisco State University*

Is Women's Philosophy Possible?
  *by Nancy J. Holland, Hamline University*

Manhood and Politics: A Feminist Reading in Political Theory
  *by Wendy L. Brown, University of California, Santa Cruz*

Mothering: Essays in Feminist Theory
  *Edited by Joyce Treblicot, Washington University*

Toward A Feminist Epistemology
  *by Jane Duran, University of California, Santa Barbara*

Uneasy Access: Privacy for Women in a Free Society
  *by Anita L. Allen, Georgetown University*

Women and Spirituality
  *by Carol Ochs, Simmons College*

Women, Militarism, and War: Essays in History, Politics, and Social Theory
  *Edited by Jean Bethke Elshtain, Vanderbilt University, and Sheila Tobias,
  University of Arizona*

Women, Sex, and the Law
  *by Rosemarie Tong, Davidson College*

# TOWARD A FEMINIST EPISTEMOLOGY

Jane Duran

Rowman & Littlefield Publishers, Inc.

ROWMAN & LITTLEFIELD PUBLISHERS, INC.

Published in the United States of America
by Rowman & Littlefield Publishers, Inc.
8705 Bollman Place, Savage, Maryland 20763

British Cataloging in Publication Information Available


**Library of Congress Cataloging-in-Publication Data**

Duran, Jane.
  Toward a feminist epistemology / Jane Duran.
    p.    cm. — (New feminist perspectives series)
  Includes bibliographical references.
    1. Feminist theory.    2. Knowledge, Theory of.
I. Title.   II. Series.
HQ1190.D87      1990
305.42—dc20      90–46615  CIP

ISBN 0–8476–7635–8 (alk. paper)




5    4    3    2    1

Printed in the United States of America


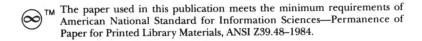 ™ The paper used in this publication meets the minimum requirements of
American National Standard for Information Sciences—Permanence of
Paper for Printed Library Materials, ANSI Z39.48–1984.

*For women knowers everywhere*

# Contents

Acknowledgments                                                    ix

Preface                                                           xi

### PART ONE: ANDROCENTRIC EPISTEMOLOGY

Introduction                                                       3

1. Analytic Theory of Knowledge                                   19

2. Naturalizing Theory of Knowledge                               43

### PART TWO: GYNOCENTRIC EPISTEMICS

3. The Feminist Theories                                          73

4. Toward a Feminist Epistemology                                103

5. The Gynocentric Model Criticized                              133

### PART THREE: OTHER FRAMEWORKS

6. French Feminist Viewpoints                                    161

7. The Gynocentric Model Expanded                                183

8. Feminist Sociology of Knowledge                               211

*Contents*

## PART FOUR: CONCLUSION

9.  The Future of the Gynocentric Model                   237

Bibliography                                              263

Index                                                    271

# Acknowledgments

It is traditional to begin acknowledgments with the statement that one cannot hope to thank everyone who should be thanked. This difficulty is more than usually present here, since it is clear to anyone working in feminist theory of knowledge that we owe an enormous amount to those who have gone before: both those who have worked recently in this field (and whose products I have cited in this work), and those who, by their personal endeavors in the sciences and other areas, showed themselves to be the early feminist epistemologists.

I can, however, name those who have been most helpful to me in the here and now. For heroic acts and supererogation, I thank Jane Braaten, Ruth Doell, Laurie Shrage, and Rosemarie Tong, all of whom read either the manuscript in its entirety or significant portions of it. I cannot be appreciative enough of their comments. Rosemarie was the best editor a writer could have, and her quiet encouragement saved me on many a day.

I thank the University of California at Santa Barbara, whose Graduate School of Education supported me with a Postdoctoral Fellowship in 1984–85, allowing me a superb start on the issues in theory of knowledge and philosophy of science that come to the fore in this work. For a wonderful class in epistemology, taught to lively and articulate seniors, I thank Hamilton College, where I visited the previous year. I am also grateful to Mount St. Mary's College in Los Angeles, where a friendly feminist atmosphere encouraged me at a much later point.

I am indebted to former colleagues on the East Coast, where offshoots of the Society for Women in Philosophy (SWIP) provided lively discussions on some of these topics, and particularly to Brian McLaughlin and John Yolton. Pacific SWIP was enormously helpful to me, and portions of the manuscript in its early stages were read there— "Androcentrism and Philosophy" in 1985 at the Los Angeles meeting, and "Gilligan's Two Voices: an Epistemological Overview" at the 1987 San Diego meeting. Finally, two prior publications, although only somewhat related, cleared the way theoretically, and I am indebted to the editors at *Philosophy in Context*, where "A Philosophical Perspective on Gender" was published in 1988, and to Mary Vetterling-Braggin, who worked with me on two related papers for Rowman & Littlefield anthologies in the late 1970s and early 1980s.

A very special thanks to everyone at the Linguistic Minority Research Project of the University of California at Santa Barbara, whose patience and fortitude were exemplary. Thank you Barbara Avery, Francisca Escobar, and Patricia Prado-Olmos; and a special thank you to Patricia for reading and commenting beyond the call of either duty or friendship. My warmest gratitude and love to my husband, Richard Duran, whose affection has sustained me not only during all of my writing projects, but throughout my adult life.

# Preface

Recent work on feminist epistemology or theory of knowledge seems to come to us, somewhat oddly perhaps, from a number of disciplines. Sociology, psychology, and political science, among others, have given birth to material that purports to spell out for us what a feminist account of knowledge entails, or what is implied by a way of knowing that pertains to women.

The trained philosopher may be somewhat puzzled by such material, since the original rubric for accounts of knowledge—theory of knowledge, epistemology, or some other categorization—springs directly from work in the heart of philosophy itself, and goes back at least to the Platonic period, if not before. If it is true (as I believe we are sometimes tempted to think when teaching) that the most valuable kinds of philosophical questions are frequently those that are most naive, the unsophisticated question that presents itself quite naturally to the philosopher examining work in feminist theory of knowledge is what precisely is it that is to count as theory of knowledge here in any interesting sense?

I began my work in this area with just such a question in mind. As an epistemologist who had already published articles in theory of knowledge, I was anxious to find what I regarded as thorough work in epistemology under the guise of feminist accounts of ways of knowing. I met with only partial success. I discovered a number of pieces that pointed one in the general direction of the development of a feminist epistemology, but did not find any one piece—whether book-length or shorter—that actually spelled out in the detail required by a supportable epistemology what a feminist theory of knowledge would entail. Interestingly enough, I found some of the most developed work falling into the somewhat different (although related, of course) category of feminist philosophy of science. Around this time, I had strengthened my own interest in the more naturalized contemporary trends in epistemology to the point where it seemed that an intersection between these two endeavors—feminist epistemology and naturalized contemporary theory of knowledge—began to emerge.

This work is an outgrowth of those beginning intellectual inquiries. My initial aim was to provide an account that would not only serve to elaborate on the possibility of a rigorous feminist epistemology, but that would also serve as something of an introduction to the androcentrism inherent in so much epistemological theorizing itself. To this end I wanted to divide my work into several parts: An opening first part would spell out, in a manner somewhat different from the overview provided by feminist philosophies of science, what has counted as epistemology in the past, and why it is androcentric. A second part would carefully and thoroughly develop a feminist theory of knowledge based on the moves in contemporary theorizing that are now available to us. A third part would attempt to tie together the feminist epistemology constructed here with other feminist views from other disciplines or modes of viewing, and a fourth part would conclude the work.

Thus the Introduction and chapters one and two provide a recapitulation of theory of knowledge up to and including recent work with a special emphasis on the epistemology of this century. The Introduction provides a general overview of the project, while chapter one focuses on the so-called normative or nonnaturalized efforts that precede the work of the past twenty years. Chapter two is a special introduction to the work of analytic epistemologists who have chosen to engage in the project of naturalizing (or at least examining the possibility of naturalizing) epistemology, a project not more than approximately two decades old.

Chapter three examines the work of feminist epistemology as it has occurred in philosophy so far, with special emphasis on feminist philosophy of science, since so little work has actually been done by epistemologists. Three thinkers are singled out for extensive commentary, and the material leads naturally into chapter four, where an attempt is made to develop a rigorous naturalized feminist epistemology based on strands of theory taken from each of the first three chapters. In chapter five I examine the intersection of the material developed in chapter four and contemporary philosophy of mind—these three chapters form the second part of the work.

The third part of the work consists of material that is intended to expand or enlarge upon the model already constructed in chapter four. In chapter six I examine work in French theory and try to show the relevance of at least the broader portions of its epistemological base to the work done here. Chapter seven illustrates what the literature tends to refer to as the "multiplicity of women's voices"—I pick several voices as roughly illustrative and comment on the applicability of the model to their general stance. In chapter eight I look at that very important area, feminist sociology of knowledge, for insight into how a feminist epistemology can ground itself without losing sight of the many-faceted views of knowledge provided for us by sociology.

Chapter nine concludes the work. I examine the arguments of the preceding chapters with some care, for they are lengthy and complex, and introduce still more new material, much of it from the most recent work in cognition and philosophy of mind, which might help us in prognosticating about the future of feminist epistemology.

The present work takes the somewhat unusual stance of assuming that epistemology, as subcategory of philosophy, has something to offer feminist theory, despite the androcentricity of its origins and much of its concern. A long section of chapter four attempts to address the tensions and contradictions inherent in such an assumption, while generally concluding that analytic epistemology has something to offer the feminist theorist, and that what it has to offer should be used. But the work ends by reminding us of how much the adoption of a feminist epistemology, or any of its precepts, relies on an attitude. The further development of feminist theory of knowledge will depend upon the adoption of a feminist worldview that alters our cores, as well as our conceptual schemes and ways of seeing.

*Part One*

# ANDROCENTRIC EPISTEMOLOGY

# Introduction

The notion of a feminist epistemology is a recurring one in the feminist scholarship and literature of the past ten to fifteen years. Interestingly enough, the phrase occurs just as frequently—or perhaps more frequently—in the work of scholars outside philosophy. Some of this usage is no doubt due to the popularity of the word "epistemology" itself, now used in many disciplines (anthropology, sociology, and so forth) in a less than technical way, but the sense that there is a specifically female mode of knowing now arises in a number of disciplines and contexts.[1]

Among professional philosophers, "epistemology" is generally shorthand for "theory of knowledge." Until fairly recently, theory of knowledge was a thoroughgoingly normative, idealized endeavor: Perhaps more so than most areas of philosophy, theory of knowledge made virtually no use of any intuitions, data, or even empirically based speculations that we might have about the way in which knowers operate—the manner in which knowers come to knowledge, if indeed they do come to knowledge. No doubt this was partly due to the unbiquitous influence of the last phrase in the previous sentence, taken as a *caveat* for investigators. For the history of epistemology has been the history of an inquiry into *whether* knowledge was possible, and seldom into the conditions producing knowledge. Philosophers often claim, when pressed, that epistemology began with Plato's *Theaetetus*, or with Descartes's *Meditations*. In both these works, especially the Cartesian work, the problem of knowledge is approached from the

3

standpoint that I may not know anything—there may not be any alleged or putative piece of knowledge that is worthy of the title "knowledge," since any claim may be open to doubt. Since philosophers have typically been attempting to carry on the work begun in this tradition, the use of the term "epistemology" in philosophy itself has in many cases been fairly far afield from the use of the term in other disciplines.

More recently, however, a few professional philosophers have begun to question the virtually entirely normative character of theory of knowledge. Several prominent professional philosophers have noted that the growth in the field of cognitive science, and they have simultaneously wondered what effect, if any, cognitive science could have on epistemology if philosophers were to make use of some of the empirical or empirically oriented data of cognitive science.[2]

This new approach to epistemology—utilizing the rubric of naturalized epistemology—is rapidly gaining acceptance, and most professional conferences that include any papers in epistemology at all now have one or more with a naturalized approach. The naturalized approach tends to assume that we can and do have knowledge. Thus, rather than attempting to answer the Cartesian question of whether there is any sentence of which I may be certain, the new approach tends to assume that we can express some of our knowledge in sentences, and that the more interesting questions revolve around *how* we obtain knowledge and what our cognitive capacities are, not how to silence the skeptic.[3]

Feminist epistemology, too, seems to assume that those we deem to be knowers actually do possess knowledge. In fact, interesting work has been done by feminist scholars on the notion that the typical questions of professional epistemology (the Cartesian sorts of questions alluded to above) are themselves the product of a male-oriented way of viewing problems that divorces the epistemic agent from the body and produces part of the evidence it seeks to evaluate. But perhaps more intriguing, at least over the long haul and at least insofar as any intersection of epistemology and cognitive science is concerned, is the notion that some of the work in naturalized epistemology might already be less androcentric than the tradition of pure epistemology, simply because there is something about the notion of descriptive adequacy and something about a correct depiction of the ways in which human knowers might know that is inherently more in tune with modes of thought that are not masculinist or male-biased. I will proceed along these lines with my work, sketching areas as I go.

Naturalized epistemology, *qua* rubric, is already a somewhat un-wieldy handle since so much has fallen into that category. A number of different emphases, not all of them related in any discernible way (except, perhaps, that they are not as idealized as the earlier strands of epistemology), comprise current work in naturalizing epistemology. Some philosophers have chosen to emphasize the social or contextual aspects of knowledge.[4] Others have written of the causal chains re-quired to produce a knowledge claim, hoping to naturalize their theo-ries with advertence to a chain of events. Still others have theorized about "reliable" computational processes that usually produce knowl-edge, these processes being, at least according to some theorists, eventually describable on the level of the physiological functioning of the brain itself.

## ANDROCENTRIC EPISTEMOLOGY

In order to develop more fully the contrast between standard analytic epistemology as practiced by professional philosophers and the newer, more naturalized epistemology, it might be worthwhile to spend some time on some of the traditional problems and orientations of analytic epistemology—the entire androcentric tradition as developed by pro-fessional philosophers.

At an earlier point I alluded to the *Theaetetus* as a possible starting point for Western epistemology, and not without reason. It is not only the case that a certain sort of definable philosophical problem arose with Plato, but for epistemology, perhaps more so than for other areas of philosophy, there has been comparatively little movement since the original formulation of the problem. Cursorily, *Theaetetus* poses for us three possible accounts of knowledge. Socrates asks us to consider the possibility that knowledge is equivalent to perception, or to the flow of information through the senses, and then that hypothesis is rejected since it is admitted that knowledge is supposed to be "incor-rigible" but perception is *not* incorrigible. Plato reminds us of the error-prone status of the senses, and this admonition about the senses retains its force in professional epistemology up to the present day. In a second, more plausible attempt, Plato has Socrates and his interlo-cutors consider the possibility that knowledge is true belief. This account at first looks more promising, and it is this central core of the attempt to define knowledge in *Theaetetus* that has been most influen-tial in the history of epistemology. It is rebutted, however, that a jury, for example, might have true belief on hearsay evidence, and that surely that would not count as knowledge. What Plato means, of course, is that if the jury believes truly, but believes for the wrong reasons, then that belief cannot count as knowledge either. Finally, in a third and still more promising tack, it is argued that knowledge is true belief "with an account." In other words, knowledge is true belief with a justification for the belief, or a provision of reasons. But for complicated reasons having to do with the Platonic metaphysics, Plato does not believe that a complete account, as it were, can be given, and *Theaetetus* ends without an adequate response to the question of what knowledge is.

Epistemologists have remained intrigued with the third portion of *Theaetetus*, for when Plato suggests that knowledge is true belief with justification, or justified true belief, it appears that he is onto something. But what constitutes the justification? Can there be such a thing as a justification that is not subject to the possibility of refutation—or even to the possibility of doubt? Can there be such a thing as epistemic certainty? Omitting for the moment the contributions of Descartes to the further elaboration of this problem, contemporary epistemologists have grappled throughout this century with the following three-part account of knowledge, originating as a philosophical problem in Plato. Knowledge is: (i) true (in accordance with the facts); (ii) believed by the alleged knower; (iii) justified, in terms of provision of reasons, by the alleged knower.

It is the third condition of the traditional three-part view that has provided by far the most difficulty philosophically, and from the standpoint of the traditional, purely normative orientation of epistemology, the impetus for such orientation. For it is obvious that there are justifications and justifications, reasons for believing and reasons for believing. Plato and Descartes both focused on the inadequacy of sensory-based reasons for belief, even in first-person accounts that would not, ordinarily speaking, be deemed as troublesome. Do I seem to know that I am here, seated by the fire with a quill in my hand? How can I be sure that I am not dreaming? How can I be sure that I am not hallucinating? To restructure the example, may I say that I know that I am looking at a kiwi fruit? I have never seen a kiwi fruit before, and am not familiar with its appearance, but my friend—whom I know to be trustworthy and reliable—just handed me a piece of fruit, indicating that it was indeed a kiwi fruit. But how can I be sure that my friend is not having perceptual difficulties? Perhaps she does not know the correct application of the label "kiwi fruit," having learned it improperly. Contemporary epistemology is full of such examples.

The fact that the original structuring of epistemological problems within the Western tradition lends itself to a virtually pure normative approach—that is, an approach in terms of what an ideal would-be knower ought to do, rather than what humans engaged in cognitive activities actually do—is obvious from the above recounting of the origins of the tradition. We frequently employ advice from friends, but can we be certain of the truth or accuracy of what our friends say? We frequently claim, on the basis of information from the five senses, to be able to distinguish between waking and dreaming, between hallucination and ordinary consciousness, but does not our very claim to be able to make the distinction beg the question?

In the last twenty-five years, professional epistemologists have been absorbed by a set of epicycles, as it were, on the original epistemological problem. In the early 1960s, counterexamples to what appeared to be tight versions of the thesis that knowledge is indeed justified true belief were found, and since then epistemologists have, in still more tightly argued and more strictly structured pieces, attempted to find "fourth" conditions, or variations on fourth conditions, that would allow us to give an account of knowledge. But a sense of repetitiousness dogs many of these accounts, and a sense on the part of some that our very survival indicates that we do indeed have knowledge, and that we ought to employ this as a point of departure in any theory of knowledge, has recently come to the fore.[5]

Now the more naturalized accounts, as I indicated earlier, want to focus on the information we can glean from the developments in cognitive science and other disciplines that *assume* we can have knowledge. Some of the more recent accounts are so fully naturalized (at least in comparison to what was being done previously) that they make an attempt to utilize only the latest and most contemporaneous work in cognitive science.[6] But feminist epistemology, however nascent and comparatively undeveloped, has always assumed that we can have knowledge.[7] The tradition that has its origins in Plato and Descartes begins with an assumption that being encased in the body, or simply being embodied, leads one to confusion. The simultaneous emphasis on reason, pure and speculative, divorced from the influence of the passions and bodily functions, and the conceptualization of woman as other, as immersed in the body, as having difficulty in—or being completely incapable of—divorcing her reason from the body, has led to a tradition in epistemology that is at once virtually exclusively normative and staggeringly androcentric.[8]

Thus feminist epistemology and the naturalization of contemporary analytic epistemology might be seen to have an intriguing and fruitful intersection. For if we can begin with an assumption that we do have knowledge, we can employ the techniques of the cognitive sciences to help us understand how all of us—adult males and females, and children—come to have knowledge. Similarly, if we can employ these sciences to help us come to see how we obtain knowledge, we can also employ them to aid in the discovery of what, if anything, is peculiar to the female knower. And the female knower, able to articulate the process of knowledge acquisition both from the standpoint of a female and from the standpoint of a person for whom the possibility of knowledge acquisition is assumed and not questioned, is at the heart of what would constitute a feminist epistemology. Thus recent advances in analytic epistemology are relevant to the development of a feminist epistemology, however androcentric and unyielding the tradition has been up to this time.

## FEMINIST THEORY AND THE ANDROCENTRIC VOICE

If we can make out the case, however roughly, that naturalized epistemology is relevant to feminist epistemology, we need now to inquire what, so far, has been broadly construed as constitutive of feminist moves in epistemology. Recent work by Evelyn Fox Keller, by Sandra Harding, and by Susan Bordo, among others, is both broadly epistemological and straightforwardly feminist. All three theorists have in common the theme we have already alluded to: There is a masculinist, androcentric tradition that yields a hypernormative, idealized, and stylistically aggressive mode of thought. At an earlier point I alluded to Plato and the importance of *Theaetetus* to the epistemological tradition as a whole. At this juncture, it might prove valuable to examine in a bit more depth some of the feminist criticism of the Platonic metaphysics and epistemology.

Keller provides an intriguing account of the relationship between what I have dubbed an androcentric epistemology in Plato and Plato's own complex philosophy of sexual love and its link to metaphysics. One ordinarily wants to start with the *Symposium* here, since it is clear in this dialogue that Plato sees instances of earthly or material-world love as instantiations of the soul's urge to come to know the immortal

Forms. Indeed, this part of Plato's work has frequently been deemed to be the most moving, and undergraduates are often introduced to Plato by way of the *Symposium*, since it is widely held that that dialogue provides an introduction to Plato's ontology and concomitant epistemology. But Keller's analysis of Plato's androcentrism is enlightening in a different sort of way. Earlier commentators have either not explicitly acknowledged or have commented little upon the obvious fact that Plato sees earthly love relationships as coming closest to mimicking the soul's quest when the relationships are male homosexual encounters. In a prefeminist era, it might have seemed irrelevant or even naive to want to comment upon the philosophical significance of this point. Keller thinks otherwise. Although it is conceded that there is no material-world sexual relation that is a truly adequate analogue of what Plato seeks to model (this being presumably part of Plato's point), some relations are better analogues than others.

> Heterosexual desire does not contribute to transcendence, for Plato, precisely because of its association with physical procreation. . . . Plato's model for spiritual begetting is the love of man for man; knowledge is a product of a divine union of kindred essences. It is a man's feeling of love for boys, not for women, that provides the first impetus for the philosopher's journey. . . . The most highly valued by far, and the only model relevant to Plato, was a relationship between an adult male (the *erastes*, or lover) and a youth of comparable social standing (the *eromenos*, or beloved).[9]

The key phrase in the above quotation is "knowledge is a product of a divine union of kindred essences." The importance for the future of epistemology of the analogy of a certain sort of male homosexual relationship to the soul's acquisition of knowledge is virtually impossible to overestimate. As Keller notes, the construction and utilization of this analogy had two important ramifications for philosophy as a whole: (1) it reinforced the notion, already implicit in Greek thought, that female nature was other than or alien to male nature, thus making it less likely that anything connected with female nature could be in any sense connected with the acquisition of knowledge, since it is clear that the acquisition of knowledge is a completely male enterprise; and (2) it furthered the split between the mind and the body, making it also unlikely that any sort of bodily function—including known functions of the brain—could be alluded to as important parts of the process of knowledge acquisition, since the model for knowledge acquisition denies the influence of the body as much as is possible for embodied beings.

Keller's insight that Plato's views on love and sex are crucial to his epistemology is an extremely important one for feminist theory, and several other feminist commentators have developed similar, although not identical, lines of thought. Susan Bordo has made a somewhat parallel argument with regard to the views that Descartes gives us in the *Meditations*.[10]   'though I cannot recapitulate the entire argument here, Bordo's point reminds us of Keller's in the broad sense that a move in philosophy that might be seen by some as a purely metaphysical or epistemological move has had much broader implications historically. Like Plato, Descartes believed that the body confuses the soul and hinders the acquisition of knowledge. The Cartesian *cogito* possesses the security it has epistemically precisely because knowledge that I exist, when arrived at by Descartes's peculiar mode of execution, is completely divorced from the senses. The overall burden of the argument with regard to the Cartesian shift in epistemology is similar to that just made for Plato.

Finally, to continue the feminist line, Harding has written, in *The Science Question in Feminism*, of more than one sort of feminist response to the androcentrism inherent in science. If we think of philosophy of science as the offspring of epistemology, we are reminded of the close connection between the two endeavors. What we now refer to as "science" is of course, in any case, the twentieth-century descendant of the "natural philosophy" of the Cartesians and other seventeenth- and eighteenth-century thinkers. At the moment I want to quote only one brief portion of the first chapter of Harding's book, since it makes the point, quite clearly, that the androcentric worldview creates the evidence by which it tends to confirm itself.

> We shall also see that a key origin of androcentric bias can be found in the selection of problems for inquiry, and in the definition of what is problematic about these phenomena. But empiricism insists that its methodological norms are meant to apply only to the "context of justification"—to the testing of hypotheses and interpretations of evidence—not to the "context of discovery" where problems are identified and defined. Thus a powerful source of social bias appears completely to escape the control of science's methodological norms. Finally, it appears that following the norms of inquiry is exactly what often results in androcentric results.[11]

In other words, all three theorists seem to agree that part of the androcentricity of the epistemological tradition, both as it manifests itself in theory of knowledge *simpliciter* and as it manifests itself in philosophy of science, is a structuring of the epistemic rules so that to do epistemology is to work only in a certain manner—a manner that produces self-confirming evidence. At a later point I want to examine this set of claims in much greater detail, but I think it is also important to investigate further what the normative tradition in contemporary analytic epistemology really amounts to.

## NATURALIZING THE ANDROCENTRIC PROJECT

Insofar as what professional philosophers dub "pure epistemology" is concerned, it makes little sense to try to demarcate between various sorts of less-androcentric and still more-androcentric styles. The project of naturalizing epistemology is a relatively recent one, and many professional epistemologists have no interest in the project precisely because they agree wholeheartedly with the older, completely normative tradition. Tersely, many professional epistemologists still feel that naturalized epistemology is no epistemology at all. So it may be helpful to my project to investigate some of the contemporary views, at least with an eye as to what constitutes epistemology, and why, by general admission, it has been and continue to be, for many, exclusively normative.

Frequent reference is currently made to Laurence BonJour's work *The Structure of Empirical Knowledge*, and the book certainly has the virtue of opening chapters that provide a clearly written and accessible overview of contemporary epistemology. The following passages from BonJour outline, I think, the sorts of distinctions that the professional epistemologist customarily makes. It is worth noting the demarcation that BonJour draws between epistemic justification and other sorts of justification, for the relevant fact is, as BonJour admits (and as some other epistemologists are at pains to point out), that epistemic justification is probably one of the least frequently employed methods of justification in ordinary daily life.

> The immediate problem is thus to distinguish epistemic justification, the species of justification appropriate or relevant to knowledge, from other actual and possible species of justification.
>
> Now it might be thought that the solution to this problem is obvious and straightforward: epistemic justification is that species of justification which is appropriate to *beliefs* or *judgments*, rather than to actions,

decisions, and so on. . . . But there are other species of justification which also can apply to beliefs, so that mere applicability to beliefs cannot be the sole distinguishing characteristic of epistemic justification. . . . A different sort of justification for believing . . . is illustrated . . . by an . . . example offered by William James. . . . James imagines a situation in which I must leap over a chasm to escape from some danger: it is uncertain whether I can jump that far, but I know that I will make a better effort and thus have a better chance at success if I believe that I can. In such a situation, he argues, I am justified in believing that I can make the leap, even though I have no real evidence that this is so.[12]

Now BonJour's point here—completely appropriate from the standpoint of contemporary analytic epistemology—is that epistemic justification is a provision of reasons for believing when the point of the exercise is to obtain truth; that is, when the point of the exercise is to rid one's justificatory set, as some epistemologists employ the term, of as many false beliefs as possible, while endeavoring to add to it as many true beliefs as possible. James's justification in the example above does not count as epistemic (BonJour calls it "pragmatic" justification) because the would-be knower is not concerned with the truth-value of the belief—rather, the point is to try to enhance action. In a similarly constructed example, BonJour tells us of a set of circumstances where I convince myself of a friend's innocence of a serious crime largely because of my esteem for my friend and because of a sensation of debt owing to him for help given in the past. In this case, too, BonJour reminds us, the justification I provide for myself with regard to the belief in question is not epistemic—here it is moral. So standard epistemology, in clarifying the distinction between epistemic justification and other sorts of justification, sets out the high standards required of epistemic justification and reminds us of the assumption by professional epistemologists that the putative knower is a truth-seeker—what Lehrer terms a "veracious inquirer."[13] But most of us, a great deal of the time, are not veracious inquirers or truth-seekers, a fact acknowledged even in the standard epistemological literature on the topic.[14] Human nature being what it is, any given day is likely to contain many more examples of James's pragmatic justification (I want to believe that my daughter can actually gain admission to Stanford or Harvard because I need that belief to motivate myself to keep working), or BonJour's moral justification (I believe that my neighbor is not deliberately destroying my eucalyptus because I think it is very unfair to my neighbor to believe otherwise), than examples of epistemic justification. So one small strand of the enterprise of contemporary epistemology, epistemic justification theory, is highlighted in its normative aspect by its very avoidance of allusion to the manner in which cognizers actually function.[15]

To return to our previous theme, the project of naturalizing epistemology, since it is in no small part descriptive, presumably will be able to make use of pragmatic and moral justification, at least on some level, in a way that normative epistemic justification theory does not. And here we see again the natural point of intersection between feminist epistemology and contemporary work in epistemology, for the feminist project, too, is concerned about the way in which knowers actually function. Indeed, one obvious analogue to the project is Carol Gilligan's work, wherein the normative moral justification typical of boys is contrasted with the individualized, more contextual moral justification of girls. Painting in broad strokes, one might almost be tempted to say that Gilligan's justice voice is the analogue of androcentric justification theory, and her care voice the analogue of a more naturalized theory. Indeed, it is interesting to note how some of the naive models employed by others in descriptions of Gilligan's work match certain sorts of lines in justification theory. It is clear that Gilligan's delineation of the female voice relies on notions like "cohering through human connection" and "a world comprised of relationships." Gilligan also notes, at one point, that girls tend to respond "contextually rather than categorically."[16]

In traditional professional epistemic terminology, coherentism has always been an alternative—sometimes a rather step-childish one—to the main line in epistemic justification theory, foundationalism. At a later point a more thorough delineation of the relationship between these two sorts of theories will be provided, but coherentism (wherein the epistemic justification for a belief or alleged claim to knowledge is provided by the belief's relationship to other held beliefs and knowledge claims, with no one of these beliefs having special status) has frequently been accused by the foundationalists of being guilty of a certain sort of circularity. Typically, a foundationalist view in epistemology has always been characterized by giving special status to one belief or one sort of belief—in the older literature the belief was frequently one of privileged access (the first-person sort of belief alluded to here earlier in my mention of Descartes).[17] The coherentist view of epistemic justification, broadly construed, has tended to be that our beliefs receive their justification from each other insofar as they cohere as a group. No one belief or knowledge claim receives special status.

Now the professional epistemologists have criticized coherentism for the theoretical difficulties caused by the size, scope, and rigor of its justificatory sets (the term "set" here refers to the set of beliefs which, coheringly, provide justification for each other at any given time).[18] But the sets employed by the coherentists, if seen through a naturalized view, need not be so rigorous nor so unwieldy.

## TOWARD A NATURALIZED AND GYNOCENTRIC VIEW

Roughly speaking, strands of naturalized epistemology may be analogous to what Gilligan characterizes as the female voice. The female voice has no doubt a somewhat different ontology to begin with, but that question does not concern us here. To further our parallel, the female voice is not, in general, concerned with questions of universalizability, normative standards, or idealized behavior. Rather, the female engaged in moral thinking (and this may be relevant to other sorts of thinking) proceeds nonfoundationally. She is instinctively a coherentist. Claims of one individual are balanced against the claims of another individual, with the goal of achieving some sort of balance within a given framework. No one standard, typically, is appealed to; this lends credence to what has been the implicit claim of the feminist theorists working on science and philosophy of science that rigorously foundationalist sorts of views are inherently androcentric.

In broad terms, the justification theory of Gilligan's female voice, insofar as it possesses one, is coherentist rather than foundationalist, and contextualist and naturalized rather than normative. That is, one may think of Gilligan's agent as working within a framework that fits her particular vision of the circumstances although that framework may by no means be adequate to a larger, more global view of the circumstances, and may in some sense be "incorrect." Employing the epistemic analogue of moral justification, Gilligan's agent is composing a justificatory set for her moral beliefs based on utterances relative to a specific situation. One could imagine that a professional epistemologist could concoct a number of Gettier-like counterexamples to this sort of functioning (that is, a number of counterexamples based on the epicycles of the justified true belief view to which I alluded at an earlier point), to show that such an agent "errs" frequently or that her mode of functioning could not be normativized to cover all sorts of cases.

Such an agent may perform the moral equivalent, for example, of the contemporary epistemologists' favorite erring epistemic agent, who believes, on the basis of what seems to be appropriate evidence, that Jones owns a Ford when, unbeknownst to him, Jones has just sold his Ford and someone else owns it.[19]

But surely this is precisely the point. Insofar as Gilligan's work is concerned, the earlier psychological theorists—Piaget, Lever, Freud— had categorized female moral functioning as failing to reach a certain standard because the functioning frequently appealed to specific cases, was too contextualized, and hence made "mistakes" (was not generalizable or universalizable in a moral sense, à la the Kantian tradition). Gilligan's work serves as a reminder to us that there are virtues in such sorts of functioning, that there are defects—failures of human relations, so to speak—in the other sort of functioning, and that to compare one sort of cognition with the other at the expense of one, is to beg the question.

In any case, I have attempted to construct an analysis of Gilligan's work along the lines of contemporary epistemic justification theory precisely because I believe that such an analysis points us in an important direction—the direction of the intersection of analytic epistemology and feminist theory. However androcentric the tradition of the professional epistemologists has been up to now, it has the virtue of being a rigorous method of inquiry and being a finely tuned philosophical apparatus. Perhaps one might say that feminist theory, or feminist epistemology up to this point, insofar as there has been an actual development of feminist epistemology, has the defect of its virtues—it is not so rigorous, not so specific, nor so finely tuned.

The question remains as to what extent feminist theory can make use of the methods and scope of professional epistemology—not to mention whether professional epistemology can and should make use of feminist theory. But my project here is more along the lines of the first endeavor than the second. The feminist critique of epistemology broadly construed is well under way, and doubtless will continue. What has yet to be constructed is a sketch of the intersection of these two endeavors in a way that might be fruitful to feminist theory itself. My project, then, is to develop a feminist epistemology along these rather underutilized and striking lines.

## NOTES

1. See, for example, Mary Field Belenky, et al., *Women's Ways of Knowing: The Development of Self, Voice and Mind* (New York: Basic Books, 1986), or the work of the sociologist Jane Flax.

2. The most prominent philosophers now working with this orientation are Alvin Goldman and Hilary Kornblith. Goldman's longest work in this vein is *Epistemology and Cognition* (Cambridge, Mass.: Harvard University Press, 1986). Kornblith's is *Naturalizing Epistemology* (Cambridge, Mass.: Bradford of MIT Press, 1985).

3. See Susan Bordo, *The Flight to Objectivity* (Albany, N.Y.: SUNY Press, 1987).

4. All of these emphases are more than adequately covered in the superb bibliography at the end of the Kornblith volume.

5. Many have referred to this movement as "evolutionary epistemology." An interesting source of papers in the area is Gerard Radnitzky and W. W. Bartley III, eds., *Evolutionary Epistemology, Rationality and the Sociology of Knowledge* La Salle, Ill.: Open Court Publishing Co., 1987).

6. One thinks, for example, of Alvin Goldman's work that has recently shifted to an emphasis on connectionist models of mind, which seem now to be outstripping the earlier computational models. See Newton Garver and Peter Hare eds., *Naturalism and Rationality* (Buffalo, N.Y.: Prometheus Books, 1986).

7. The epistemic tradition of classical skepticism has not strongly influenced what currently falls under the rubric of "feminist epistemology." What is meant by "feminist skepticism" has more to do, crudely speaking, with attacking the validity of the male tradition. See, again, Bordo; and see also Sandra Harding, *The Science Question in Feminism* (Ithaca: Cornell University Press, 1986).

8. Evelyn Fox Keller, among others, has written extensively on the relation between abnegation of the body, exaltation of pure reason, rejection of women or of the feminine, and the idealized male homoeroticism that occurs in Plato. See Keller's *Reflections on Gender and Science* (New Haven, Conn.: Yale University Press, 1985), especially chapter one, "Love and Sex in Plato's Epistemology."

9. Keller, *Reflections on Gender*, 24–25.

10. Susan Bordo, "The Cartesian Masculinization of Thought," *Signs* 11, no. 3 (1988):619–29.

11. Harding, *The Science Question*, 25–26.

12. Laurence BonJour, *The Structure of Empirical Knowledge* (Cambridge, Mass.: Harvard University Press, 1985) 6–7.

13. Keith Lehrer, *Knowledge* (Oxford: Clarendon Press, 1974), passim.

14. Richard Feldman, "Lehrer's Theory of Justification," *Australasian Journal of Philosophy* 57, no. 3 (1979):266–73.

15. See Daniel Kahneman, Paul Slovic, and Amos Tversky, *Judgment Under Uncertainty: Heuristics and Biases* (Cambridge, U.K.: Cambridge University Press, 1982).

16. Carol Gilligan, *In a Different Voice* (Cambridge, Ill.: Harvard University Press, 1982). The two phrases in the preceding sentence are from p. 29; the "contextually" phrase is from p. 38.

17. See Frederick Suppe, *The Structure of Scientific Theories* (Urbana-Champaign: University of Illinois Press, 1977), for an excellent section on the importance of foundationalism in the earlier, positivistic philosophy of science.

18. James W. Cornman, "Foundational vs. Nonfoundational Theories of Epistemic Justification," in *Essays on Knowledge and Justification,* ed. George S. Pappas and Marshall Swain (Ithaca: Cornell University Press, 1978), 229–52.

19. This example is based on Gettier's original piece, "Is Justified True Belief Knowledge?" in *Analysis* 23, no. 7 (1963):122–23.

## Chapter One

# Analytic Theory of Knowledge

Any assertion about the normative and hyperidealized nature of contemporary analytic epistemology requires some support. Although a cursory look at the tradition might go some way toward provision of such support, it is in the detailed epistemic analysis of problems of knowledge and knowledge assumption that analytic epistemology most clearly manifests its normative nature. Epistemology as a subarea of endeavor for philosophy as a whole is, I have contended, as old as the Platonic dialogues—and, indeed, this is how the notion of epistemology is generally introduced to students. But if this large area of questioning is one of the first to emerge in the Western philosophical tradition, as textbooks are only too happy to inform us,[1] it is also true that it is only in the modern (post-Cartesian) period that epistemology has achieved anything like its present status, and probably only in the twentieth century that it has pursued the narrowly defined sorts of questions now characteristic of it as an area of expertise: questions with regard to the establishment of a "fourth" condition for knowledge, the correct delineation of the epistemic status of what the foundationalists term basic statements, and so forth.[2]

Although Russell's *A History of Western Philosophy* lacks the scholarly precision of many other such histories, it is widely cited and an excellent source of summarizations of the Anglo-American philosophical viewpoint on many issues. I want to utilize Russell as a source with respect to the epistemic tradition, and then go on to cite Russell's own work. Russell, like others, appears to believe that the contemporary interest in matters epistemic begins with Descartes:

> This passage [the *cogito*] is the kernel of Descartes' theory of knowledge, and contains what is most important in his philosophy. Most philosophers since Descartes have attached importance to the theory of knowledge, and their doing so is largely due to him. "I think, therefore I am" makes mind more certain than matter, and my mind (for me) more certain than the minds of others. There is thus, in all philosophy derived from Descartes, a tendency to subjectivism, and to regarding matter as something only knowable, if at all, by inference from what is known of mind.[3]

What is important about the preceding passage is not so much the emphasis on Descartes himself, but the emphasis on the subjectivity of certain knowledge, or as Russell has it, fact that "my mind (for me) [is] more certain than the minds of others." For this emphasis on the mirroring of the contents of one's mind by one's thoughts is at the heart of contemporary epistemology, at least insofar as many of its leading theoretical offshoots are concerned.

Descartes's project was an attempt to establish something of which he could be certain in order to provide himself with an epistemic criterion. The *Meditations* begins with Descartes easily able to cast doubt on alleged knowledge acquired through the senses, since the tradition dating back to Plato had exhibited a fondness for demonstrating how simply the senses could be made to err. But knowledge only of my own existence is of little use, and the architectonic structure of the *Meditations* is clearly designed to provide us with a passageway back to knowledge of the external world. The precise nature of the passageway is not important, but the manner of achieving the end result is, for as Russell has remarked, it is the emphasis on my knowledge of the contents of my own mind that provides the impetus for a good deal of the consequent work in epistemology.

## LOGICAL ATOMISM

In attempting to demonstrate the extremely normative nature of contemporary epistemology, particularly epistemic justification theory, I aim at being able to provide a basis for the development of more naturalized, and more overtly feminist, strains of thought at a later point. But some sort of an overview of twentieth-century epistemology

is required, so I intend to sketch in this chapter some work leading up
to the current lines of debate to provide a large-scale canvas. Bertrand
Russell is usefully cited again in this context, for some of Russell's
work in epistemology—particularly when seen in the context of the
sense-data theorists—is helpful in elucidating the influence of the mind-
first model.

Russell's "The Philosophy of Logical Atomism" is important not
only for its delineation of the intersection of early philosophy of
language and metaphysics but for its implicit epistemology as well,
since the tradition upon which Russell commented in the previous
quotation manifests itself here in his work, and in a way which
foreshadows a good deal of the history of twentieth-century epistemology. In a series of lectures delivered in 1918, Russell developed what
is now a somewhat celebrated doctrine about the usage of words to
name particulars:

> The only kind of word that is theoretically capable of standing for a
> particular is a proper name, and the whole matter of *proper names* is
> rather curious.
> Proper names = df words for particulars.
> . . . The names that we commonly use, like "Socrates," are really
> abbreviations for descriptions; not only that, but what they describe are
> not particulars but complicated systems of classes or series. . . . The only
> words which one does use as names in the logical sense are words like
> "this" or "that."[4]

Russell went on to elaborate changes in his doctrine, some of which
appear in *An Inquiry into Meaning and Truth,* but the doctrine as it
first appears in the lectures was enormously influential for decades to
come in Western philosophy. Tersely, Russell's contention that names
that we commonly use, like "Socrates," are "really abbreviations for
descriptions" rests on the notion that a "particular" must be thought
of in terms of the sense-datum that we would denominate. At a later
point in the lectures, Russell offers the assertion that a particular, or
sense-datum, can only be kept going for two to three minutes at most.

Here the historical influence of the Cartesian insistence on the
primacy of the mental-as-I-experience it ("privileged access")—to
which Russell himself had alluded, as we saw—is clearly manifest. The
sense-datum that I call "Socrates," or "Ronald Reagan" for that
matter, can be described by me as a rather elongated figure, with a
whitish patch of thus-and-so length (perhaps somewhat toga-like, in

the case of Socrates), topped by a roundish patch of such-and-such characteristics . . . and so forth. Any number of occurrences generally prevent me from maintaining this sense-datum with its original set of properties for more than a minute or two, but even if, hypothetically, the Socrates of my datum were to remain still and unmoving, physiological changes undergone by me, including the tearing of the eye, natural tendencies to blink, distractions, and so forth, make it highly unlikely that I could maintain this datum for a longer period of time than the brief period originally mentioned by Russell. And it is the datum to which the name refers, since any underlying substance, material or otherwise, which might give rise to the datum is (in this view) only a construct that we have a tendency to make, based on the appearance to us of a series of such data over a period of time that tend to resemble each other. This last, rather Humean point, is a point about ontology and thus somewhat removed from our area of inquiry. But the Cartesian point remains, and there are in fact passages in the *Meditations* that foreshadow, so to speak, this very line of argument.

The desire to have true beliefs, susceptible of rigorous justification, which might then be counted as knowledge, manifests itself in this pared-down phenomenal account of Russell's as to what it is that the logically proper names (demonstratives such as "this" and "that") actually name. Since the home of the sense-datum *qua* datum is the mind, it is unlikely that one could be in error about the nature of the datum as long as one maintained the same datum (that is, as I have just indicated, the temporally brief datum with the identical properties) and as long as one was cautious in characterization of the datum. The interiority of the datum also provides a foundation against which other claims can be measured, and here Russell is at least crudely foundationalist.

These two strands of argument—the primacy of the datum as a mental construct, or at least a construct with an origin internal to the self rather than external to it, and the hedged nature of assertions about the datum—became crucial for the next few decades in analytic epistemology. For the datum here has a role analogous to that of the doubting something of the Cartesian *cogito*. The analogy is in some ways rough, but the parallel is an important one for epistemology. Critical commentary on the *cogito* has focused on the notion that the *cogito* seems to work only while one is actually doing it.[5] While one is aware that one is doubting one can be assured of one's existence, insofar as one can be identified with a thing that doubts. While one is aware of a given datum, one can be as completely sure of the existence of the datum and qualifiedly, at least, as sure of its properties (". . . it appears to be whitish") as one can be of any empirical fact. It is an often repeated platitude that Descartes, as a mathematician, wished to employ the methods of mathematics and the sciences, so as to give as certain a basis as possible for knowledge that seems to proceed from the external world.[6] The desire to place empirical knowledge on a footing equal to nonempirical or deductively ascertainable knowledge continues in the twentieth-century analytic quest, inaugurated at least in part by Russell, to establish a basis of irrefutability for sense-based contentions, beginning with the deployment of logically proper names. W. V. O. Quine noted that Russell had been given credit for "explaining [entities] away in favor of nothing more than a nominalistic view of particulars and notations."[7] The virtue of this view, here characterized in blunt terms, is that it allows one a greater degree of assurance about any statements of propositions made with regard to the particulars in question.

The early view of Russell's that I have just presented here was only the opening gambit, so to speak, in a line of moves, each of which was designed to enable the professional epistemologist to give a tighter and tighter account of knowledge, or claims to knowledge, derived through the senses. If the difficulty was that empirical data seemed on less sure ground from the outset than deductively certain propositions, great care was taken to try to ensure the success of a view that would establish certainty for claims based on perceptual data. Commonly, the sensory mode taken as paradigmatic in the literature was seeing, and the problem of visual sense-data became acute. The philosophical benefit to be derived from Russell's logical atomism was that a pared-down, time-slice view of particulars made the epistemic status of the particular more certain and less susceptible to doubt. The success of the view opened the way in the 1920s and 1930s to a wide variety of similar sorts of views, each of which tried to be as precise as possible about what it was, ontologically, that one experienced when one was confronted with a sense-datum, and where one stood epistemically with regard to such a datum.

## SENSE-DATA VIEWS: NORMATIVE THEORIES OF PRIVILEGED ACCESS

Preliminarily, the path of least resistance seemed to be to suggest that one never sees directly what the ordinary, philosophically untutored individual would call a physical object. Instead, one is always confronted with sense-data, the characteristics and properties of which one could be certain of if statements about them were sufficiently qualified or hedged. The permutations of such a view are so numerous that I can cite only one or two examples. Remarkably, G. E. Moore, associated with a "commonsense" view of the ontological questions (in other words, with the view that there really are such things as material objects, rather than with a strictly phenomenalist account that would deny or cast doubt on the existence of material objects) wrote several pieces that are among the most closely reasoned but at the same time the most difficult exemplars of this particular tradition. If one bears in mind that the epistemic goal here is certainty with regard to knowledge claims based on sensory-originated data, the tangles of argument become somewhat easier to unravel:

> It seems to me quite plain that one of the commonest senses in which the word "see" can be correctly used in English, perhaps the commonest of all, is that in which a particular person can be said, at a particular time, to be "seeing" such objects as, *e.g.*, a particular penny, a particular chair. . . . I have, indeed, once met a philosopher who told me I was making a great mistake in thinking that such objects are ever seen. But I think this philosopher was wrong. . . .
>
> [However], . . . I think it is true that I so use the phrase "visual sense-datum" that, from the fact that any entity is "directly seen," in the sense explained, that entity *is* a visual sense-datum. . . .
>
> [And, it is also the case that] But I have to own that, I now think I was mistaken in supposing that, in the case of "seeing" an opaque object, where in seeing it you are seeing only one visual sense-datum, the sense-datum can possibly be identical with that part of the opaque object's surface which you are seeing.[8]

In other words, what one actually sees, according to Moore, is the sense-datum, which, as he goes on to explain, has some relation $R$ to the object in question, but the relation is not one of identity.[9] The squeamishness with which such a view—which is essentially what came to be known as a "sense-data view"—was greeted at the time was no doubt at least partly related to the fears I have alluded to in my citation of Russell's Ockhamish ontology in the preceding paragraphs. Here epistemic precision has the upper hand at the expense of any sort of naturalistic ontology, and one has the uneasy sensation that one has brought, philosophically, a pig in a poke. If it is not possible to spell out the relation that the sense-datum bears to the surface of the object (and part of the philosophical difficulty here, of course, is that every individual who looks at the object sees a slightly different datum, even when angles and so forth are taken into account), then one might as well deny that one does in fact see the object in the usual, common sense, everyday vein.

The Oxford and Cambridge philosophers associated with these sorts of views did, in fact, refer to nonphilosophical views about the status of mundane objects as views of "the plain man," or "the common man." In fact, J. L. Austin, in attempting to refute Ayer's view—which was, at least in the Austinian interpretation, somewhat more extreme than Moore's view cited above—referred to the move from the physical object ontology of the common man to the (according to Ayer) correct, philosophical account that Ayer expounded as "the bottom, one might perhaps call it, of the garden path. In these paragraphs we already seem to see the plain man, here under the implausible aspect of Ayer himself, dribbling briskly into position in front of his own goal, and squaring up to encompass his own destruction."[10]

The sense-data theorists, in an effort to obtain epistemic certainty, sacrificed most of what would pass for an adequate ontology, and in the process did, indeed, begin to encompass their own destruction. The backlash against a view like Moore's, or like Ayer's view in *Foundations of Empirical Knowledge*, where he attempts to argue that we never directly perceive anything other than sense-data, was perhaps inevitable. Austin himself led most of the way in attempting to show that much of the argument leading to the sense-data position was based on dubious usage of ordinary English-language locutions such as "looks," and "seems," divorced from their normal context and asked to do strenuous philosophical duty in an ontological or epistemic framework. The employment of these terms was originally related to attempts to hedge one's assertions about the data one was seeing. In a previous example I noted that one could approach—or even obtain, according to some thinkers—certainty on a knowledge claim about visual sense-data if one described one's datum in terms such as "It appears to me to be. . . ."

But Austin noted, quite forcefully, that such locutions already have standard English meanings with which we, as native speakers, are all familiar from their regular usage, and that to employ them in a more recherché manner is to do violence to them. The point then was quite in line with Wittgenstein's frequently cited remark about philosophical problems that seem to arise from language having gone "on holiday."[11] One portion of Austin's *Sense and Sensibilia*, in an effort to dislodge the position of the sense-data theorists, actually catalogues various of the "looks" locutions that occur in everyday British English ("It looks blue." "He looks a gentleman." "She looks chic,"). [12] But this particular set of moves in epistemology—the atomistic view, the sense-data view, and the rejection of the sense-data view by ordinary-language arguments—was not to prove the most tortured of recent attempts to come to grips with knowledge. Very shortly after the Austinian sorts of objections undid the precision of the sense-data views, American philosophers began to tackle the conditions for knowledge from the standpoint of analytically tight necessary and sufficient conditions. This line of approach had the virtue of precision—as did, indeed, the sense-data approach—but also the virtue of obviating the necessity to speak of knowledge simply on empirically derived grounds. Approaching the question of knowledge from the standpoint of necessary and sufficient conditions for knowledge simultaneously placed all cases of knowledge, whether empirically derived or not, on the same footing.

## AMERICAN ANALYTIC EPISTEMOLOGY

In a piece published in the British journal *Analysis* in 1963—perhaps the single most celebrated piece in postwar Anglo-American epistemology—Edmund Gettier concocted a number of specifically constructed counterexamples to the thesis that justified true belief constitutes knowledge. I intend to examine his material and the replies to it at some length, as it is essential to my larger argument about the nature of twentieth-century epistemology. The flavor of the counterexamples helps to illustrate the point I have just made: The new moves in epistemology, however far away from sense-data theories they may have been, lacked nothing in precision or analytic thoroughness. The Gettier article drives a wedge between justification and the evidence that would ordinarily constitute the basis for justification. Briefly, I may hold a belief *p*, and be justified in holding *p* according to my own epistemic standards and the standards of those around me, but I may be right about *p* for reasons that are not at all related to the grounds of my justification, or, unbeknownst to me (or anyone else in a position to comment on my grounds), it may simply be the case that I am mistaken about the grounds of justification because there are still other facts, of which I am unaware, that do damage to my original basis for justification.

A quote from Gettier shows us how intricately constructed the examples were:

> Let us suppose that Smith has strong evidence for the following proposition:
>     (f) Jones owns a Ford.
> Smith's evidence might be that Jones has at all times in the past within Smith's memory owned a car, and always a Ford, and that Jones has just offered Smith a ride while driving a Ford. Let us imagine, now, that Smith has another friend, Brown, of whose whereabouts he is totally ignorant. Smith selects three place names quite at random, and constructs the following three propositions:
>     (g) Either Jones owns a Ford, or Brown is in Boston;
>     (h) Either Jones owns a Ford, or Brown is in Barcelona;
>     (i) Either Jones owns a Ford, or Brown is in Brest-Litovsk.
> Each of these propositions is entailed by (f). Imagine that Brown realizes the entailment of each of these propositions he has constructed by (f), and proceeds to accept (g), (h), and (i) on the basis of (f). Smith has correctly inferred (g), (h), and (i) from a proposition for which he has strong evidence. Smith is therefore completely justified in believing each of these three propositions. Smith, of course, has no idea where Brown is.
> But imagine now that two further conditions hold. First, Jones does *not* own a Ford, but is at present driving a rented car. And secondly, by the sheerest coincidence, and entirely unknown to Smith, the place mentioned in proposition (h) happens really to be the place where Brown is. If these two conditions hold, then Smith does *not* know that (h) is true, even though (i) (h) is true, (ii) Smith does believe that (h) is true, and (iii) Smith is justified in believing that (h) is true.[13]

This Gettier example accomplishes two things at once. It forces on the reader the realization that logical relationships between propositions necessitate a disjunction's being true if only one of its disjuncts is true. Although a common sense analysis of our use of language, sans logic classes, supports this as an everyday notion, the epistemological twist here is that the first sort of relationship alluded to in the example is one of logical entailment, and is not an empirical relationship.

But the second move made is a convenient rendering of the sort of thing for which "Gettier examples," as they came to be called, were known, and is also important for an overview of theory of knowledge. It turns out that the proposition is true, but for accidental sorts of reasons. If Jones has always owned a Ford, never anything else, and I have known Jones a good many years, it may never occur to me to wonder whether Jones actually owns the Ford that I see him driving right now. So what would ordinarily constitute adequate empirical evidence for the first disjunct—that I see Jones driving a Ford—collapses because intervening events, of which I was not aware, have taken away Jones's former Ford and left him with a Ford rental that he does not, of course, own. So the first disjunct is false. Now if both disjuncts are false the disjunction as a whole cannot be true, so in order to save the disjunction the second disjunct must be true.

But how was I to have any evidence that Brown was in Barcelona? I haven't had any contact with Brown in ages. Lacking what would ordinarily be called adequate evidence, I have accidentally hit upon the right location for Brown, who just left on an extensive vacation in Andalusia last week. So the second disjunct is true—although I had no justification for it—and the proposition as a whole is true. Hence, as Gettier remarks, something seems to be wrong with the tripartite analysis of knowledge, since I would not ordinarily say that I did know that (h) was true, were I apprised of the actual facts of the situation.

How does one account for this lacuna? Proceeding epistemically, the problem seems to be with the accidentalness, as it were, of the second disjunct of the proposition. If I had even flimsy evidence that Brown was in Barcelona—a postcard with some dates, for example—we might not go along with Gettier's analysis. So it appears that in order for the epistemic agent to be justified, the justification must be linked to the knower in some way such that the linkage does not break down. The problem with Brown's being in Barcelona is that there is no such linkage between that fact and the epistemic agent, and the problem with Jones's owning a Ford is that the supposed linkage is more apparent than real—in other words, if the epistemic agent had access to still more facts she would realize that the Ford she thought Jones owned was temporarily acquired by Jones under another arrangement (if, for example, she had by chance been at the Hertz rental desk when the car was obtained). These lines of reasoning are typical of those that came to dominate epistemology, and underscore its logical relations and airtight, normative nature.

## REPLIES TO THE COUNTEREXAMPLES: TWO STRANDS

The response to the Gettier counterexamples by professional philosophers was swift and far from unanimous. Responses tended to break down into two sorts of accounts. The first account strove to br try to make clear what the conditions would be for a causal linkage between knower and alleged facts of justification such that the links could not be broken. In other words, if Brown were really in Barcelona and I had received the postcard from him (and not from someone posing as Brown to throw me off the track), then it should be possible to trace the causal linkage between Brown's actually writing the postcard, mailing it, the card's being on a plane, being delivered to me, my seeing it under the appropriate conditions, etc. In the Jones case, one should be able to trace back Jones's physically being in that particular car to Jones's purchase of the car, etc. Alvin Goldman and other epistemologists developed such theories, and they were at the time referred to as "causal" theories. Another sort of analysis of the difficulties posed by the counterexamples focused on the availability of propositions stating facts that, if such propositions were known to the agent, would alter the agent's response to the original alleged knowledge claim. For instance, "Jones does not currently own any car and Jones is renting a Ford" is a proposition with a truth value of true, according to the constructed example, and is the sort of proposition that when conjoined with (h) has the effect of defeating the first disjunct of (h). Such analyses were called defeasibility analyses, since it was clear that in order for a proposition to count as a piece of knowledge it would have to be (borrowing from legal language) indefeasible.

Now in setting out the moves in American thought that led from the prewar and postwar sense-data theories to theories more contemporary, I have tried to focus on major examples to provide an adequate account of the structure of professional epistemology. What is immediately noticeable from all of these examples (and perhaps most noticeable, interestingly enough, in the Gettier examples) is the lack of descriptive or even cognitively regulative elements in the exemplary situations. One does not want to proceed completely naively here: If it is true, no doubt, that few persons other than professional philosophers and those highly trained in artificial languages tend to construct propositions by disjoining, the obvious rejoinder is that part of the force of philosophical argument is its concern with that which is logically possible; so the fact that Gettier's example deals with a rather nonintuitive manner of arriving at propositions is not even, standardly, the larger part of the problem. However, one wants to ask, given that one might in fact construct propositions by disjoining—or by staring at a patch on the wall, shutting one's eyes, and letting the patch become an after-image—what sorts of facts about cognitive and neural functioning are relevant? One wants to inquire why it is that elements of memory storage, retrieval from memory, sensory retention of images, capacity for inferring logical structure, and other sorts of cognitive capacities—all relevant to the sorts of examples utilized—are never referred to in the theories or relevant counterexamples? The fact that epistemological theory had originated in a completely apsychological manner (and retained its apsychological character well into the 1960s and 1970s) was a source of worry for some epistemologists and the source of still another important move in theory of knowledge, as I shall sketch shortly.

Before passing on to the more naturalized material, preparatory to our larger project, I want to spend a bit more time on the Gettier examples and the responses to them, as it has been this sort of work that has been most characteristic of postwar American epistemology. At an earlier point I indicated that the replies to the examples fell into two main groups: The first sort of reply was a causal theory and the second sort of reply fell under the rubric of defeasibility theory. The first sort of reply is perhaps more important for my project here because it is in itself somewhat more naturalized than many of the lines that preceded it.

To provide an overview, it will be recalled from the Gettier example above that one of the chief difficulties posed by the examples was giving an account of justification such that the adequate evidence clause of the tripartite knowledge condition (set forth here in my allusion to *Theaetetus* in the Introduction) was not divorced from the belief clause, nor from the events that ordinarily would have been thought to have preceded the evidence clause. If I believe that Jones owns a Ford, it is because I have mistaken this Ford rental for other Fords he has owned in the past (so, from the standpoint of general conditions, if I had a superb memory and had kept all relevant factors in mind, I would realize that this was not one of the previous Fords), or because, realizing it is not one of the previous Fords, I have assumed it is a newly purchased Ford. But if I know that Jones is somewhat hard up and if I did not actually see Jones purchase the Ford, perhaps I would not be so hasty in my judgment. And, of course, if I had actually seen Jones purchase the Ford, the linkage would not break down. The problem with the alleged justification in the example is that a trace in linkages would reveal that Jones acquired the Ford, temporarily, through a Hertz rental desk.

In "A Causal Theory of Knowing," originally printed in *Journal of Philosophy* in 1967, Alvin Goldman tries to establish a view that would get one past the sort of Gettier example just recounted. Using precisely the same Gettier example used here, Goldman writes:

> Notice that what *makes p* ["Jones owns a Ford or Brown is in Barcelona"] true is the fact that Brown is in Barcelona, but that this fact has nothing to do with Smith's believing *p*. That is, there is no causal connection between the fact that Brown is in Barcelona and Smith's believing *p*. . . . Thus one thing that seems to be missing in this example is a causal connection between the fact that makes *p* true (or simply: the fact that *p*) and Smith's belief of *p*. The requirement of such a causal connection is what I wish to add to the traditional analysis.[14]

Goldman's complete analysis goes on to cite example after example, and is of course too lengthy to be fully fleshed out here. But something still more interesting about Goldman's analysis, for our purposes, is his awareness of the sorts of psychological considerations that would have to be adduced in order for a fully causal theory to make sense, since awareness of causality is presumably related to other cognitive factors—such as memory, for one. Toward the end of his article, Goldman notes that:

> Probably there are some mental states that are clearly distinct from the subject's belief that he is in such a state. If so, then there is presumably a causal process connecting the existence of such states with the subject's belief thereof. We may add this kind of process to the list of "appropriate" causal processes. The more difficult cases are those in which the state is hardly distinguishable from the subject's believing that he is in that state.[15]

Here Goldman demonstrates an awareness of the fact that it is mental processes themselves, presumably, that need to be accounted for in any fully causal account. But a general awareness of this in epistemology was still several years off at the time of the publication of his article. More to the point, and helpful in drawing a line between the work that preceded it and the work of 1967, is Goldman's comment toward the end of the quotation above that "the state which is hardly distinguishable from the subject's believing that he is in that state" is a difficult case. That state is, of course, one of first-person privileged access, and is thus completely in line with the sorts of states to which philosophers had always sought recourse when in an epistemic pinch (as the sort of view found in the sense-data theories indicated). The recurring nature of the privileged material cannot be overemphasized, and is of the utmost importance when attempting to come to grips with the tradition as a whole.

The Goldmanian response to the Gettier examples represented just one sort of response, and the sort of answer that, as I have indicated, would over the long run lead to more naturalized views, which I will examine at a later point. But another sort of response to the Gettier counterexamples also appeared on the scene, and the second response is worth some examination. The causal theory responses at least tried to indicate that a more naturalistic view of how the agent comes into contact with the material for justification would emphasize a sequence of events, the agent's sensory awareness of the sequence, and so forth. But the earlier tradition of twentieth-century epistemology—the sort of tradition perhaps best exemplified by the excerpt from Russell, and the one that bespeaks most clearly its normative nature—is concerned almost exclusively with a logical analysis of epistemic relations, since this analysis is the sort of scrutiny that is required to create rigorously tight conditions. Marshall Swain and others prepared responses to the Gettier examples that emphasized what came to be referred to as "epistemic defeasibility"—the notion that one could possess evidence that would lead to one's complete justification (and hence to knowledge) only if one possessed evidence that was indefeasible, that is, that could not be defeated. This somewhat legalistic language was quite appropriate for the sort of analysis it labeled, since Swain's view and the views of the other defeasibility theorists placed almost exclusive emphasis on the logical relations between propositions, rather than any material-world causal relations between states of affairs that might give rise to propositions.

The difference between these two sorts of analyses is not a trivial one and is worth remarking on. In a sense, the defeasibility analyses are almost more important for my purposes, since it is clear a tradition that emphasizes logical relations is a tradition that yields the sort of normative, universalizable thinking that feminist theory has characterized as androcentric, and that we will examine more closely at a later point. To repeat, Goldman sees the problem with the examples proposed by Gettier as essentially being one of a break in the linkage between the series of facts that would ordinarily give rise to a certain justification and the justification itself. In other words, if I believe (to pull out the example once more) that Jones owns a Ford because I have seen him driving one and because I know that he has owned Fords in the past, I have overlooked the possible break in the putative linkage between his being in this Ford and his being the owner of this

Ford. But it is possible to ignore causal linkage altogether and to focus instead on a logical analysis of propositions that contain information. One could, in fact, think of the Gettier examples as situations in which the epistemic agent is deprived of knowledge because of the existence of "defeating" propositions. Propositions themselves have long been philosophically suspect, but that is somewhat beyond the point here.[16] For a no counterexamples, all-cases-covered sort of epistemology, what one perhaps ought to do is to focus on a set of necessary and sufficient conditions that would prevent the existence of "defeating" propositions to one's knowledge claim—or to phrase the matter more precisely, would render any such defeating propositions otiose. This is what the defeasibility theorists tried to do, and it is this sort of move that, in many ways, carries on the rigorous, normative, and Cartesian tradition in twentieth-century American epistemology, for the analysis of propositions required for defeasibility theory has absolutely nothing to do with cognitive functioning.

Swain's article "Epistemic Defeasibility" may serve as an exemplar of this sort of analysis.[17] Interestingly enough, Swain remarks at several points in his analysis that he is not interested in the "pipe-dream," idealized versions of knowledge bases familiar to contemporary readers of epistemology.[18] What Swain says that he means by this is that he is not interested in a sort of "God's eye view." But in fact his analysis does illustrate the sort of theorizing of which I have been writing.

At an early point in the article, Swain proposes a definition of indefeasible knowledge that will serve our purpose (though it goes through several emendations, since it is heavily counterexampled by Swain himself) as an illustration of a logical, rather than causal, analysis of the problems posed by Gettier's 1963 counterexamples.

> (ivc) $S$'s justification for $h$ is indefeasible (that is, there is no true body of evidence $e'$ such that (a) $e$ justifies $S$ in believing that $e'$ is false and (b) the conjunction of $e$ and $e'$ fails to justify $h$).[19]

Here one wants to note the phrasing of the definition. The key term is "conjunction." It is not the availability of the evidence itself that worries the epistemologist so much as the conjunction of the evidence, stated in proposition $e'$, with some defeating sentence or proposition $e$. The conjunction thus formed fails to justify $h$, the original knowledge claim, if $h$ id defeasible. In other words, if Smith were to come across the proposition "Jones now is driving a Hertz rental car" $(e)$, then the conjunction of that proposition with other propositions would defeat the original proposition "Jones owns a Ford." But this analysis completely leaves out any of the material-world conditions surrounding the knowledge claim, or any remote appeal to how—through what sensory processes—Smith came across the evidence with regard to Jones in the first place.

I will include only one more version of Swain's conditions for indefeasibility: it provides further evidence that the tightening of conditions to provide for indefeasibility is done through a restructuring of logical relations. After several more counterexamples and somewhat differing versions of the conditions—the counterexamples including examples of instantaneous paralysis under statistically unusual conditions, the sorts of concoctions that some have dubbed "philosophers' wonderland"[20]—Swain makes the following move:

> In all of these examples, where there is some negative counterevidence it consists of some proposition or set of propositions that the person $S$ is *in fact* justified in believing to be *false*. . . .
>
> A more promising approach is to consider what would happen if a man were to become justified in believing to be true *all* of those true propositions that he is in fact justified in believing to be false, and where the remainder of his epistemic situation changes only in some minimal way required to preserve consistency. We can specify what such a situation would look like by defining a type of alternative, which I shall call an *evidence-restricted* alternative:
>
> Fs* is an evidence-restricted alternative to an epistemic framework Fs if and only if (i) for every true proposition q such that "$S$ is justified in believing not-$q$" is a member of the evidence component of FS, "$S$ is justified in believing $q$" is a member of the evidence component of Fs*, (ii) for some subset C of members of Fs such that C is maximally consistent epistemically with the members generated in (i), every member of C is a member of Fs*, and (iii) no other propositions are members of Fs* except those that are implied epistemically by the members generated in (i) and (ii).
>
> . . . We can make defeasibility dependent on what would happen if one's epistemic position were to improve in just this carefully defined way by replacing our earlier condition (ive) with:
>
> (ivf) $S$'s justification for $h$ is indefeasible (that is, there is an evidence-restricted alternative Fs* to $S$'s epistemic framework Fs such that "$S$ is justified in believing that $h$" is epistemically derivable from the other members of the evidence component of Fs*).[21]

Fortunately for the analysis here, we do not need to comment on Swain's lengthy set of conditions in a way beyond the obvious: the setting up of the evidence-restricted alternative involves taking each proposition that would ordinarily have been rendered false by *h* (an example would be "Jones is driving a Hertz rental car"), assigning it a truth-value of true, placing all such propositions together in one set, and then seeing if "*S* is justified in believing that *h*" is still derivable from it. In most cases, of course, it would not be, but in the case where such a move could be made, *h* has been rendered—by analysis of the logical relations of propositions—indefeasible. The conditions are, *ex hypothesi*, universalizable and rigorously normative, and according to the tradition, this is what an account of knowledge ought to be.

I have set out two types of replies to the Gettier counterexamples because each type of reply exemplifies trends in contemporary American epistemology. As I indicated at an earlier point, there is a sense in which Swain's defeasibility response (and the other defeasibility responses generated at about the same time) stands more closely in line with the tradition as a whole than does Goldman's causal relations response, although it may be somewhat gratuitous to harp on the distinction. But if the logical relations analysis that Swain's reply typifies is at the core of much of contemporary epistemology, it is also true that shortly after the causal theories appeared in the literature a completely new tack in epistemology began to emerge—a tack that we will find to be a welcome one.


## A NATURALIZED THEORY OF KNOWLEDGE

The causal theories at least alluded, however briefly, to cognitive processes, and the nature of the theories themselves—with their emphasis on material-world relations between objects that might come to the attention of the epistemic agent through the use of the senses—lent itself to further reference to the actual functioning of intellectual and cognitive faculties. In addition, the late 1960s and early 1970s saw an enormous rise in the development of what came to be known as "cognitive science"—the intersection of areas such as psychology, linguistics, artificial intelligence, computer simulation, and computer science itself. Although there was initially little response from professional philosophers to this material, it was clear from the outset that the material was immediately relevant to issues in philosophy of mind (and, of course, in its most formal aspects, to work in pure logic itself, although that does not concern us here).[22] Epistemologists were indeed tardy in giving professional notice to the development and rise of cognitive science, but by the late 1970s the situation had begun to change. Not surprisingly, one of the first pieces by an epistemologist to suggest that the new material was not irrelevant to professional analytic epistemology was by Goldman, and soon afterward a spate of such publications appeared.[23] The first steps were tentative: The title of an early piece by Hilary Kornblith is "Beyond Foundationalism and the Coherence Theory." But longer pieces soon appeared, and finally books.[24] It may well be that some of the initial resistance on the part of many epistemologists was a desire to avoid the possibility of seeming to advocate reduction—after all, Quine in a much earlier piece entitled "Epistemology Naturalized" had seemed to recommend the replacement of epistemology by the natural and social sciences.[25] But the new wave advocated, in general, not so much the replacement of epistemology as the recognition by epistemology (or the taking into account by epistemology) of work that clearly is related to the possibility of knowledge acquisition. It is to this work that we now turn.

At a much later point, I will examine in detail the major contention that naturalized epistemology is less androcentric. Certainly it is less normative. In "Beyond Foundationalism and the Coherence Theory," which first appeared in *Journal of Philosophy* in 1980, Hilary Kornblith straightforwardly addressed the question of whether or not the actual cognitive functioning of agents could be relevant to epistemology as practiced by professional philosophers. He acknowledges that the tendency has been to believe that an "apsychologistic" approach is best, but forcefully argues that this is a mistake. He notes that traditional approaches to the theory of knowledge may be viewed as "two sides of a Kantian antinomy."[26] I intend to quote him at some length here, as I believe his initial piece is one of the most important introductions to the topic.

> One of the legacies of epistemology is a tendency to divorce epistemological questions from psychological questions. Epistemology is a normative discipline; it is concerned, among other things, with questions about how reasoning ought to proceed. Such questions can be answered, we are told, independently of investigation into the processes that in fact occur when reasoning takes place. Questions about justified belief are thus translated from the mental realm—"What kinds of transitions between mental states make for justified belief?"—to the logical realm—"What

kinds of arguments are "good" arguments?" This approach to epistemological questions pervades much of contemporary philosophy. . . . Once
this false presupposition is rejected, the insights of both foundationalism
and the coherence theory may be joined in a single unified theory of
justification.[27]

Kornblith reminds us here of the dichotomy that I claim first began
to manifest itself most clearly in contemporary philosophy in the split
between causal theories of knowledge and defeasibility theories, which
we have just examined. What is particularly noteworthy about Kornblith's wording of the situation is that the phrase "translated from the
mental realm" is especially felicitous, since it draws attention to the
fact that justification is a mental process, and that it requires some sort
of move, or translation, to take the mental process of justification
outside is natural arena and to theorize about it in terms of logical
conditions.

Kornblith goes on to assert that the standard accounts of justification
present us with criteria for what is constitutive of a good argument.
Again, these are logical criteria, or criteria structured within the
framework of logical conditions, and he calls the thesis that ventures
to claim that this is a philosophically correct account of justification
the *arguments-on-paper thesis*.

In a brief argument that reminds us of a situation with which we
should be all too familiar (if we have taught undergraduate logic),
Kornblith asserts that the fact that someone has been taught modus
ponens and the fact that this same person may know that certain
inferences follow from premises on the basis of modus ponens—or any
other tenet of derivation—does not really mean that the person will be
justified in the sentence that is supposed to constitute the modus
ponens-validated inference. As Kornblith says, justification can only
be accounted for in terms of the belief states of persons and the
relations between them.[28]

Now to see how crucial this insight is requires that we pause briefly
to recapitulate some important points that form the backdrop for the
novelty of Kornblith's thesis. I began my overview of twentieth-
century epistemology by characterizing Russell's logical atomism as
an important step in contemporary theory of knowledge, since it paved
the way for a great deal of what followed. Russell's work was important, I argued, because his delineation of the referent of logically
proper names reduced the referent to no more than a sense-datum—an
aspect of the phenomenal that could be kept going, Russell estimated,
for a couple of minutes.

It is not merely the fact that a sense-datum was alluded to that makes the structure of logical atomism important, but rather it is the emphasis on the immediacy and comparative certainty of the data when they are divorced from attempts at underlying metaphysics that is crucial. If Socrates was himself no more than a series of appearances, and if (to cite our former example) any given referent of the name "Socrates" (when employed by a speaker) was a patch or datum in the speaker's visual field, the interiority of the phenomenon and its immediacy clearly make error much less likely than it would be if one insisted on a more substantial ontology as support for the usage of names.

Russell's logical atomism gave way to Moore's work (and the work of others following sense-data lines) largely because, as I claimed earlier, it was these lines that seemed the most likely to lead to the possibility of irrefutable or incorrigible propositions. And the irrefutable or incorrigible propositions, according to Austin in his succinct analysis of the work of Ayer, Price, and others, were (if they existed at all) hedged propositions about the nature of individual sense-data as perceived by a given perceiver.

Thus the goal of epistemology was at least temporarily met. But the price paid was enormously high. It mattered perhaps comparatively little in the earlier portion of this century that epistemology was completely severed from any adequate account of cognition, since accounts of cognition were at that time relatively impoverished. But as the two decades after the war saw theory of knowledge done continuously in the same sort of way—with the closely argued, logically structured Gettier examples and their responses (particularly, again, defeasibility theory)—it became more regrettable that epistemological accounts of knowledge could not in general be instantiated in agents.

Thus, Kornblith's move (and others formulated at approximately the same time) is perhaps more of a break than one might first be inclined to think, if one did not already have access to the history of contemporary theory of knowledge. Kornblith goes on to write of the role of background beliefs in determining an agent's set of beliefs, and to provide a semi-reliabilist account of knowledge.[29] Before moving on with still more material from the naturalization of epistemology, however, I want to develop one last distinction that has been important for contemporary theory of knowledge but that I have somewhat neglected here.

The title of Kornblith's article is "Beyond Foundationalism and the Coherence Theory," and that particular distinction has been crucial in the epistemological literature of the last twenty or thirty years. I alluded to the distinction to some extent in the Introduction and employed the term "foundationalist" when discussing the Russellian atomism and sense-data theories.

Properly, foundationalism is more a theory of epistemic justification than a theory of knowledge *simpliciter*, since it is largely an attempt to explicate what would constitute justification for one's knowledge claim. (It is true, however, that many foundationalists have referred to their theories as "theories of knowledge.") Foundationalism is related to the material I have already covered, at least insofar as putative ancestry is concerned, in just this way: The foundationalist claims that a knowledge claim can be justified in a chain, or a series of chains, by basing each claim—including the original—on some other claim judged to be epistemically prior, and then finding a basic claim or stopping point beyond which, epistemically, one cannot go. This stopping point is alleged to have special epistemic status, and for most foundationalists dealing with empirical knowledge (rather than the deductive knowledge of mathematics and related fields) the stopping point has been a sentence or proposition of privileged access—in other words, precisely the sort of sentence or proposition mentioned earlier with regard to sense-data theory. If I make some sort of claim about my own inner state, such as "I seem to see a whitish patch," it is difficult (although according to many not impossible) to imagine how I could be wrong.[30] Some have glossed this as how I could be "refuted," or taking "incorrigible" as the handy phrase, how I could be corrected. After all, I have taken no great risk in claiming that "I seem to see. . . ." How could anyone else possibly know what I seem to see? And I have not claimed that the patch is white—simply whitish. And so forth. In any case, this sort of model of epistemic justification gave rise to numerous sorts of foundationalist theories, and until recently foundationalism was perhaps the theory of epistemic justification par excellence.[31] But there has always been at least one other major contender among theories of justification, and as Kornblith has indicated by giving his piece a certain title, the other contender is coherentism.

It might seem a more intuitive grasp of epistemic justification to think of our beliefs or knowledge claims as forming a web or network, where no one claim has special status but where each claim is justified simply by its place in the scheme. Coherentists have typically been concerned with consistency and other more technical sorts of problems, but the criticisms of foundationalism eventually came to be legion and coherentism has recently come to the fore.[32] We can learn

something then from examining, however briefly, these two rival theories, since it is clear, again, that each theory (as formulated classically)
is apsychological. Each theory tells us nothing about the functioning
of epistemic agents, and each theoretical stance may be thought of as
a recommendation for the way in which epistemic agents should
perform the task of justification, if that task were to be performed
ideally. But human agents rarely perform epistemic tasks in an ideal
manner.

# NOTES

1. See, for example, David Stewart and H. Gene Blocker, eds., *Fundamentals of Philosophy* (New York: Macmillan, 1987).

2. Russell, among others, feels constrained to mention the comparatively recent emergence of epistemology as eminent among the subdisciplines of philosophy. See his *A History of Western Philosophy* (New York: Simon and Schuster, 1960), especially the chapter on Descartes.

3. Ibid., 564.

4. Bertrand Russell, "The Philosophy of Logical Atomism," in *Bertrand Russell: Logic and Knowledge,* ed. Robert C. Marsh (New York: G. P. Putnam & Sons, 1971), 200–01.

5. See Jaakko Hintikka, "*Cogito, Ergo Sum:* Inference or Performance?", in *Descartes: A Collection of Critical Essays,* ed. Willis Doney (Garden City, N.Y.: Anchor/Doubleday, 1967).

6. This is a virtual platitude of the commentary on Descartes and is, of course, a point made by Descartes himself. See Descartes's *Rules;* see Russell, *A History,* 568.

7. W. V. O. Quine, "Russell's Ontological Development," in *Essays on Bertrand Russell,* ed. E. D. Klemke (Urbana-Champaign: University of Illinois Press, 1970), 8.

8. G. E. Moore, "Visual Sense-Data," in *Perceiving, Sensing and Knowing,* ed. Robert J. Swartz (Garden City, N.Y.: Doubleday Anchor, 1965), 130, 134, and 136, respectively.

9. Ibid., 136.

10. J. L. Austin, *Sense and Sensibilia* (New York: Oxford University Press, 1964), 6.

11. Ludwig Wittgenstein, *Philosophical Investigations*, 6th ed., trans. G. E. M. Anscombe (New York: Macmillan, 1953), Remark 38, p. 18e.

12. Austin, *Sense,* 34–35.

13. Edmund Gettier, "Is Justified True Belief Knowledge?," *Analysis* 23, no. 7 (1963):122–123.

14. Alvin I. Goldman, "A Causal Theory of Knowing," reprinted in *Essays on Knowledge and Justification* (Ithaca: Cornell University Press, 1978), 68.

15. Ibid., 84.

16. The origins of this view are usually associated with Quine. See, for example, the essays in his *From a Logical Point of View* (Cambridge, Mass.: Harvard University Press, 1953).

17. Reprinted in Pappas and Swain, *Essays,* 160–83.

18. Ibid., 168.

19. Ibid., 166.

20. Ibid., 167.

21. Ibid., 175–77.

22. The exception here, of course, is the work of Hubert Dreyfus, *What*

*Computers Can't Do: A Critique of Artificial Reason* (New York: Harper and Row, 1972).

23. Goldman's "Epistemics: The Regulative Theory of Cognition," appeared in *Journal of Philosophy* 75, no. 10 (1978):509–23.

24. Cf. fn. 2, *Introduction*.

25. Quine is typically read in this manner. This piece is reprinted in Kornblith *Naturalizing Epistemology* 1985b.

26. Reprinted in Kornblith, *Naturalizing Epistemology,* 115–29. This particular phrase occurs on p. 115.

27. Ibid., 115–16.

28. Ibid., 119.

29. Ibid., see 122–27 especially.

30. See Austin, in *Sense,* 111–13.

31. Even attacks on foundationalism seem to acknowledge its longtime leadership role. Mark Pastin, in attempting to construct a new version of foundationalism, seems to implicitly acknowledge both foundationalism's importance and the odd sort of respect it has received from its opponents, in "Modest Foundationalism and Self-Warrant," reprinted in Pappas and Swain, *Essays,* 279–88. See especially 280–81.

32. For an account of coherentism and the classical objections to it, see Cornman, "Foundational."

# Chapter Two

# Naturalizing Theory of Knowledge

The preceding discussion of twentieth-century analytic epistemology has provided a backdrop for the introduction of naturalized epistemology—a necessary backdrop, for the advances made in recent years in merging lines of research in the cognitive sciences with epistemology itself can only be appreciated when it is understood how deeply, according to some, these advances go against the grain.

In particular, I emphasized during my development of the contrast between the two sorts of responses to the Gettier examples (causal theories and defeasibility theories) how fully analytic and traditionally epistemological defeasibility responses were. With their concern for an analysis of the concept of knowledge in terms of necessary and sufficient conditions that would leave no room for counterexampling, the defeasibility analyses had the virtue of standing in the mainstream of American analytic epistemology while possessing all the flaws that such an analysis, devoid of adversion to cognitive functioning, could exemplify.

In this chapter I hope to provide an overview of recent developments in the naturalization of epistemology, similar to the overview of contemporary Anglo-American theory of knowledge that was provided in the previous chapter. So far I have sketched the positions, while providing comparatively little commentary on the androcentric nature of the theorizing itself (see the Introduction). Although that is essentially the task of the next chapter, certain strands of argument should be fairly clear at this point and need to be kept in mind if the larger project is to unfold clearly. In my outline of analytic epistemology, the very sorts of theoretical traits I have just mentioned as consistently coming to the fore—analysis in terms of logically necessary and sufficient conditions, lack of allusion to descriptively adequate models, the importance of counterexampling, putative universalizability of the conditions, and so forth—are in fact the sorts of traits that the feminist theorists have dubbed androcentric. It is important to bear this in mind, since my later development of a naturalized and gynocentric model will depend significantly on contrast with the nonnaturalized, androcentric models that precede it.

If contemporary analytic epistemology may be thought of as nonnaturalized and androcentric, the current naturalization of theory of knowledge at least strikes the positive note of moving in another direction. If, as some theorists have contended, gynocentric thinking tends to concern itself with the particular and the contextualized (or as Bordo has it, the "View From Everywhere"), the newer naturalized material is already somewhat less androcentric simply insofar as it is more context sensitive and less concerned with a highly idealized universalizability.[1] It comes as no surprise, however, that the naturalized material began to come to the fore in epistemology because of moves made within the established body of theory itself.

Broadly speaking, the origins of the project of naturalization seem to lie in two, somewhat disparate, theoretical areas. The first has already been examined here: The structure of the Gettier examples was such that allusion to causal processes was a likely response, and such allusion is, of course, allusion to conditions that can be empirically confirmed and hence that stand apart from logically structured conditions. But the second locus of generation for naturalizing epistemology appears to fall more under the rubric of sociology of philosophy, or perhaps sociology of the sciences, to the extent that philosophy intersects with them. The sheer ubiquitousness and frequency of citations to the progress of cognitive science in many disciplines made it more-or-less inevitable that philosophers concerned with the problem of knowledge would at least come across such material, even if their initial reaction was to declaim the irrelevancy of cognitive psychology or computer simulation to theory of knowledge.

## GOLDMANIAN NATURALIZATION

As I indicated earlier, Alvin Goldman's work was among the first to appear in major journals that made use of the new material. In the preceding chapter I argued that the move from a causal theory of knowledge, as a reply to the failure of the tripartite traditional theory, to a still more naturalized view of epistemology was an easy and fluid one, given the nature of previous theorizing. Nevertheless, Goldman's first articles in this area (and pieces published around the same time by other philosophers as well) typically contain several paragraphs of introductory explanation, as it were, on the importance and relevance of cognitive science to epistemology.

An early piece in *The Monist*, published in 1978 and entitled "Epistemology and the Psychology of Belief" contains this argument:

> Epistemology has always been concerned with mental states, especially doxastic states, such as belief, suspension of judgment, and the like. A significant part of epistemology is the attempt to evaluate, appraise, or criticize alternative procedures for the formation of belief and other doxastic attitudes. . . . What epistemology has not done—at least 20th century analytic epistemology hasn't done it—is to seek help from experimental psychology in choosing its doxastic categories. . . . If epistemology is in the business of saying what psychological states a cognizer should be in in various circumstances, or what states it would be rational or intelligent for him to be in, we need as good a specification as possible of the range of psychological states open to him. . . . One might well suspect that systematic pursuit of cognitive psychology might yield a richer and more accurate set of doxastic descriptions than intuitive thought alone can do.[2]

Apparently Goldman feels it necessary to explain—over and over again—why epistemology can and should utilize empirical material from the cognitive sciences. In this comparatively early piece, Goldman is quite specific about the subareas of theory of knowledge that might be aided by cognitive psychology. He lists them as (1) the relationships of belief to consciousness, (2) the structure of beliefs, (3) alternative representational codes, and (4) the strength of beliefs.[3]

Since we are at the beginning of our view of naturalized epistemology, it might be helpful to see more precisely what Goldman means. Painting in broad strokes, any material having to do with belief acquisition should be relevant to epistemology because the tripartite framework (and the criticisms of it) all contain or examine a belief clause. Goldman notes that even traditional theory of knowledge has made use of some distinctions regarding beliefs, such as what had previously been dubbed "occurrent" and "dispositional" beliefs.[4] But as he also notes, this distinction has its more empirically accurate home in the distinction that psychologists would label as that between STM and LTM—between short-term and long-term memory. As in so many other areas relevant to an overview of knowledge acquisition, much work had already been done in this area by the later 1970s, most of it either unavailable to philosophers, or more importantly, unnoticed by philosophers even when it was available. As Goldman asserts, work on memory and belief would make some portions of the belief clauses of various epistemological theories more sophisticated, were they to be incorporated, and on the other hand such empirical work might vitiate or alter what philosophers had taken to be crucial epistemic distinctions. He states,

> The degree of accessibility or retrievability from long-term memory varies from item to item. . . . What seems important for epistemology is to recognize the range of psychological states that we can broadly think of as bearing or carrying "information," states that have some potential usefulness for interacting with other cognitions and ultimately guiding behavior. . . . In particular, why should normative or regulative episte- mology be concerned with these matters? One reason is simply that normative epistemology's principles or injunctions will be ambiguous unless these distinctions are observed.[5]

In other words, as Goldman is at pains to point out, if our epistemo- logical theory tells us that we ought to believe *p*, we need more information on what sort of belief state for *p* is actually being enjoined. A century ago, when psychology and philosophy were more-or-less in the same harness, such information could not have been made avail- able. But the information is here now, and the onus is on the episte- mologist to make use of it, on pain of theorizing incoherently about cognitive states.

Goldman goes on to point out how each of the remaining three subareas listed above could be made more theoretically precise through the use of material from cognitive psychology. Later articles in *Synthese* and *Midwest Studies in Philosophy* developed these no- tions still further, and finally a book, *Epistemology and Cognition*, resulted.[6] Although I cannot go into the particulars of the theory in much greater detail here, a cursory look at some of the topics covered in the book is helpful in creating an outline of areas pertinent to naturalized epistemology. The legacy of previous work in analytic theory of knowledge was a large one, so some topics for naturalized epistemology were a direct outgrowth of previous theorizing.[7] *Episte-*

*mology and Cognition* contains chapter titles such as "Problem Solving, Power and Speed" (ch. 6), "Constraints on Representation" (ch. 11), and "Internal Codes" (ch. 12). There are also chapters with more traditional titles, such as "Skepticism" (ch. 2) and "Perception" (ch. 9). The large section title for Part II of the work is "Assessing our Cognitive Resources." By the time this work appeared, almost a decade after the earliest journal article cited above, the naturalization of epistemology was well under way.

My focus thus far has been on analytic epistemology, specifically its origins and contemporary work, naturalized though it may be, that might still fall into that category. There is another area of analytic philosophy, however, that itself intersects easily with epistemology, and in which some of the naturalized material made its first inroads. I refer, of course, to philosophy of mind. The computational model of mind developed from work in cognitive science meshed quite naturally with already functionalist accounts of mind that have gained currency in the past twenty years, and philosophers of mind could scarcely escape utilization of the more empirical material. With any sort of empirical work on the mind/brain at a premium, one pattern that emerged during the move toward naturalization in epistemology was that an issue was picked up first in philosophy of mind and then in theory of knowledge. For some issues—such as belief—inchoate theory was replaced by more sophisticated, developed lines only after several rounds of interchange between cognitive scientists (including, of course, linguists, anthropologists, computer scientists, psychologists, and so forth), philosophers of mind, and epistemologists. I want to turn next to more work by Kornblith, some of whose work I examined in the previous chapter, before moving on to work in philosophy of mind that has an obvious impact on the naturalization of epistemology.

## KORNBLITH AND THE EMPHASIS
## ON SOCIAL CONSTRUCTION

As opposed to Goldman's work, which has tended to emphasize the categories of cognitive science and even artificial intelligence (AI) in developing lines for the naturalization of epistemology, the work of Hilary Kornblith has focused more on the social interactions of individuals and their cognitive and epistemological ramifications. In a recent journal piece, "Some Social Features of Cognition," Kornblith argues that there are important dispositions, social in practice and effect, with regard to our interactions with others and the weight of their opinions upon us.[8] Like much of the work that has preceded it, this article is an important break with the genealogy of mainstream theory of knowledge. As recently as a decade ago, epistemologists almost never emphasized the social features of knowledge—indeed, to do so would have been to violate the sacrosanct, since it was understood that the goal of epistemology was to give an account consonant with truth and the avoidance of error, none of which has anything to do with the social aspects of knowledge acquisition. More importantly for our purposes, Kornblith's account not only deals with the social features of knowledge acquisition but also points out that there is such a thing as justification from an internal perspective that would not count at all as justification from an external truth-seeking (God's eye) perspective.

Kornblith begins his piece by noting that the social features of cognition are evident from an early age:

> From birth, each person in our society is exposed to a vast quantity of information. A significant source of a child's belief is the child's parents. At least early on, children accept what their parents tell them at face value and uncritically. Children do not accept what their parents say because they have found them to be generally reliable sources of information on mundane matters; at least early on, children are incapable of running such checks on their parents. The fact is that children merely do accept what their parents say, and this uncritical attitude serves them well.[9]

Note the last two sentences in the above quotation. They are very much in contrast to what we have seen of epistemology up to now. Kornblith actually goes so far as to say that the uncritical attitude of children to what their parents say "serves them well." Until recently, the standard epistemological approach to such material would have emphasized concern about the truth-values of statements that might be uttered to small children, and the child's seeming lack of capacity (admitted by Kornblith) to make those sorts of distinctions. Presumably, an agent so young as to be unable to perform the requisite distinctions is no epistemic agent at all—or so the argument would have gone until a few years ago. But Kornblith is utilizing two or three recent trends in epistemology and developing new lines of argument based on these trends.

The first trend strikingly employed is reference to "reliable sources of information." "Reliable" is a term now in common usage because of reliabilist theories of knowledge, an offshoot of the causal theories examined earlier, and also associated with Goldman. A second significant trend, a manifestation of the social emphasis, is the use of other persons (here the parents) as sources of information, rather than some more neutral source—environmental pickup, the senses operating on discrete contexts, and so forth. The third trend, already discussed, is the tacit admission that despite the fact that an epistemic agent may be unable to run a check on a source of information, the source is not necessarily unutilizable or epistemically unworthy. These three trends, taken together, represent enormous changes in the last decade in epistemology.

Kornblith's article goes on to cite various experiments, familiar from psychology courses, that provide empirical evidence for the contention that adults frequently modify their beliefs to cohere with the beliefs of other adults, even where such modification is manifestly a move toward falsity.[10] Now where previous epistemologists would have spoken of "veracious inquirers" and the paucity of evidence to support the move of an adult confused by, say, some optical illusion about which she is receiving false information, Kornblith's point in the citation of such information is to reinforce the notion that, in general, our tendencies to acquire the beliefs of others serve us well, not poorly. Such a line of argument is particularly unusual when one recalls the numerous examples in the recent literature of addled epistemic agents who believe, for all the wrong reasons, in such phenomena as clairvoyance and precognition. If it is clear that the tendency to believe in such phenomena is reinforced in our society on an everyday basis by the popularity of reports about the alleged phenomena and the ubiquitousness of celebrities purporting to be true believers, one can scarcely say anything more epistemically heterodox than to assert that our tendencies to believe what others believe serve us well.

Now Kornblith makes these points because he wants to remind us of "the lack of integration . . . between the ways we acquire our beliefs and our beliefs about the way we do and ought to acquire our beliefs."[11] But, to repeat, to say so much is to say something new within theory of knowledge. It is clear that at this juncture in the literature the sway of the highly normative has somewhat palled, and descriptive tendencies have come to the fore in epistemology as well as in other areas that have been affected by cognitive science.

In two other journal articles, "The Psychological Turn" and "Ever Since Descartes," Kornblith details further what the naturalization of epistemology might amount to.[12] In "Ever Since Descartes," Kornblith notes that "questions which Descartes treated as interchangeable will have to be separated by naturalistically-minded epistemologists."[13] Throughout the paper, he reminds us that some questions the Cartesian tradition has treated as normatively epistemological are in fact susceptible to empirical answer, and that to fail to take empirical responses to these questions into consideration when doing epistemology is to miss a very important point. For example, Kornblith notes that Descartes was attempting (in contemporary formulation) to answer such questions as "How ought we, objectively speaking, to arrive at our beliefs? What processes available to us, if any, are conducive to truth?" But, Kornblith responds, "the question of the reliability of various belief-acquisition processes is a straightforward empirical question."[14] The Cartesian tradition, Kornblith argues, has insisted that we describe every idealized move of the epistemic agent in terms of whether or not the move is available internally to the agent and whether it is something that fits the agent's subjective (internally felt) scheme. However, as Kornblith contends, many reliable mental processes have no internally felt analogues (a point made in the paper I described earlier), and the agent may still nevertheless be epistemically justified in every respect if such justification is seen from a perspective other than the internal.

In "The Psychological Turn," he is still more precise about the advantage such a turn may have for epistemology in the long run.

> An apsychologistic theory of knowledge is characterized by a rule for determining a privileged class of beliefs, and a set of epistemic rules. Given the set of an agent's beliefs at a particular time, we first apply the rule for determining the privileged class of beliefs, the result of which, of course, is a set of beliefs. To this set of beliefs we apply the various epistemic rules. The set of beliefs thus determined are those which the agent is justified in believing at the time in question. An agent is justified in believing a particular proposition at a particular time just in case that proposition is a member of the set determined by applying epistemic rules to the privileged class of beliefs for that agent at that time.[15]

With this description Kornblith characterizes succinctly the rule-bound, logically structured nature of normative epistemology, with the rules here being, of course, the formal rules for set determination, completely divorced from rules of cognitive functioning (whether those rules be determined by the computational model or some other model).

Kornblith goes on to argue, at length and quite forcefully, that epistemology requires naturalization and "[a] complete rethink[ing] of the motivation for our epistemological projects," because we owe it to ourselves as cognizers to rid ourselves of bad epistemic habits.[16] Furthermore, the portrayal of cognitive processes has advanced so rapidly that we are in as much position to utilize empirical knowledge to rid ourselves of poor epistemic habits and attitudes as we are, say, to rid ourselves of poor driving habits and attitudes.

Kornblith's work has been extremely important in setting out the ways in which epistemology can be naturalized, and perhaps more importantly, delineating the ways in which, in the past, it has failed to be naturalistic. If one thinks of the process of answering the question about epistemic justification—the process of theorizing about the hoary third condition of the traditional tripartite view of knowledge that we have already examined—simply as an exercise in specifying the logical, deductive (or inductive) rules that an agent might follow under idealized conditions to yield a justified true belief, one works within the framework of the Platonic and Cartesian traditions. But if one attempts to answer this question in a manner that takes into account our empirical knowledge of how agents actually do go about justifying claims, one is failing to do epistemology, according to the more traditional theorists of knowledge. It is this sort of response that Kornblith's work attempts to put to rest. The assumption—motivated by whatever considerations—that naturalized material is irrelevant to epistemology is an assumption that, according to Kornblith, Goldman, and other theorists, is damaging epistemology. If, as I shall argue at length at a later point, naturalized epistemology is more than relevant to feminist theory, the work of those who have insisted on the naturalization of epistemology is at the forefront of what feminist theory needs to master.

## PHILOSOPHY OF MIND AND THE TURN TOWARD THE NATURALIZED

At an earlier point I made the distinction between recent work in epistemology, naturalized or nonnaturalized, and work in other areas of analytic philosophy that might prove relevant to theory of knowledge, such as philosophy of mind. This distinction is particularly important for my project here, since some of the most valuable work that might be utilized in any naturalization of epistemology has appeared in contemporary analytic philosophy first in philosophy of mind and/or philosophy of psychology. This is, of course, not at all surprising, since it is this area of philosophical endeavor that is most closely linked to the work being done in cognitive psychology and the cognitive sciences as a whole.

I want to turn now to some of the more recent work on mind, both philosophical and nonphilosophical, with the hope that the tie-in to naturalized epistemology will become more obvious as I sketch the outlines of the theoretical work. The cognitive revolution, as it has been called, is now so well known in most areas of academic effort as to need no introduction. It is a revolution that took place in the 1950s and 1960s, roughly speaking, as behavioristic models in psychology, sociology, anthropology, and the social sciences in general began to give way to models more mentalistic in origin. The new mentalism, however, bore little or no resemblance to the old dualistic mentalism of the past (itself, of course, an offspring of Cartesian views). The new cognitive or mentalistic outlook was essentially monistic (materialistic), and hence required no metaphysical or ontological split to establish itself. More importantly for psychological theorizing, the original impetus behind the cognitive move in psychology was to avoid some of the problems associated with the old stimulus–response, behavioristic patterns. Since these patterns were frequently associated with a die-hard positivistic stance, and since that stance itself became discredited (due to the work of Quine and others) around this same period, a theoretical replacement was sorely needed.

The notion that it might be possible to develop a model of cognitive functioning that did not require an unnecessarily burdensome metaphysics and that was more in line with advances made in the still-nascent computer science began to take root over thirty years ago. The history of the revolution has been repeated in numerous publications (entire books have been devoted to the early years of cognitive science), so I will not reiterate it here.[17] By the late 1960s the emphasis in psychology had changed from behaviorism to the computational model of mind, and cognitive psychology, once pushed to the wayside or ignored, had become predominant among the subdisciplines of psychology.

This material first made its appearance in philosophy of mind in the functionalist accounts associated with Putnam and others. The notion that mental functions could be specified, independent of the mental strata in which they were embedded, was an important one and has been crucial to further developments in philosophy of mind. Not that mind/brain identity has not been assumed—it has been assumed, but it is part and parcel of most of the contemporary models that the account specified could be instantiated in any "hardware." Brain matter, computers, tin cans, and clockwork devices all count as hardware, and the model is indifferent as to which hardware might be employed.

Most importantly, philosophy of mind has tended to be concerned with a critique of the computational model of mind, the model borrowed directly from cognitive science, which asserts that the mind functions with neuronal flip-flops, à la a computer or computational device, and that the logical relations of these flip-flops (the syntax) combined with appropriate representations (the interpretational semantics) constitute the language of thought. Daniel Dennett, Stephen Stich, and Owen Flanagan have done recent important books that examine the philosophical questions surrounding the computational model (what inherent inconsistencies, if any, does it possess? is it consistent with a primitive notion, left over from homespun psychologizing, such as "belief?"), its history, and so forth.[18] One area related to such theorizing had until recently been left unexplored, however. The actual neurophysiological relations inherent in the brain itself had in general not been captured by the computational model because of the model's insistence on being above mere matters of instantiation. Neuropsychology and the neurological sciences continued to advance, however, and it soon became clear (again) that sufficient empirical progress had been made so that to attempt to avoid mention of the structure of the brain was to attempt to avoid the obvious.

## CHURCHLAND AND NEUROPHILOSOPHY

One of the most important recent advances in philosophy of mind is the work done in Patricia Smith Churchland's *Neurophilosophy*; here she assumes that the structure of the brain is not irrelevant to questions in philosophy of mind, and more importantly, she argues that the question of the instantiation of mind models is an important one. Specifically, the book argues for a position that is essentially reductionist: The mind is the brain (not just any piece of hardware that one chooses to regard as an appropriate vehicle for the computational model), and the computational model itself, with some modifications, is susceptible to reduction to neurophysiological relations. The book argues forcefully that the nonreductionist view of some cognitive psychologists and other theorists of the mind is now out of date and beside the point.

This argument is, of course, pro-naturalistic and then some for epistemology, since it would seem to imply not only that epistemologists cannot afford to ignore cognitive functioning, but that there is already extant specific material about cognitive functioning that is model-specific (i.e., brain-specific) and that is already reduced, insofar as specification of neuronal processes is a reduction from a non-neuronal model. With regard to the computational model of mind and its relationship to research done by physiologists, doctors of medicine, and others on the brain itself, Churchland writes:

> In most variations on this anti-reductionist theme, [functionalist or computational accounts], the computer metaphor is prominent, for a variety of reasons. . . . By contrast, neurobiology is assumed to address neither of these levels [logical relations or semantic constraints] but rather to be focused on the architecture—that is, on the level of the mechanism.[19]

In other words, despite the importance of the hardware [architecture], recent accounts of mind have tended to dismiss it or ignore it. Although this nonspecific move might at one point have represented some sort of advance in the social sciences, since for years the anti-mentalistic behavioristic forces held sway, it can hardly be unimportant to address the issue of instantiation now, since we have access to so much more research on the brain, and since the notion of a mentalistic model is already assumed in so many areas of psychological theorizing.

Churchland's reductionism is important not only for the issues it raises that might be helpful to the project of naturalizing epistemology, but also because the question of reducibility forces us to examine more closely the computational model of mind. Crudely speaking, the computational model is concerned with syntax—that is, the structure of the language of thought, the neuronal flip-flops that are the analogue of the computer's 1's and 0's—only at the level of hardware, or architecture (hence the question of instantiation, with which we were just concerned). But more intriguingly for issues in philosophy of mind and theory of knowledge both, intentionality itself—the aspect of the mental that is deemed most characteristic of human functioning and that might almost be considered a hallmark of the mental—is at the heart of the computational model, although in a rather odd way.

Any intentional state or propositional attitude—any mental state that takes an object, whether that object is deemed to be a sentence, a material-world object, or still another mental state—may be thought of, under the computational model, as a set of representations. The representation is simply that which is semantically encoded; it is the interpretation thrown up by the syntax of the language of thought. Part and parcel of the original theoretical impetus behind the notion of representation was the desire to account for what appeared, in initial theorizing, to be a gap in the causal chain. We are still not at a level in physicalistic theorizing that would allow us to describe the causal chain that leads, presumably, directly from neuronal firing at synapses to everyday activities like driving a car or writing a paper. The computational model, not at all concerned with the material instantiation of its features, was designed at least partially to try to account for this causal lacuna. Zenon Pylyshyn had originally described the motivation in these terms:

> [There is a distinction] between processes governed by semantic principles (which I call "cognitive processes") and those realized in what I call the "functional architecture" of the system. . . . According to the position I have taken, processes carried out in the functional architecture are processes whose behavior requires no explanation in terms of semantic regularities. . . . Plainly, what is going on is, my behavior is being caused by certain states of my brain. Yet—and this is the crux of the problem— the only way to explain why those states caused me to type the specific sentences about walking, writing, the mountains and so on is to say that these states are in some way related to the things referred to (writing, walking, mountains). . . . My brain states are not, as we have noted, causally connected in appropriate ways to walking and to mountains. The relationship must be one of content: a semantic, not a causal, relation.[20]

The original point of the model, then, was to correlate the symbolic codes—codes actually embedded in the hardware, so to speak—with the appropriate semantic interpretations to obtain the brain state that is "about" the requisite intentional object (mountains, ice cream, automobiles). The goal was to provide an account of mental functioning that would enable one to make the theoretical move between the realm of mundane activities we all inhabit and the brain states that we would like to believe are at the causal root of the activities, even though we cannot, at this point, specify the causal process. Thus Churchland's work is crucially important, since she is arguing forcefully that we can, in the long run in any case, be much more specific about the architecture—the brain states—than we have been in the past. Her point is that the logical/semantic relations that have been deemed to constitute the core of the computational model are in principle reducible to states in the brain, and that we are moving in the direction of such reduction rather sooner than some might have thought.

One is constrained to note also the analogy between the logical–semantic relationships posed by the computational model of mind (and adhered to religiously by those who argue against in-principle reducibility) and the sorts of relationships between propositions or between propositions and an epistemic agent posed by the highly normative epistemological theories examined in the previous chapter. It has in general been characteristic of twentieth-century analytic philosophy that problems are thought of in terms of logical relations; this pretheoretical stance, which may to some extent beg the question, prohibits theoreticians from seeing that there are any other possible approaches to the problem. In other words, a move toward naturalization, whether in philosophy of mind, epistemology, or some other area of philosophy, is always suspect. As I have argued previously, this is true at least in part because the problems have been formulated in such a way as to preclude a move outside the realm of the straightforwardly logical. All of the foregoing is, of course, consonant with the style of androcentric theorizing that has been examined by feminist theorists and others concerned with the theoretical imbalance inherent in the rigidly analytic approaches. How far such an approach may go, and to what extent such an approach might be thought to be androcentric to the point of bias from the outset is itself an area for investigation, but the relation between the sort of theorizing that Churchland criticizes for its failure to recognize the possibility of naturalization and the sort of theorizing in epistemology *simpliciter* that I have portrayed in the previous chapter is a striking one.

Churchland addresses, somewhat obliquely, this sort of tendency in theorizing when she spells out the anti-reductionist stance and the motivations that have fueled it.

> The real obstacle to reduction, it is claimed, is the intentionality of mental states; that is, the fact that they have content. For explanations at the intentional level are of a radically different nature from those at levels that do not advert to representations and content. . . . Where the idea [the anti-reductionist idea] does get support is (1) from the venerable tradition in philosophy according to which the logical-meaningful dimension of mental business cannot be explained naturalistically, and (2) from unjustified assumptions about limitations of neuroscience.[21]

Here Churchland articulates my point, and also makes the larger point that there is nothing in contemporary neuroscience that leads in the direction of precluding reduction; rather, the argument is the other way around.

The final effect of Churchland's effort is to remind us of the importance of acquainting ourselves as rigorously and thoroughly as possible with material in the cognitive sciences that might aid us in the task of providing an account of knowledge. The objection, held by the traditional theorists, that empirical material is not relevant to the sorts of questions about knowledge and epistemic justification asked by philosophers, cannot be sustained, and it is philosophical argument by those trained in the analytic tradition that is moving forcefully against it.

The upshot of the naturalization of views of the mental for further theorizing is that an empirically accurate model of the way in which agents actually function will almost doubtlessly reveal trends in behavior that are more consonant with several lines of endeavor suggested by feminist theorists. The foregoing will provide us with fructifying material for review at a later point, but it will suffice now to mention the following: All that we know currently about input/output conditions, both from the standpoint of the neurosciences themselves, and from the standpoint of non-instantiated models, such as the computational model, suggests that input conditions for cognitive functioning are affected markedly by environment, and in such a way as to render the abstracted, environmentally irrelevant theorizing of the traditional epistemologists otiose. Earlier I cited Kornblith's appraisal of the Asch experiments (showing suggestibility of agents, in accordance with social conditions) as an example of more recent epistemological trends that are contextually sensitive and naturalized. Kornblith's work, as well as Goldman's, is noteworthy precisely because it deems social factors to be relevant; more importantly, the greater part of what is known about cognitive functioning within and without the neurosciences backs up Kornblith's claim and reinforces the contention that contextually neutralized thinking is out of date and wrong-headed.

The point to be made more forcefully later on is that the strain in feminist thinking that has emphasized the contextual grounding of gynocentric models may be more accurate for all humans than even some feminist theorists are initially prepared to admit. In other words, what we are learning about human cognitive functioning reveals all agents as contextually bound figures sensitive to input–output constraints. The androcentric normative models are just that—idealized models, created by men and in the masculine style, which are empirically inadequate. Feminist or gynocentric models that emphasize environmental influence and the effects of social interaction on the general epistemologial functioning of humans (whether scientists, office workers, or children playing hop-scotch) are turning out to be more complete and appropriate than could initially have been imagined.

## BAKER AND THE SALVATION OF BELIEF

Still further work on the computational model and philosophy of mind in general reveals interesting theoretical permutations and epicycles, many of which are relevant to theory of knowledge. Lynne Rudder Baker, in *Saving Belief*, sketches four sorts of stances held by those who are doing contemporary work in philosophy of mind; each stance is related not only to empirical work in cognitive science, but also to problems of knowledge acquisition and justification.

Roughly speaking, the stances depicted by Baker comprise possible theoretical positions with regard to one of the questions posed earlier, the question of whether or not "folk-theoretical" notions such as belief can survive scrutiny and live within a computational model of mind. Here is part of Baker's depiction of the four standpoints:

> I shall consider these possible outcomes of physicalist psychology:
>
> (i) First is the approach to physicalistic psychology most hospitable to the common-sense conception. On this approach, the common-sense concepts of beliefs and other attitudes are considered largely correct (by physicalistic standards) and able to be rendered suitable for the explanatory purposes of science. . . .
>
> (ii) An approach less hospitable to the common-sense conception, but one that still leaves room for particular attributions of attitudes—the approach I call "weakly reductive"—holds that the common-sense concepts are incorrect but that they are extensionally equivalent to correct ones. . . .
>
> (iii) The third approach repudiates the common-sense conception altogether. According to it, common-sense concepts are incorrect and extensionally non-equivalent to the concepts in terms of which human behavior is truly explained, and the incompatibility between common-sense concepts and the correct scientific concepts render the common-sense concepts illegitimate. . . .
>
> (iv) The final, instrumentalistic approach deems the common-sense conception to be empirically false, yet worthy of retention. . . . Because

of their convenience and practical value, they [the common-sense concepts] retain a kind of legitimacy.[22]

Baker goes on to argue for an essentially moderate position. Physicalistic theory cannot save or vindicate common-sense concepts such as belief in any full-blooded sense, but we cannot do without them either. What is most helpful about the thoroughness of Baker's approach is the extent to which the various positions with regard to folk psychological concepts sketched in her account of contemporary philosophy of mind help us to come to grips with the notion of a naturalized epistemology. Positions (ii) and (iii), as sketched above, are particularly important, since they are in the forefront currently and since (iii), in particular, seems to be related to questions of reductionism.

In her overview, Baker identifies (ii) and (iii) both, at times, with positions of Paul Churchland and Stephen Stich. If (ii) is, as she claims, rightly titled "weakly reductive," then surely (iii) is "strongly reductive." And if, as was claimed in the preceding section under the discussion of Patricia Smith Churchland's *Neurophilosophy*, most of what is currently known about the mind is in-principle reducible at some later point to neuronal functioning, then (iii) is a very important position indeed. Position (iii) is, of course, eliminativist, and Baker also notes with regard to this particular position that "On this view, no sentence of the form '*S* believes that *p*' expresses, or has ever expressed, a truth, and no such sentence can explain anything."[23] Since there is no extensional equivalence between propositional attitudes and the relevant brain states (in completed theory, of course—a state at which we have yet to arrive) there can be no ascertainment of the truth conditions inherent in a sentence that assigns belief states, wish states, or any other propositional attitudes, and the best that could be said of such sentences is that they are nonconfirmable. Since they are, *ex hypothesi*, nonconfirmable, they cannot figure in any interesting empirical view of the mind, or in any established scientific cognitive theory.

More importantly, it is precisely these states that have always played a paramount role in theory of knowledge since, of course, it is the belief condition that is the propositional attitude condition relevant to knowledge claims. If *p* is known, on the tripartite account, it is not merely the case (for example) that *S* wishes that *p* were true, since wishing clearly is not a strong enough condition to impart the forceful cognitive state characteristic of "knowledge." (It does, in fact, carry with it a connotation that the epistemic agent has a suspicion that $p$ is not the case.) What is required, of course, is that $S$ believe that $p$ is true, and if the future neuroscience that one might desire to employ for the naturalization of epistemology casts doubt on (or deems irrelevant) belief statements, traditional epistemology is gone.

But this is, as a matter of fact, the likely future of epistemology. Assuming that neuroscience proceeds apace, and assuming the correctness of (iii), the traditional language of anything like a theory of knowledge would have to be altered. "Belief" would have no place; specification of relevant brain states would.[24] Even more moderate positions like (ii) do normative epistemology great damage, and position (iv) is a tacit admission that the worth of propositional attitude terms lies in their non-nomological use.[25] The only view that would vindicate, in any substantial way, contemporary epistemology belief talk is view (i), which Baker associates with Fodor. But it is perhaps the least popular of the four views, and in any case, it is not clear precisely what "rendered suitable for the explanatory purposes of science" means in this context.

The further one pursues the project of examining contemporary philosophy of mind for its relevance to the project of naturalizing epistemology, the more one is struck by the difficulty of formulating anything like the tripartite theory of knowledge in terms that would satisfy contemporary models of mind. It is not just (as Goldman has suggested) that the belief condition is unspecific (what sort of belief?), and not simply, as Kornblith has asked us to consider, that the belief condition as usually formulated leaves out many of the contextual circumstances of belief acquisition, including the social ones. It is, more importantly, that it is not clear, based on trends in contemporary cognitive science, that belief talk, wish talk, desire talk, or similar sorts of attudinal talk really mean anything within the framework of an empirically developed model of mind. The fact that leading theoreticians cannot agree on this does not, of course, offer us any aid and comfort if we would like to pretend, in a craven way, that disagreement saves the folk model. The amount of controversy on the topic indicates that the demise of the folk model is very near, if indeed it has not already occurred. The normative epistemology based on logical relations that we examined in the preceding chapter relied for its impact on an assumption that everyone knew what belief was, for, after all, one has the ordinary uses of the term, and so forth. (One can, in fact, see here the somewhat obvious hand of a thinker like Austin, who would have been much more easily able to say, in 1949, that we all knew what we meant by "belief.")

What this sort of epistemology could not have foreseen—and might not have cared about, in any case—was the rise and development of nomological models of mind that were empirically confirmable and that gave us precise information on the hardware in which they were instantiated. If the initial impact of the computational model was partly due to its lack of specificity about instantiation, that glow wore off to some extent and has been replaced by an even stronger ambience—the ambience due to certitude of instantiation in the neural networks of the brain. Once the various theses of mind functioning have passed through the alembic of brain instantiation, one is left with an extremely specific and extremely reduced model that, it appears, will have no use for the language of folk psychology.

At an earlier point in the text I indicated that the position dubbed by Baker (i) is the position that offers the most hope for a naturalized epistemology or account of mind in which something like our ordinary notion of belief could figure. But, as it happens, Baker does a good job of arguing against this position in her work, and the force and clarity of her argument help to impress upon us the necessity of acquainting ourselves with and accepting on some level positions (ii) and (iii). I want to take time now to examine Baker's analysis of (i) (as exemplified by the work of Fodor), for I hope it will show the detailed philosophy of mind that is necessary for a naturalized epistemology, and the difficulty of retaining a folk psychology that would be concomitant to it.

Baker devotes the first full chapter of her work ("Belief in Cognitive Science") to a detailed account of the position that would purport to save propositional attitudes in something like their full-fledged sense within a computational model of mind.[26] She notes at the outset that "Fodor sees himself as heir to seventeenth- and eighteenth century representational conceptions of the mind. . . . The task of cognitive science, on such a view, is to bring a version of that conception up to date."[27] Tersely, what Fodor tries to do is to create an account of belief and other propositional attitudes that is consonant with at least one version of the computational model by ascribing to contentful mental states (propositional attitudes) a causal role in the production of behavior. Now as we saw at an earlier point in examining Patricia Smith Churchland's work, the motivation for the ascription of logical relations status (rather than causal relations status) to representations and the mind is the desire to avoid leaving representations out of the account altogether, since according to many thinkers, their role clearly could not be causal.[28] Thus the very fact that Fodor wants to assign a causal status to representations, the semantically interpreted analogues of the syntactical flip-flopping in the computational model, should be a sign to us of the originality of his view and the problems it faces. Baker's move is to show that there are counterexamples to his notion of the sort of role representations can play. Since the argument is sophisticated and somewhat difficult here, it is necessary to quote Baker at length:

> Fodor has taken cognitive science to be defined by two theses:
> (1) *The content condition.* Mental states are relations to representations, and mental processes are operations on representations, which are identified "opaquely" by "that"-clauses.
> (2) The formality condition. Mental processes are "formal," in that they apply to representations by virtue of their nonsemantic (e.g., syntactic, computational, functional, physical) properties.
> Fodor's argument for the content condition is that attributions of beliefs and the like, via "that"-clauses, are required for explaining action.[29]

Now in a complicated but easily understood counterexample, Baker manages to destroy most of Fodor's assumptions and his place for folk psychology as well. What Baker tries to do is to show that we can find a counterexample to the thesis that what is referred to as the identity of "type-type relations" goes through. In other words, part of Fodor's argument that there is a place for folk psychological terms in an empirical science of the mind—because propositional attitudes do causal work that is consistent with the nomological bent of the sciences themselves—is that mental states can be identified by content (i.e., semantic type or propositional attitude type) and that, so identified, they play a syntactic (formal) role in the functioning of the mind. Baker's counterexample is designed to show that it is not true that in every case where a mental state can be differentiated from another by semantic type or content (a given belief, say), it can still be differentiated by syntactic role. Some states that are syntactically identical (or of the same formal type) will not be semantically or attitudinally identical (of the same semantic type). Baker's case here is a superb exemplar of analytic theorizing put to a use that ultimately seems to vindicate at least some of the more naturalized work of other areas of theory. The example is too lengthy to quote in its entirety, but I will quote a generously sized excerpt in order to provide the flavor of the counterexampling technique employed.

The first thought experiment is aimed at refuting the view that classification of mental state tokens by their actual causal relations coincides with classification of mental state tokens by restricted semantic type. . . .

Imagine a documentary movie that compares subjects in psychology experiments. Each subject is shown videotapes of violent episodes and is asked to classify the incidents. The subjects are encouraged to reason aloud. In the case of non-English-speaking subjects, what we hear is the narrator's translation of the subject's utterances.

In the first scene, a non-English-speaking subject, identified as Subject N, is speaking. We hear the voice-over: "Was the incident one of simple assault or of provoked assault? Provoked assault is serious, more serious than simple assault. Since a two-hundred-pound man is not endangered by a child's insults and the assault was particularly fierce, it was serious enough to be provoked assault. So, I'll check the box for provoked assault."

Later in the film, an English-speaking subject, identified as Subject E, has seen the same incident. We hear: "Was the incident one of simple assault or of aggravated assault? Aggravated assault is serious, more serious than simple assault. Since a two-hundred-pound man is not endangered by a child's insults and the assault was particularly fierce, it was serious enough to be aggravated assault. So, I'll check the box for aggravated assault."[30]

The example proceeds to fill in the blanks in the following way: In the thought experiment, Subject N speaks a dialect wherein it so happens that every phoneme uttered is indistinguishable from English, but of course the meanings do not coincide. Subject N's society does not have the notion of aggravated assault as a legal concept, and so, as Baker remarks, "None of Subject N's current thoughts can correctly be translated into English as thoughts concerning aggravated assault."[31] And yet, to continue to fill in the example, all of the behavioral output evidence (including motions of the hand, production of phonemes, etc.) from the two subjects is identical, and by hypothesis, because the production of identical phonemes would presumably call upon syntactically identical portions of cerebral structure, all of the causal relations embedded in the two subjects are identical. And still—the point of the counterexample—the meaningful content produced by these two sets of identical relations is not identical. Hence identification of mental content or propositional attitudes (the belief states) with symbolic relations type cannot coherently be retained within a computational model that would rely at some level on formality of relations for its nomological import.

I have chosen to dwell at length on this example from Baker's work not only for its import for philosophy of mind (and hence the naturalization of epistemology) in general, but also because it is a surpassingly well constructed exemplar of analytic theorizing. Nevertheless, whatever the merits of Lynne Rudder Baker's specific counterexample to Fodor's thesis, the primogeniture of folk psychological constructs, both in philosophy of mind and epistemology, seems to be a thing of the past. If the newer, more naturalized epistemic material continues to take hold, both the rigidly normative and wildly idealized theories of epistemology itself and the somewhat unreduced views of mind that would still accord a place to the belief condition in theory of knowledge have outlived their usefulness. Naturalized epistemology demands a naturalized philosophy of mind, and the latter takes most of its impetus from whatever contender is the frontrunner among mental models or theories of mind in cognitive science. Most recently, the computational model has itself been overtaken by connectionist models, and it is to these that I now turn.

## CONNECTIONISM AND NATURALIZATION

The connectionism material is still so new that a project that is essentially epistemological may be forgiven for making only passing allusion to it. Nevertheless, it threatens to overtake the computational model of mind in the long run, so some acquaintance with it seems necessary if we are to obtain a full-bodied view of what analytic epistemology and the attempts to naturalize are currently about. Although a number of researchers have been at work on noncomputational models, I will refer here largely to the work of David E. Rumelhart, James L. McClelland, and others in what is known as the PDP Research Group.[32]

The title of the group refers to the notion that parallel distributed processing (PDP) models, rather than the computational model, which favors serial, nonparallel processing, have something valuable to contribute to our account of cognition. In general, and speaking in crude terms so as to better capture the flavor of the dispute between the two models, the PDP model (or connectionist view, as it is now known) has the virtue that it seems to accord, almost isomorphically as it were, with what we now know of neuroscience. Tersely, this is due to the fact that the model relies on notions that seem to mimic the connectionist structures of brain tissue with its tangle of neurons and synapses. In more precise terms, the model is able to provide better micro-modeling of phenomena ranging from skilled typing to forced monocular vision because it relies on the notion of interaction between many units simultaneously.[33]

Now continuing through with the line I have developed throughout this chapter, I want to make the following two points: One wants to be aware of the in-principle reducibility of any model to material more thoroughly neuroscientific (as Patricia Smith Churchland has argued), since so much of a truly naturalized epistemology would hang on this. Inevitably, the reduction would be relevant to the epistemologist when and if the actual reduction occurred. Secondarily, insofar as the naturalizing epistemologist is in the process of adducing material from cognitive science to follow through on the notion of "ought implies can," the epistemologist wants to make use of relevant, up-to-date material. In this sense, the computational model, while by no means discredited, is now on the wane in some circles and hence is not as relevant to the project of naturalization as it was a few years ago.

My general argument here—simply that the naturalizing epistemologist needs to be aware of recent developments in cognitive science and psychology—is, I take it, indisputable and not particularly interesting. More to the point, of course, any epistemologist or philosopher interested in the intersection of philosophy of mind/epistemology/philosophy of psychology might well inquire precisely what, if anything, from the connectionist model is now available and useful.

Now it might be useful for our purposes, as we wind up our overview of naturalized contemporary analytic epistemology, to look briefly at the PDP modeling of a cognitive-cum-motor process such as typing. No previous computational models have attempted in-depth portrayals of such activities, for the serial processing of the computational models cannot adequately give us the extreme speed exhibited by competent typists. Hence, McClelland, Rumelhart, and G. E. Hinton note in the opening chapter of their two-volume work that:

> As Feldman and Ballard (1982) have pointed out, the biological hardware is just too sluggish for sequential models of the microstructure to provide a plausible account at least of the microstructure of human thought. And the time limitation only gets worse, not better, when consequential mechanisms try to take large numbers of constraints into account.
>
> Parallel distributed processing models offer alternatives to serial models of the microstructure of cognition. They do not deny that there is a macrostructure, just as the study of subatomic particles does not deny

the existence of interactions between atoms. What PDP models do is describe the internal structure of the larger units, just as subatomic physics describes the internal structure of the atoms that form the constituents of larger units of chemical structure.[34]

Thus, speaking in general terms, the model provides a smaller and more accurate portrayal of the processing of a typist, for example, because it is able to focus on the simultaneous interaction of and inhibitory/excitatory status of many small parts. When a poised finger is within striking range of a given key, a pressing movement is triggered—but we know from our common-sense observations of functioning typists that a great deal more, involving other fingers simultaneously and pressing/suppressing motions, is going on.[35] The model allows for an inhibitory signal to pass between the unit responsible for the letter just typed and the relevant finger, and virtually simultaneously an excitatory or activating signal to pass to the unit responsible for the next letter to be typed. As Rumelhart and McClelland state, "In this model the sequential structure of typing emerges from the interaction of the excitatory and inhibitory influences among the processing units."[36]

The cursory overview of connectionist models that I have provided above is intended only as the briefest introduction, but some introduction is necessary if epistemology is to keep up with cognitive science and the newer material in philosophy of mind. The point of this chapter has been to try to develop material that might be constitutive of naturalized epistemology and to show, at least to some extent, how this material sprang from the broad trends in analytic epistemology in this century that I sketched in the previous chapter. In some respects the movements have been rather obvious ones: Causal theories, designed to respond to the Gettier examples, have given way to Goldman's later work and to a number of theories labeled "reliabilist." Kornblith's work, like Goldman's, takes as its obvious point of departure the completely apsychological nature of much of the previous theorizing—an apsychological nature so obvious that it leaps out, so to speak, at the working theorist as he or she prepares to develop new and original lines of thought.

But the material that I have adduced, which more properly falls under the rubric of "philosophy of mind" (Churchland's work, and Baker's) can be tied into epistemology only in the more general sense that if work like Goldman's and Kornblith's is to continue, then the epistemologist must be aware of movements in philosophy of mind itself. Finally, the connectionist model is straight from contemporary work in cognitive science, although it has already found a place in some of the newer epistemology.[37]

What we require at this point to develop a feminist epistemology that takes into account contemporary analytic theorizing, is an overview of much of the work that has been deemed epistemological in contemporary feminist theory. I have alluded to the work of Keller, Harding, Bordo, and others without providing a large-scale background for their work, and without discussing it in detail. In the next chapter I will show how their work intersects with the trends I have discussed in chapters one and two, before developing a theory in chapter four that will make use of all of the contemporary epistemic material, overtly feminist and nonfeminist alike.

## NOTES

1. See Belenky, Clinchy, Goldberger, and Tarule, *Women's Ways;* or Keller, *Reflections on Gender.*

2. Alvin Goldman, "Epistemology and the Psychology of Belief," *The Monist* 61, no. 4 (1978):525.

3. Ibid., 526.

4. Ibid.

5. Ibid., 526–27.

6. See Goldman's "The Relation between Epistemology and Psychology," *Synthese* 64, no. 1 (1985):29–68; "Epistemology and Problem Solving," *Synthese* 55, no. 1 (1983):21–48; "The Internalist Conception of Justification," in *Midwest Studies in Philosophy,* vol. 5, ed. Peter A. French, Theodore E. Uehling, Jr., and Howard K. Wettstein (Minneapolis, Minn.: University of Minnesota Press, 1980); and Goldman, *Epistemology and Cognition.*

7. See Goldman, *Epistemology and Cognition,* Table of Contents, p. ix.

8. Hilary Kornblith, "Some Social Features of Cognition," *Synthese,* 73, no. 1 (1987):27–41.

9. Ibid., 28.

10. Ibid., 29. (He is citing Asch's work, originally to be found in Solomon Asch, *Social Psychology* [Englewood Cliffs, N.J.: Prentice-Hall, 1952].)

11. Ibid., 35.

12. Hilary Kornblith, "The Psychological Turn," *Australasian Journal of Philosophy* 60, no. 3 (1982):238–53; "Ever Since Descartes," *The Monist* 68, no. 2 (1985):264–76.

13. Hilary Kornblith, "Ever Since Descartes," *The Monist* 68, no. 2 (1985):264.

14. Ibid.

15. Kornblith, "Psychological Turn," 238.

16. Ibid., 253.

17. See, e.g., Pamela McCorduck, *Machines Who Think* (San Francisco, Calif.: W. H. Freeman & Co., 1979). This is perhaps the most accessible of the recent books.

18. See Daniel Dennett, *Brainstorms* (Montgomery, Vt.: Bradford Press, 1978); Stephen Stich, *From Folk Psychology to Cognitive Science* (Cambridge, Mass.: Bradford of MIT Press, 1983); and Owen Flanagan, *The Science of the Mind* (Cambridge, Mass.: Bradford of MIT Press, 1984).

19. See Patricia Smith Churchland, *Neurophilosophy* (Cambridge, Mass.: Bradford of MIT Press, 1986).

20. Zenon Pylyshyn, *Computation and Cognition* (Cambridge, Mass.: Bradford of MIT Press, 1983), 130, 27.

21. Churchland, *Neurophilosophy,* 378, 381.

22. Lynne Rudder Baker, *Saving Belief* (Princeton: Princeton University Press, 1987), 13–14.

23. Ibid., 13.

24. This has long been an issue in philosophy of mind. Churchland, in *Neurophilosophy,* and Stich in *From Folk Psychology,* address it directly.

25. As Baker formulates this position, and as she ascribes it to Dennett, one of the main uses of such a position is to bolster the *moral* value of the employment of propositional attitude terms.

26. Baker, *Saving Belief,* 23–42.

27. Ibid., 23.

28. Cf. fn. 19; Pylyshyn provides an adumbration of this view.

29. Baker, *Saving Belief,* 24–25.

30. Ibid., 30.

31. Ibid., 31.

32. Some of the most important work produced by the group is to be found in two volumes: David E. Rumelhart and James L. McClelland, eds., *Parallel Distributed Processing: Explorations in the Microstructure of Cognition* (Cambridge, Mass.: Bradford of MIT Press, 1986, vol. 1, 1:3–44 and vol. 2:24, 471–502. One of the shorter introductions to the volumes comes in the form of a review by Stephen Palmer of the University of California at Berkeley in *Contemporary Psychology* 32, no. 11.

33. Within the Rumelhart and McClelland work, see vol. 1 chap. 1 ("The Appeal of PDP") for an account of modeling skilled typing, and vol. 2, chap. 24 ("State Dependent Factors Influencing Neural Plasticity," by P. W. Munro) for an account of the plasticity patterns in binocular and monocular vision.

34. Rumelhart and McClelland, *Parallel Distributed Processing,* 12.

35. Ibid., 16.

36. Ibid.

37. See Goldman in Garver and Hare, *Naturalism,* 79–98.

*Part Two*

# GYNOCENTRIC EPISTEMICS

# Chapter Three

# The Feminist Theories

The recent literature on feminist epistemology reveals that the word "epistemology" has been construed in the broadest possible sense, as I indicated in the Introduction. To construe the term in this way is not, of course, to do it violence: A broader construction for the term may be a more philosophically interesting one, since it may draw our attention, theoretically, to areas previously left untouched. But an area of intrigue for theorizing, both at the microlevel and the macrolevel, is the area where what has been called feminist epistemology intersects with contemporary analytic epistemology. This area is more-or-less unexamined in the literature, although it would seem, from the outset, to have innumerable possibilities and to be the sort of intersection that might prove enormously fruitful.[1]

To be more precise about the intersection requires that the work done by the feminist theorists be examined more closely, just as we examined the work of the naturalizing epistemologists in the previous chapter. Three thinkers have done work of paramount importance, and many others have contributed journal pieces and articles that have received wide circulation.[2] One of the most salient features of the work done in feminist theory so far that might fall broadly under the rubric of epistemology is that a great deal of the work has actually focused on science and philosophy of science. If one thinks of philosophy of science as the twentieth-century child of epistemology, this is not so surprising, but it is surprising that so much feminist work should fall in this area when it might be thought to be more straightforward, so to speak, to work on epistemology itself or to attack some of the precepts of contemporary theory of knowledge.

In any case, Evelyn Fox Keller and Sandra Harding have done important work, widely circulated within and outside of feminist circles, on science and the philosophical overview of science. Susan Bordo's work falls mainly into the category of philosophical and cultural history, yet it has been very useful for delineating the extent to which the Cartesian overview, which I have mentioned in the previous two chapters, has affected the development of philosophy as a whole and especially those areas of philosophy that might be related to epistemology. Still other work has been done that might be categorized, roughly, as along the lines of Continental theory of knowledge from a feminist perspective.[3] Although in general I will not be citing such work in this chapter, since Continental philosophy has traditionally had little to say to Anglo-American analytic philosophy (and vice versa, of course), I will cite some of the work related to the development of the thought associated with Lacan, Irigaray, and Cixous from time to time, where it might seem to be pertinent for larger strands of theory, and I will go into it at somewhat greater length at a later point in the text. The discourse on feminist epistemology from the Continental perspective has been a promising one and will no doubt continue, even if it is not always obviously relevant to more analytic constructions of the problems of theory of knowledge.

## KELLER AND ANDROCENTRISM

Evelyn Fox Keller's work has been of the utmost importance in coming to grips with what a feminist analysis of science and/or philosophy of science might amount to. Her books *Reflections on Gender and Science* and *A Feeling for the Organism* have been particularly helpful, and a spate of journal articles has helped refine her point of view and simultaneously ensure that it has received broad dissemination. I cited Keller at an earlier point when I wanted to give a sketch of the androcentric nature of traditional theorizing, and I will examine her views more fully now, since her work has been crucial.[4]

Briefly, Keller has tried to portray androcentrism in the development of the sciences and theory of knowledge broadly construed as at least partially and significantly the result of the development of male gender structure during childhood and adolescence. Such a view necessarily relies on the theorizing of the psychoanalytically oriented developmentalists, and is at least partially the result of schools of thought that were originally Freudian, since they in turn rely on object-relations theory for their impact. (Following common usage of such theory, which may be somewhat confusing to some readers, the "object" in object-relations theory is, in most salient cases, another person, and refers to the infant's development of a sense of self and a sense of object-others as a process that begins most importantly when the infant starts to separate herself or himself from the all-encompassing mother during the first few months of life. The mother then becomes the first "object"—first entity outside the self—with which the infant is familar.)

The importance of Keller's work lies in her articulation of the aggression that the male child employs to separate himself from the mother—completely and thoroughly, so that gender-identity problems are avoided as conventional social life would require—as a construct that becomes a feature of the male child's life and that carries over into other areas of endeavor.[5] The hypothesis of object-relations theory has been that the male child becomes gradually aware during the earliest years of life of his gender separateness from his mother and his gender identity with other males. But, as is the case for the vast majority of children all over the world, if he is being cared for by his mother or other adult female figure, his first bonding and emotional attachment comes with someone whose gender identity is radically different. Thus the child's natural tendency to want to merge completely with the adult figure must be fought against—and fought against forcefully as he becomes older—in order to avoid a merger of gender identity that would leave him non-male in personality structure.[6] Sketching in broad strokes, the male child pulls away from the female nurturing figure by separating himself psychologically from the figure and by devaluing females and female-oriented activities insofar as that is possible. That this happens quite easily and rapidly in most Western societies is an empirically confirmable fact that one can see instantiated in the play and roughhouse of any group of kindergarten children.

In *Reflections on Gender and Science*, Keller depicts the androcentrism of science in a series of essays that examine particular instances of bias in theorizing or of gender-related distortions in scientific models. I cited some of her work on the importance of male homosexuality in the Platonic tradition and in Western thought in general at an earlier point, and I want now to examine some of her work on male aggression.[7] The insight that the aggression and dynamism required for the young male to break free of the pull of the mother shows up or recurs in our society in a number of different ways, both in the overall devaluation of females and the feminine, and in areas of theorizing—whether political, scientific, or religious—is a valuable one, and has been crucially important for feminist theory. Significantly, Keller is herself a trained scientist, and the rigor of her attack on various sorts of biases is extremely helpful for the project of feminist epistemology, in no small sense precisely because it is so clearly done. The voices of feminist theory from the Continental tradition, or from the overviews of literary theory and cultural history, have been of aid in articulating broad general trends, but feminist theory has often seemed, until recently, to lack a surer grounding in epistemology and scientifically oriented thinking. Keller's work remedies this defect to a great extent and helps prepare feminist theory for its amelioration by still more tightly constructed strands of thought drawn from analytic philosophy.

Here is Keller on male aggression:

> Aggression, of course, has many meanings, many sources, and many forms of expression. Here I mean to refer only to the form underlying the impulse toward domination. I invoke psychoanalytic theory to help illuminate the forms of expression that impulse finds in science as a whole, and its relation to objectification in particular. The same questions I asked about the child I can also ask about science. Under what circumstances is scientific knowledge sought for the pleasure of knowing, for the increased competence it grants us, for the increased mastery (real or imagined) over our own fate, and under what circumstances is it fair to say that science seeks to dominate nature? Is there a meaningful distinction to be made here?[8]

This passage helps us come to grips with the central and recurring theme of Keller's work: the extent to which science has become infused with a desire to approach natural phenomena—Nature herself—to continue the metaphor—as if the relationship were adversarial. The striving for autonomy in the child, particularly the male child, becomes a quest for mastery and objectification. The objectification, in turn, provides the basis for still another epistemological stance, and that is the stance of perceiving phenomena in isolation.

These two themes—the importance of dominance and mastery, both linked to an adversarial view, and the importance of objectification and nonrelational stances—form the core of Keller's critique of the sciences. From the standpoint of epistemology *simpliciter*, Keller's work is remarkable for the precision with which she has articulated how science is informed by these points of view. The book *Reflections on Gender and Science* contains not only essays on the historical context in which our Western view of scientific endeavor arose, but essays on how objectificationist and adversarial strands of thought have affected the history of certain specific scientific projects. Two chapters in the work, in particular, focus on scientific inquiries and the overview that has been operative during their performance. "Cognitive Repression in Contemporary Physics" and "The Force of the Pacemaker Concept in Theories of Aggregation in Cellular Slime Mold"[9] are superb examples of feminist philosophy of science, since they are attuned to specific controversies within physics and biology.

Like most of the work I will examine in this chapter, Keller's work makes little overt use of the categories of contemporary analytic epistemology that I have examined in the preceding chapters. This does not mean that those categories are irrelevant to Keller's project, however, nor does it mean that her project has no natural area of intersection with such work. I will address the issue again at a later point, but cursorily one can delineate the intersection as follows: Contemporary philosophy of science (and in some respects science itself) is the outgrowth of the earlier rigidly positivistic philosophy of science of the 1930s and 1940s. That view of science, however outmoded at this point, was extremely influential and relied on analytic epistemology in the sense that the distinction between sentences of science known *a priori* (analytic sentences) and the observationally based confirmable sentences (synthetic sentences) was tied into a foundationalist epistemology. As I indicated briefly in the first chapter, the foundationalist epistemology—which developed at least partially from the sense-data theories, with their emphasis on the incorrigibly known, epistemically privileged data—served its purpose, during its heyday, as a basis for other work in epistemology and philosophy of science.

Now Keller's work is explicitly responding to some views current in philosophy of science and scientific endeavor that are the epistemic offspring of these older, positivistic, foundationalist views. If the Quinean attack on the analytic–synthetic distinction[10] and the repeated attacks on incorrigibility (some of which, as I indicated earlier, are traceable to Austin) helped to destroy the positivist model, with its correspondence rules linking the observation sentences to sentences in theory, it is still true that the consequent models in philosophy of science tended to be informed by the strict hierarchical nature of such views.[11] In this sense, Keller's work (insofar as it criticizes these models in physics and biology) is completely linked to other work in philosophy of science, and indeed to epistemology itself. Thus we see how closely theory of knowledge itself is aligned with the work feminist theorists criticize.

Keller explicitly acknowledges this relationship in chapter six of her work, "Dynamic Objectivity: Love, Power and Knowledge," where she cites other work in philosophy of science and sketches the areas of intersection between what some have labeled the "*weltanschauungen*" accounts[12] and her own feminist (but also somewhat *weltanschauungen*) account:

> Inevitably, the question is not simply which theory offers the fullest explanation, the best prediction, but also which theory best satisfies that host of unspecifiable "aesthetic" criteria (see, for example, Kuhn 1962; Hanson 1958)—including which theory is most consonant with one's implicit ideological and emotional expectations. If erotic themes have tended to be submerged in the history of science, they have been submerged by a rhetoric and ideology of aggression, which, though never binding, has been critically formative in the development of both scientists and science.[13]

If it is true, then, that Kuhn's work, with its emphasis on paradigms (and hence, to the chagrin of some, its implicit emphasis on the sociology of science) is in some sense descriptive and, as Keller indicates, ideologically aware and interactionally sophisticated, then Keller's work itself takes off from the work of Kuhn and the other social coherence views, and differs from them more in her emphasis on masculinism and androcentrism as operative concepts, rather than, say, popularity of a given paradigm.

To cite Keller on specific topics in biology or physics is, I think, to present her work in fullest flavor. Since Keller is herself a mathematical biologist, her analysis of the explanatory power given certain constructs in the slime mold controversy is particularly acute. Keller writes:

> Nonetheless, shortly after Segel and I published our model (Keller and Segel, 1970) [which offered "an alternative to the widespread view that special (sometimes called founder) cells were needed to initiate aggregation"], the initiator cell view was revived by Cohen and Robertson (1971a) with a considerably more detailed description of the relay of signals emitted by pacemaker cells [cells with special properties which govern or dominate the processes of the cells around them] through a population of

relay competent cells. . . . These properties became the central focus of research for many investigators. . . . The assumption of pacemaker cells was felt to be so natural, it so readily explained the phenomena, that the question I had begun with simply disappeared.[14]

Here Keller cites specific slime mold research and the manner in which the adversarial, objectified style of which she has been writing manifests itself in biological paradigms. The sort of model that might allow for aggregation of slime mold cells in a more reciprocally focused, equitably interactionist manner was buried by the onslaught of views that attempted to account for aggregation and differentiation by the force of a "dominant," leader-like cell.

By my lights, the exemplary quality of Keller's work lies in the precision of its articulation and the force of its use of scientific material. I plan to turn now to work of a somewhat different theoretic stripe, but I will return to Keller again as the need arises. Her work in feminist philosophy of science moves naturally into the categories of traditional philosophy of science and twentieth century epistemology, thus creating an obvious point of departure for the development of a feminist epistemology that is aware of and draws on analytic episte- mology itself.[15]

## HARDING'S *SCIENCE QUESTION*

Sandra Harding's *The Science Question in Feminism* is perhaps the single most influential volume among those that have been produced on feminist philosophy of science or feminist epistemology. Harding's work draws on multiple strands of theory and analysis: contemporary Continental philosophy, literary theory, analytic philosophy, and work in the social sciences proper all find a home in Harding's work, and Harding does a masterful job of weaving these strands into an entire fabric. Whereas Keller, for example, analyzes the "text" of science more from the standpoint of psychoanalytic object-relations theory, and to some extent from the standpoint of previous theoretical moves in philosophy of science itself (the Kuhnian, or more broadly speaking, *weltanschauungen* moves of which I have written earlier), Harding tends to rely more fully on threads of analysis drawn from the literary and Continental traditions. It is another virtue of Harding's work that she makes use of almost all of the feminist material in philosophy of science and the feminist critique of science that had preceded her work; little is omitted, and her bibliography alone provides a powerful diagnostic tool for those who would attempt to come to grips with the ills of science or who would attempt to ameliorate the scientific syndrome.

Harding divides work done previously in the feminist critique of science into five stages and then tries to show how further work developed from the five, emerging in three strands that she regards as particularly salient. Cursorily, the three projects that she identifies as "feminist epistemologies" are feminist empiricism, feminist standpoint epistemologies, and feminist postmodernism. Harding identifies problems for each of these projects, although one is left with a residual impression that she has identified feminist postmodernism (an off-shoot, of course, of Continental categories and of largely Continental theorizing) as the project that has the most hopeful future, precisely because it is the one project that seems to be most aware of the plethora of women's voices.

Before I turn to Harding directly, however, I think it is important to articulate precisely what it is about Harding's labeling and categorization that is so intriguing and valuable for the feminist project as a whole, and, at least according to some, somewhat problematic from the viewpoint of theory.[16] Preliminarily, one would like to be able to assay the use of the term "epistemology" here, since it is important not only for an analysis of Harding's work, of course, but also for my own project, since I focus on epistemology more narrowly construed.

To return briefly to a point made at the opening of this work, "epistemology" is a word now used in many disciplines, and even within philosophy itself, more than one voice and more than one style of theorizing has employed the term. Bluntly, "epistemology" in disciplines other than philosophy, and in the nonanalytic portions of contemporary philosophy, has come to mean "ways of knowing." I think it is important to develop the contrast here between the standard use of the term epistemology in analytic philosophy and the uses to which it is being put by those not in analytic philosophy, for much will turn on this. As we saw in the preceding chapters, the analytic tradition has large skeptical components, both as a holdover from Plato and as part of the Cartesian tradition, however generously that phrase is taken. Thus the analytic point of view has never assumed that we do, as cognizers, have knowledge; on the contrary, the assumption has frequently been that the status of "knowledge" is problematic. In addition, as chapter one pointed out, the struggle to try to create a foundation or incorrigible basis for knowledge, at least from roughly the early twentieth century on, resulted in ever more rigorous, tighter, and more complex analyses of knowledge, many of which would have been incomprehensible to anyone not a trained philosopher (and not trained in the analytic tradition). But the new, nonanalytic use of "epistemology" assumes, in general, that we do have knowledge, and seems more concerned with displaying the manner of acquisition of the knowledge, or the cognitive style of the knower, than with answering skeptical challenges. Indeed, insofar as feminist critique has been concerned, these more timeworn approaches of the analytic tradition have been virtually ignored.

Having said this, it is important to get clear on Harding's use of the term "epistemology." When Harding writes of the "feminist epistemologies," her phrase may be taken as shorthand for "feminist ways of knowing" or for "feminist critiques of traditional accounts of ways of knowing." For the moment I will eschew discussion of the very great difference between these two phrases, as I believe further discussion of Harding will show precisely where the differences lie. What Harding means by "feminist empiricism," for example, is that an account of the functioning of the sciences that has accepted, in general, empiricist (and even quasi-positivist) portrayals of knowledge acquisition as beyond criticism has tended to focus on rather more straightforward issues of women's role within the sciences, such as the number of women functioning in scientific endeavors, and the effect that the training of greater numbers of women would have on the sciences. This emphasis has been at the cost of examining what some would regard as deeper, underlying issues in the structures of the sciences themselves (issues that have, of course, been addressed by Keller, for one).

By "feminist standpoint epistemologies," Harding means those lines of feminist critique that have in general taken a post-Marxist view of the division of labor on our planet, and that have argued that women are privileged to have an epistemically different perspective from males by virtue of the state of their oppression and the tasks that, as members of an oppressed group, they are asked to perform. Here the term "epistemology" is virtually completely divorced from its use in the analytic tradition and does duty in the Marxist sense that what is taken for knowledge, or what passes for knowledge and information within a given society, is largely a social construct. Finally, by "feminist postmodernism," Harding means those strands of feminist analysis, influenced by such thinkers as Lacan, Foucault, Cixous, Heidegger, and Derrida, that are fixed firmly within the Continental tradition and that see the pretended unity of science, society, and indeed Western culture itself as a shattered or fragmented pattern that never had the authority it purported to have.[17]

Thus our discussion of Harding will be our first major point of departure from a discussion of epistemology as a standardly defined subarea of philosophy. Nevertheless, the Harding material is extremely fruitful for an analysis that sees an intriguing intersection between some of the work in naturalized epistemology and the feminist critique itself, since Harding's work is so wide-ranging, and since at least one of the three feminist projects that constitute the major themes of her book is a direct offshoot of standard analytic philosophy of science and the twentieth-century American epistemological tradition (I refer here, of course, to feminist empiricism). In the following discussion, I plan to provide a brief view of Harding's analysis of these three projects, and at the same time to pull out from them the material relevant to a later construction of an analytically based feminist epistemology.

Harding's critique of feminist empiricism is most salient for our purposes, and it is to this construction that I now turn. There is an inevitable *lex talionis* in any such overview of feminist theory, for the feminist critique of empiricism must, if it is to stay within the terms of the argument, accept at least some of the tenets of empiricism itself, and Harding is well aware of this difficulty. Harding's point of commencement in her analysis of feminist empiricism is that it

> argues that sexism and androcentrism are social biases correctable by stricter adherence to the existing methodological norms of scientific inquiry. . . . [It] is appealing for a number of reasons, not the least because it appears to leave unchallenged the existing methodological norms of science. It is easier to gain acceptance of feminist claims through this kind of argument, for it identifies only bad science as the problem, not science as usual.

In other words, what Harding characterizes as feminist empiricism amounts, in general, to arguments about the exclusion of women from science and to subarguments about what women, as scientists, could contribute to scientific endeavors. Feminist empiricism is, if one will buy the terminology, a rather middle-of-the-road critique (as opposed to a more radical critique), since it seems to assume that the canons of science may stand as they are and that redress of numbers and attention paid to inequities of participation will go a long way toward solving any problems that have arisen in the conduct of science itself.

What Harding finds dubious about the feminist empiricist critiques of science is that they are, on one level, somewhat inconsistent and incoherent, and on another level they fail to address some of the difficulties of bias in science that exist in the mode of theorizing itself. As Harding points out, if strict empiricism were correct, the canons of scientific inquiry would be so user-blind that it would not make any difference whether there were women scientists or not. In other words, if science were as "objective" and "neutral" as it purports to be, gender or sex of investigator or participant would be irrelevant.[19] What difference could it make, the argument goes, whether a male or female is involved in searching for a planet beyond Pluto, or in the quest to discover still more subatomic particles? Thus a flat inconsistency arises for feminist empiricism at a basic level, since empiricism, strictly read, subverts the very feminist empiricist project. More importantly, however, Harding writes:

> . . . though empiricism holds that scientific method is sufficient to account for historical increases in the objectivity of the picture of the world that science presents, one can argue that history shows otherwise. It is movements for social liberation that have most increased the objectivity of science, not the norms of science as they have in fact been practiced, or as philosophers have rationally reconstructed them. . . .
>
> We shall also see that a key origin of androcentric bias can be found in the selection of problems for inquiry, and in the definition of what is problematic about these phenomena. But empiricism insists that its methodological norms are meant to apply only to the "context of justification"—to the testing of hypotheses and the interpretation of evidence—not to the "context of discovery" where problems are identified and defined.[20]

Thus, according to Harding, feminist empiricism fails from the outset in two important ways.

Although a full-scale view of Harding's critique of the three feminist projects is beyond the scope of what I hope to accomplish here, it is important to look at Harding's appraisal of the other two projects, the feminist standpoint epistemologies and feminist postmodernism. It is crucially urgent in the sense that much of what has been dubbed "feminist epistemology" has, in fact, fallen under these rubrics.[21] If we are to become clear on what many, if not the preponderant majority, have deemed to constitute feminist epistemology, we must examine Harding's account of these two projects in some detail.

Harding's account of the feminist standpoint epistemologies relies on the work of four major thinkers: Hilary Rose, Nancy Hartsock, Jane Flax, and Dorothy Smith. Of these four, two—Hartsock and Flax—are paradigmatic, and I will try to provide a brief summary of Harding's responses to them. Harding is in general favorably impressed by the standpoint theorists, but she finds internal inconsistencies and incoherences in their work, just as in the work of the feminist empiricists. What may very well clearly distinguish feminist empiricism from the standpoint work for Harding is the fact that the empiricist view has the defect of already working within an androcentric tradition. This particular defect is, of course, precisely what the standpoint epistemologies aim to remedy.

Now the standpoint epistemologies *in toto*, according to Harding, move in the following direction:

> They try instead [unlike feminist empiricism] to arrive at hypotheses that are free of gender loyalties. It is true that first we often have to formulate a "woman-centered" hypothesis in order even to comprehend a gender-free one. But the goal of feminist knowledge-seeking is to achieve theories that accurately represent women's activities as fully social, and social relations between the genders as a real—an explanatorily important—component in human history. . . . From the perspective of feminist history, it is traditional thought that is subjective in its distortion by androcentrism—a claim that feminists are willing to defend on traditional objectivist grounds.[22]

In other words, the claim is that the special perspective of women is an epistemic perspective that yields its own theory of knowledge (and ontology as well).

By this time the reader can probably anticipate the intersection that I would establish between this use of the term "epistemology" and the more standard employment that I have cited so frequently in the preceding pages: The inner-centered, incorrigible, privileged access point of departure for traditional epistemology (foundationalist epistemology, certainly) is androcentric precisely because it has cut context off from the knower in a stupefyingly sharp manner. That *qualia* which are known to me solely by introspection (internal sense-data) should become the classic cases of *qualia* which serve as subjects for incorrigible sentences or propositions is epistemically odd, to say the least, and would not be taken for granted by us had we not come, through the entire history ranging from Plato to Descartes and beyond, to accept the divorce of in-the-bodiness from knowing.

The feminist response to the articulation of this tradition is, of course, that it is no accident that it is associated with, and articulated by, thinkers who are overwhelmingly male. The response, if fully set out, would go deeper: It would claim that it is highly unlikely that a female thinker would have come up with such a theoretical framework or viewpoint. Numerous reasons, some arcane, and some not so arcane, have been given for this contention, but the standpoint theorists (and here Harding cites both Hartsock and Flax) make frequent mention of the greater ties to the body of the female, particularly through childbirth, menstruation, and the caregiving roles traditionally assigned to women.[23]

It is here, then, that the two uses of "epistemology" come together in a way most susceptible to clear explanation. Not only did Plato and other thinkers emphasize a mode of knowing that was divorced from the body because the senses were prone to err, but the entire mode of being-in-the-body experienced by males is such that it lends itself to a greater separation of the realm of the mental from the realm of the physical. Thus androcentric or masculinist epistemology does indeed have a "standpoint": the standpoint of the incorrigibly mental (and hence, according to some theorists, the utterly incorrigible). This is also, as Harding has written in an earlier passage, the standpoint of the "entire scientific methodological ethos of objectivity, value-neutrality, dispassionate inquiry, and the like."[24] It is objective because it is applicable, supposedly, to all (since divorced from context and bodily being); value-neutral for the same sorts of reasons (one may also employ the term "universalizable" here); and, finally, dispassionate because it is contextual awareness and particularities of circumstance that tend to make inquiry biased, passionate, particularized, and less than universal. The standpoint of the female or the gynocentric view is then subjective, bodily, passionate, and valued. It is, no doubt, more "error prone," since its particularity makes it not useful as a point of departure for Truth-with-a-capital T—but then, many theorists (by no means all female!) have inquired, what can we make of the concept of truth?

Hartsock's particular standpoint epistemology (and neither Hartsock nor Flax is a philosopher by training) relies heavily on a neo-Marxist approach to the concept of gender-driven division of labor. Hartsock sees the standpoint of the female as based on women's distinctive practices and domestic labor.[25] Hartsock writes of the feminist standpoint as:

. . . an interested social location ("interested" in the sense of "engaged," not "biased"), the conditions for which bestow upon its occupants scientific and epistemic advantage. The subjugation of women's sensuous, concrete, relational activity permits women to grasp aspects of nature and social life that are not accessible to inquiries grounded in men's characteristic activities. The vision based on men's activities is both partial and perverse—"perverse" because it systematically reverses the proper order of things: it substitutes abstract for concrete reality; for example, it makes death-risking rather than the reproduction of our species form of life the paradigmatically human act.[26]

Thus, according to Hartsock, a more realistic worldview—ontology and epistemology—is concomitant with developing notions of knowing and acting that are less androcentric.

Flax, on the other hand, is a social scientist whose view of the female standpoint is mainly informed by psychoanalytically oriented theory (object-relations theory, again) and sociological views of its prominence in intellectual history. Harding quotes Flax as writing that "Feminist philosophy thus represents the return of the repressed" and Flax reads the masculine sense of self—which informs all theory, since all theory is male-dominated—as originating in the pull of the male away from the mother.[27] This point, also made by Keller, reveals the male to be in an "arrested stage of development."[28] Flax sees male theorizing about the world as being largely informed by unresolved and denied issues of separation and individuation. Harding writes of Flax's view:

We can move toward a feminist epistemology through exposing the infantile social dilemmas repressed by adult men, the "resolutions" of which reappear in abstract or universalizing form as both the collective motive for and the subject matter of patriarchal epistemology. The feminine dimensions of experience tend to disappear in all thinking within patriarchies.[29]

But valuable as Harding finds the standpoint epistemologies to be, she is perplexed and puzzled by the female viewpoint theorists' apparent inability to formulate a position that does not deny that Truth is up for grabs and simultaneously assert a truth or truths about the female point of view. Furthermore, it is no small defect of a feminist standpoint theory that the multitudinous ways in which women divide themselves—the varieties of ways in which they appear on the planet, so to speak—appear to be overlooked or disregarded by such a theory.

Harding closes by enjoining us to grapple with the message of postmodernism (and here, of course, she borrows from Lacan, Derrida, DeLeuze, Cixous, Kristeva, and so forth) and to celebrate the fracturedness of women's being on the planet. To do so requires further advances in feminist epistemology, above and beyond the standpoint epistemologies, and certainly beyond the (by Harding's standards) rather limited point of view of feminist empiricism. Harding's closing remarks extol an epistemology that is alive to its inconsistencies and that does not claim to have a lock on truth. Thus, one might add, we have come 180 degrees, since part of the original task of an epistemology was to help us come to grips with the ways in which our belief statements and pieces of evidence for them were related to the truth, or the ultimate facts of the matter. In Harding's view, any developed feminist epistemology must assimilate the point that there are no ultimate facts of the matter.

I have focused extensively on Harding because her work has been so influential, and because her delineation of the three main projects (feminist empiricism, feminist standpoint epistemologies, and feminist postmodernism) constitutes an encyclopaedic overview of what has been categorized as feminist epistemology. But Harding makes few moves herself in the direction of developing a more fully articulated postmodern feminist epistemology, aware of and joyful in its base of fractured identities. Rather, she serves to point us in that direction while delegating that task to other theorists.

Perhaps most intriguing about Harding's work, in the long run, is the rather short shrift given to feminist empiricism. This more conservative view—at least within Harding's categories—is the one view of the three that has the most in common with epistemology's traditional philosophical heritage, while also being the one that is the least developed from the point of view of feminism, since it is guilty of employing devices that are already stigmatized as masculinist and androcentric.

But, one may object, this much is true, at least to some extent, of the other projects as well. If the standpoint epistemologies do not fall within the analytic or empiricist framework, and if they perhaps give the appearance of being less androcentric in their origins, it is largely because they draw on Continental strands of theory. These theoretical points of view, however, are themselves the product of overtly male exercises in thinking (Marx, Lacan, etc.). Postmodernism is probably the least androcentric of these three enterprises and yet is again very much related to male theorizing (Freud is, after all, a precursor to

Lacan), and in any case some threads of postmodernism seem to deny the possibility of a genuinely female voice. Harding is, of course, aware of all these peculiarities, yet one is constrained to say that she may have thrown the baby out with the bathwater (which she claimed not to want to do) when she gave tacit dismissal to feminist empiricism.[30] How feminist empiricism can be made more coherent and less androcentric is a later, and larger, task for this work.

I turn now to the work of Susan Bordo, the theorist whose writings are probably the least closely related to the standard analytic tradition. For this reason her work may not prove as overtly relevant to our later theorizing as the work of Keller or Harding, and yet Bordo's work has been enormously influential because the very Cartesian tradition to which I have alluded is painted by her in careful, textured strokes.

## BORDO AND CARTESIAN OBJECTIVITY

Bordo's work is particularly alluring within the framework of what I have discussed so far in this chapter because she cuts across and intersects at least two of the themes with which we have been engrossed. Bordo acknowledges the importance of views like Keller's and Harding's (which in turn, at least insofar as object-relations theory is concerned, rely on the work of Chodorow), by her implicit use of a psychoanalytic construction of childhood in her development of Cartesianism.[31] Of still greater importance, however, is Bordo's use of frameworks of intellectual and cultural history that provide us with an apposite overview of the seventeenth century. Bordo is quick to point out that Descartes's personal intellectual peregrination, as depicted particularly in the *Meditations*, is a journey of thought unlikely to have been taken by any thinker living much before Descartes's time, since the inwardness manifested in the *Meditations*—and, as Bordo has it, Descartes's epistemic anxiety—is a product of the loss of the medieval worldview and its comforting organicity as much as it is a product of the individual's (here Descartes's) development. In other words, Bordo's analysis of Descartes's *Meditations* in her work *The Flight to Objectivity* is simultaneously an analysis of the psychological wanderings of an individual and an analysis of the dislocation of a culture, the European culture of the Middle Ages. Thus Bordo sheds light on (and to some extent disagrees with) the thesis I have tried to sustain here, which has claimed that masculine theorizing has a long tradition, within Western culture, of divorce from the body. Bordo acknowledges problems for the senses and the body itself, as disorienting prison, in the writings of Plato and other thinkers. But it is part of Bordo's argument that the deemphasis on the body originating with Descartes is particular to his time (and possibly, in its vexed form, particular to him within his time).

Thus it may be the case that it is a fair move, in developing the thesis that Western epistemology has tended to exclude the body from its origins, to stretch a line of devaluation of the senses back to the ancients, and to cite passages in Platonic works. But Bordo sees the emphasis placed by Descartes on *res cogitans* as a rather abrupt shift, and one that shows European thinking cut off, in the seventeenth century, from the organic unity with the world and the universe as a whole that had preceded it.

With regard to the Platonic tradition and its contrast to Descartes's fervid denunciation of the body, Bordo writes:

In Plato and Aristotle, the lines simply cannot be drawn in so stark a fashion. In the *Symposium*, we should remember, the love of the body is the first, and necessary, step on the spiritual ladder which leads to the glimpsing of the eternal form of beauty. For the Greek philosophers, the body is not simply an impediment to knowledge; it may also function as a spur to spiritual growth. Its passions may motivate the quest for knowledge and beauty. . . . For the Greeks, then, there are definite limits to the human intellect. For Descartes, on the other hand, epistemological hubris knows few bounds. The dream of purity is realizable during one's lifetime. For, given the right method, one can transcend the body."

Descartes, of course, wants to rid himself of the influence of the body because he views knowledge as stemming from the possession of clear and distinct ideas, and these are ideas that have no sensory origin. But we are already familiar with Descartes's motivations, both from his own writings and from the mammoth commentary upon them. What is new and exciting about Bordo's approach to the interpretation of the *Meditations* within cultural context is that it provides superb support for the assumption that a certain sort of masculinist distancing actually became more pronounced in European culture—and hence in European thought as a whole—over a period of time. Indeed the origins of Western philosophy may have been androcentric but its important subdisciplines grew still more androcentric as European thought and culture proceeded, through a variety of currents, to distance itself from the world of the senses.

In chapter four of her work, "Individuation and Locatedness: A Cultural Drama of Parturition," Bordo describes the worldview of the Middle Ages as the "infancy" of Western culture. Like the infant bound to the mother, as described by the object-relations theorists, the medieval European felt at home in the world, organically united to it, and in some sense unable to distance herself or himself from it, even in imagination. This perception of one's self in the world was manifest, according to Bordo and some of the theorist whose work she cites, even in medieval art, with its lack of perspective and its quality of "absorption." Characteristically, perspective in the visual arts is an invention of and accomplishment of the Renaissance, when heightened individual self-consciousness was mirrored in every facet of culture.

Bordo remarks on the art of the Middle Ages:

> It seems clear that for the medieval aesthetic imagination, absorption in the world rather than locatedness in the world was central. It is the latter mode of experience—of the self as discretely located in space and geometrically related to other objects so located—that the perspective painting tries to recreate on the "illusionist" space of the canvas, through the adoption of the "fiction" of the fixed observer and the plotting out of the objects to be represented as more or less remote from that observer.[33]

If the medieval thinker found himself absorbed in the organic unity of the world, he was unlikely to attempt to adopt perspective in his artwork. And, absorbed in the world, he was unlikely to suffer from Descartes's "epistemological insecurity,"[34] nor was he likely to suffer from what some have dubbed Descartes's schizoid depersonalization—a sense of unreality and lack of, or confusion over, personal boundary so strong that it resulted in the *cogito*.[35] When in epistemological panic, the reality of the mind may indeed seem greater than the reality of the external world, and epistemological fear is concomitant with a worldview that finds itself increasingly beset by cognitive categorization breakdown as the result of greater knowledge acquisition. The man of the Middle Ages, Bordo quotes the historian of science Burtt as noting, had no problem with knowledge; the world was "intelligible . . . and explicitly taken for granted."[36] But Galileo, Copernicus, and the shattering experiences of coming into contact with other cultures (especially the Chinese) had destroyed the givenness of the world for the post-Renaissance person and rendered it strange and unfamiliar.[37] Thus was epistemological uncertainty born, and thus was a redoubtable assault made on the certainty of knowledge acquired through sense perception.

Bordo makes particularly poignant Descartes's personal quest as she untangles knots in the culture of the transitional seventeenth century. More importantly from our perspective, one might well theorize Descartes (and many of the male thinkers who followed him) as victims of a double distancing. Forced to wrench themselves from the world of their mothers in order to become socialized males, theorists working in the post-Renaissance, rise-of-science period had the profoundly distinctive experience of seeing their worldview destroyed at the same time that they developed—through the technological means of the culture as a whole—the capacity to·articulate it. This dual rupture had the effect on more thoughtful individuals (surely, one supposes, the very philosophers whose work has now come down to us, and many thinkers—both female and male—whose work was not saved) of distancing them from their heritage, their parentage, their emotional lives, and themselves. Small wonder that Descartes took pleasure in setting mathematical problems for his colleagues that he knew could not be solved.

Bordo's work, then, brings us full circle, since it seems to turn us naturally toward the object-relations theory with which we began our discussion of Keller. Before obtaining closure on the work of contemporary feminist epistemology, however, I want to examine briefly some of the work of other theorists whose pieces have appeared in antholo gies and journal articles.


## SLICES OF FEMINIST THEORY

Because of the prominence of work in feminist theory at this time, several journals have devoted entire issues to it (among these, *Cana dian Journal of Philosophy* and *Australasian Journal of Philosophy* have figured heavily), and there remains, of course, *Hypatia*, the one philosophy journal devoted to feminist philosophy. It is no accident that many of the writers in these and other journals echo strains that I have already sketched here, since all of the writers in the field have been affected by the work of Keller, Harding, Bordo, and a few other figures. Nevertheless, each theorist has a different slant, and it would be strikingly unfair to fail to mention some of the pieces—and authors—that are relevant to this endeavor, and relevant in an important way.

*Hypatia* recently published two issues on "Feminism and Science," and several of the articles in these issues tie immediately into my epistemological themes. Writing in the second of the two issues, Ruth Hubbard, in "Science, Facts and Feminism,"[38] reminds us that

> Natural scientists obtain their objectivity by looking upon nature (including other people) in small chunks and as isolated objects. They usually deny, or at least do not acknowledge, their relationships to the "objects" they study. In other words, natural scientists describe their activities as though they existed in a vacuum. The way language is used in scientific writing reinforces this illusion because it implicitly denies the relevance of time, place, social context, authorship and personal responsibility.[39]

In other words, as I have remarked in this chapter at several places, the language of androcentric epistemology and/or philosophy of science takes as the norm for theorizing a stance that is explicitly divorced from context—so cut off from context, that in other employment one might deem the stance pathological. Hubbard is reminding us not only that the androcentric voice is structured in this way, but that it achieves only an "illusion" of distancing, since no human can be fully distanced from the world, and since each human is a product of context to a greater or lesser extent. Thus part of Hubbard's point is that contemporary science's failure to acknowledge that it, too, is driven by social forces beyond its control and is responsive to social conditions that it pretends to ignore leaves us with science-as-lie. (This theme was also a central point of focus for Sandra Harding's work.)

Hubbard continues, "This removes relevance of time and place, and implies that the observation did not originate in the head of a human observer, specifically my head, but out there in the world. . . . The problem is that the context-stripping that worked reasonably well for the classical physics of falling bodies has become the model for how to do every kind of science."[40] Even within philosophy of science itself, it has long been held by many that a degree of preposterousness attaches to the social sciences' pretension (if indeed they have any such pretension) to the "objectivity" of the natural sciences. What has seldom been acknowledged to date is that the natural sciences do not have the objectivity to which they pretend.

Hubbard asks rhetorically if it is possible for us to envision a new sort of science, and then cites the sort of movement that produced the collectivist effort *The New Our Bodies, Ourselves*.[41] Others have frequently cited the work of the Nobelist Barbara McClintock in this regard, at least partially, no doubt, since she is the focus of a work by Evelyn Fox Keller and since she is one of the few women scientists in

recent times who have obtained such recognition. Keller is quick to
point out that the less detached, more involved methods employed by
McClintock could be employed by anyone, male or female, and indeed
have been employed at various times by male workers. Nevertheless,
by the same token, Keller and other observers are struck by the fact
that McClintock's patient attention to each individual corn plant and
assiduous observation of corn plants over a period of time gave birth
to the theory of genetic transposition at a time when other workers in
the field, almost entirely male, ridiculed or ignored the time-consuming
efforts employed. It may be no accident that McClintock is a woman
and that her methods, by her own account, have been remarkably
different from those of other geneticists of her generation.[42]

Writing in the companion issue of *Hypatia*, the feminist philosopher
Helen Longino draws our attention to complexities in the theorizing
about gynocentric or feminist epistemologies that need further consideration. In this chapter I have frequently conflated what might constitute a gynocentric view with what Harding herself has depicted as the
larger project—an ultimately ungendered, or gender-free view that is
somehow true to the realities of gender as they operate in human
societies. The conflation, although it is not deliberate, is almost unavoidable, for it appears throughout the literature. This is one reason,
presumably, why Harding mentioned that "It is true that first we often
have to formulate a 'woman-centered' hypothesis in order to comprehend a gender-free one."[43] But Longino asks us to be still more careful
about what the notion of a "feminist science" could mean:

> The hope for a feminist theoretical natural science has concealed an
> ambiguity between content and practice. In the content sense the idea of
> a feminist science involves a number of assumptions and calls a number
> of visions to mind. Some theorists have written as though a feminist
> science is one the theories of which encode a particular worldview,
> characterized by complexity, interaction and wholism. Such a science is
> said to be feminist because it is the expression and valorization of a
> female sensibility or cognitive temperament. Alternatively, it is claimed
> that women have certain traits (dispositions to attend to particulars,
> interactive rather than individualist and controlling social attitudes and
> behaviors) that enable them to understand the true character of natural
> processes (which are complex and interactive). While proponents of this
> interactionist view see it as an improvement over most of contemporary
> science, it has also been branded as soft—misdescribed as non-mathe-
> matical. . . . I think that the interactionist view can be defended against
> this response. . . . However, I also think that the characterization of

feminist science as the expression of a distinctive female cognitive temperament has other drawbacks. It first conflates feminine with feminist.
While it is important to reject the traditional derogation of the virtues
assigned to women, it is also important to remember that women are
constructed to occupy positions of social subordinates. We should not
uncritically embrace the feminine.[44]

Longino is reminding us here of the difficulty that first made itself
explicit during our discussion of Harding's work. Any sort of science—
masculine, feminine, androcentric, gynocentric, or of some other
sort—must adhere to certain sorts of canons and tenets of theorizing
if it is to be considered a science. My desire to read the Tarot might
possibly be considered evocative of gynocentric patterns of behavior
in certain circles, since the Tarot employs archetypes that lend themselves to a holistic account of living and life on the planet in general.
But my employment of the Tarot for serious purposes of prognostication is not, and can never be (without the most radical sorts of changes
in our auxiliary beliefs) scientific. There is nothing in the Tarot that
lends itself to prediction and explanation consonant with the rest of
our knowledge about the world. As Longino remarks, to hypothesize
that a less androcentric or more female-centered science, philosophy
of science, or epistemology would be notably less rigorous, or "non-
mathematical," is to make a serious mistake.

Longino ends her piece with a call for feminists to practice science
and, at least tacitly, with a call for science to alter its structure
sufficiently so as to make the feminist practice of science possible. But
what is most important about Longino's piece is its recognition of the
necessity to bear in mind what it is that we are talking about when we
discuss a "feminist science," or, for that matter, a "feminist epistemology." If conditions are so radically altered in the conceptualization
of a science or an epistemology that the project is no longer recognizable as falling under that rubric, then relevant distinctions, necessary
for the operation of a science or an epistemology, can no longer be
made. This is one of the reasons, no doubt, why Elizabeth Prior and
Robert Pargetter, writing in the special issue of *Australasian Journal
of Philosophy* devoted to feminist themes, note that "[a certain kind
of feminist] employs the ultimate weapon—a meta-Wittgensteinian
strategy. She not only refuses to play a language game. She refuses to
play the logic game."[45] In the next chapter I hope to explore some of
the reasons why it is still of some use to feminist theory to play the
logic game (or a given language game), and to examine some views

that would run contra the hypothesis that the logic game is useful for a feminist epistemology.

Finally, two other thinkers, Lorraine Code and Alison Wylie, have explored certain themes that have recurred in this chapter in articles published in the recent issue of *Canadian Journal of Philosophy* devoted to "Science, Morality and Feminist Theory." In an article entitled "Second Persons," Code argues that autonomy—a notion frequently employed in ethics—is related to the epistemological distancing characteristic of androcentric epistemology that we have explored in this chapter and that it is overemphasized in philosophical thinking as a whole. Its alternative is what she refers to as the "second person view"—a view that pays attention to interpersonal relationships in an important way and that could serve as the basis for further epistemological or moral theorizing. In this view, the self is not thought of in terms of a definition that would cut it off from others or attempt to detach it from others; rather, the self is thought of or defined in terms of its relationship to others. Code's article is largely concerned with the effects for moral theorizing of such a stance, but she also makes some vivid points with respect to the notion of a relationally defined self and the more classical questions of epistemology:

> Whereas the autonomous *moral* agent makes his most unequivocal appearance as the hero of Kantian moral discourse, the autonomous epistemic agent is perhaps most strikingly visible as the pursuer of the Cartesian "project of pure enquiry." A follower of Descartes' method is radically independent, pursuing the method in a process of solitary rational endeavour, and embarking upon that pursuit by freeing *himself* both from his previously accumulated beliefs and habits of mind, and from the influence of his own material being. . . .
>
> [But] Baier moves to the notion of second personhood in her discussion of "*Cartesian* Persons" by showing that, although Descartes distrusts language as it contrasts with the certainty attainable in pure thought, nonetheless, when they move out of the theoretical mode, "Cartesian persons and embodied Cartesian thinkers *speak* . . ." Descartes himself would not have accorded epistemic significance to the learning processes of infancy and childhood. . . . But Baier argues that "Without earlier confusion to reflect on, a Cartesian intellect would have no purpose. Its ends, like ours, are set by its beginnings."[46]

Here Code makes the valuable point that it is not only in-the-bodiness that is missing from many traditional accounts: There is also a relatedness to others that is missing, even insofar as it might have something to do with the epistemic or cognitive development that is in question. As Code puts it, perception and memory are typically accorded an exaggeratedly large role in most traditional empiricist epistemology.[47]

Alison Wylie's piece "The Philosophy of Ambivalence" is a critical discussion of Harding's work, and I find Wylie's work important because she articulates certain points made here in the discussion of Harding in a fresh and insightful way. Wylie writes that "On balance, it is unavoidable that Harding recommends, at best, a qualified tolerance of incoherence in our theories."[48] But Wylie sees the greatest value in Harding's project in her "clear identification of the constructive tensions that emerge in feminist critiques of science," and in the tacit call of her work continually to attempt to move beyond the limitations and fragmentations of the theories that speak to a specific point of view, or the standpoint theories.[49] How this could be done is, of course, another question.


## FEMINIST EPISTEMICS AND CONSOLIDATION

In this chapter I have attempted to provide an overview of the main strands of argument in what is currently known as feminist epistemology, or perhaps more correctly, the feminist critique of science. The analytically trained philosopher is struck from the outset by the variations in epistemological thinking and conceptualization evident in the voices of feminist theory. Perhaps most intriguing to the analytically trained epistemologist is the comparative paucity of material in the feminist critique that ties directly into the strong twentieth-century epistemological tradition, or which utilizes any of the more technical work in epistemology, philosophy of science, or philosophy of mind in any sort of straightforward and obvious way. What appears at first to be a lacuna to the philosopher most comfortable with analysis is, of course, a lacuna with a point and certainly no accident. The very style of analytic philosophy and epistemology is, as we have seen, androcentric, and although such a style could be employed in endeavors that are feminist at heart, it might appear to be theoretically inconsistent to do so.

On the other hand, the argument can easily be made that no epistemology can divorce itself entirely from its philosophal heritage, or from some of the more traditional sorts of questions with which epistemology has always had to grapple. The coming two chapters, the next in particular, are explicitly devoted to trying to make some sense of the very deep problem at the intersection of contemporary epistemology, philosophy of science, philosophy of mind, and feminist theory. To what extent can feminist theory divorce itself from traditional canons of theorizing (particularly when the theory is not overtly Continental in its antecedents)? Does it make sense to give the title "epistemology" to epistemologies that are far from fully developed, and that (in some instances) bear precious little resemblance to traditional theories of knowledge? If the latter question can be answered in the affirmative, what is the theoretical base of such an epistemology? If the questions ought to be answered in the negative, what new sort of theorizing can emerge that would provide a more structurally sound foundation for feminist attempts to come to grips with questions regarding knowledge and knowledge acquisition?

In the preceding pages we have examined the work of Evelyn Fox Keller, Sandra Harding, and Susan Bordo, with a brief excursion into essays and responses developed by other theorists. Several major theoretical points are iterated by each theorist, and reiterations only enforce the striking quality of such points as they speak to feminist theory as a whole. The important work done by Dorothy Dinnerstein and Nancy Chodorow over a decade ago, detailing how child-rearing practices affect the development of the individual, and of males in particular, has now become one of the foci of feminist theory.[50] As I indicated during the discussion of Keller, the tendency has been to refer to this focus as "object-relations theory," but this rather simplified appellation, derived, as has been indicated, from classical Freudian theory and its offshoots, does not do full justice to the importance of these notions for feminist theory. One might rather refer to gender development theory, or individual gender role theory. In any case, the notion that males and females are reared differently, acquire their respective gender roles (on the whole) in a different manner, and that this manner of acquisition has far-reaching cultural manifestations that can scarcely be overstated has been one of the most salient points of feminist theory.

It is a peculiar and emphatic virtue of Keller's work that she is able to utilize this heavily plowed area in a way such that its ramifications are ably articulated and made admirably clear. Keller does not oversimplify, nor is she satisfied with the sort of coarse dichotomizing that the anti-feminists are only too happy to attribute, however incorrectly, to feminism.[51] The varying cognitive styles delineated by Keller can and do occur over a wide range of individuals, and only the broadest sorts of strokes enable us to refer to the styles as "masculinist" or "gynocentric." Because Keller is able to cite specific examples of the styles at work in the natural sciences, her work is made all the more valuable, and some objections are vanquished from the outset.

Sandra Harding's work is perhaps the most detailed, and certainly the most encyclopaedic in its scope and outlook. I have focused on Harding's assessment of the three projects that she specifically selects for critical targeting, feminist empiricism, feminist standpoint epistemologies, and feminist postmodernism, because since Harding's work was published these three rubrics have fallen into common use, and also because Harding does such a thorough job of investigating them. As Alison Wylie has written, Harding identifies "constructive tensions," and does so in a way that allows the reader to come to her or his own conclusions.[52] Nevertheless, I find the most intriguing paradox uncovered by Harding to be the very area that has received perhaps the least attention in the literature: the paradox of feminist empiricism. The standpoint epistemologies and the postmodernist view now have their able exponents, and (one hypothesizes) because their paradoxes are not quite so evident nor so overt they seem to have emerged with a popularity that does not attach to even more sophisticated versions of feminist empiricism. The specific tensions that adhere to varieties of feminist empiricism will be the focus of much of the remainder of this work, and part of the project of this text is to articulate more fully the paradox of feminist empiricism and to attempt to come to some sort of resolution with regard to it.

Susan Bordo's work has most carefully and fully developed notions that provide a cultural and intellectual history for the kind of conceptualization that, above, I have labeled "gender development theory." If the birth and development of the individual is recapitulated in some way in the birth and development of contemporary post-Renaissance and postindustrial society, this phylogeny-recapitulates-ontogeny sort of cultural view needs to be fully set out, and Bordo has done so. Thus her work on Descartes not only forces us to look at the idiosyncrasies of temperament displayed by one who seemingly employs depersonalization for theoretical purposes, but also asks us to clarify our notions of the development of European culture as a whole at that time. Thus, as I indicated, we are left with a portrait of Descartes (and many of his contemporaries) as individuals who displayed in their thinking some of the characteristics that gender development theory asks us to assert as consequent to the development of male gender, and we are also left with a portrait of these thinkers as culturally displaced individuals whose intellectual groundings were in the process of being shaken and liquefied. Thus the notion of the double rupture; thus also, thanks to Bordo, a clearer overview of the development of later Western thought.

Finally, I have highlighted some small portions of the work of Ruth Hubbard, Helen Longino, Elizabeth Prior and Robert Pargetter, Lorraine Code, and Alison Wylie to provide some of the flavor of journal pieces and shorter articles that have been and are part of the feminist critique. All of the pieces deal in some way with the baby-and-the-bathwater question, the question Harding labeled "the science question in feminism," but that might best be labeled here "the knowledge question in feminism." Contemporary analytic philosophy provides us with a lengthy, elegant, and detailed history of precise work in epistemology. But the very viewpoints that have characterized much of the work have been dubbed androcentric, and rightly so. Is it possible to utilize these androcentric tools to perform feminist tasks? It is to this question that I now turn.

# NOTES

1. Lorraine Code has examined this area to some extent. See her *Epistemic Responsibility* (Hanover, N.H.: University Press of New England, 1987).

2. The journal of feminist philosophy, *Hypatia,* has made an enormous contribution here, particularly with its special double issue on feminism and science (vol. 2, no. 3 [1987], and vol. 3, no. 1 [1988]).

3. See, for example, Luce Irigaray's "Le Sujet de Science: Est-il Sexué?", translated by Carol Mastrangelo Bové as "Is the Subject of Science Sexed?" and appearing in *Hypatia* 2, no. 3 (1987):65–87. There is, of course, a great deal of other work in this tradition, some of which will be investigated in chap. six.

4. Keller's work has been of the utmost importance, no doubt at least partly because she is herself a trained scientist. *Reflections on Gender and Science* was preceded by several journal pieces that had already received wide circulation in feminist circles.

5. The major works on this topic, for feminist theory, have been Nancy Chodorow's *The Reproduction of Mothering* (Berkeley: University of California Press, 1976), and Dorothy Dinnerstein's *The Mermaid and the Minotaur* (New York: Harper and Row, 1976).

6. It has been hypothesized that males are more prone to gender-identity difficulties (as they are currently defined by the medical and social sciences) and females to core- or ego-identity problems for these very sorts of reasons. One school of thought has it that this sort of object-relations view helps account for the comparative paucity of female transsexuals to male transsexuals, for example. Some of these problems (insofar as males are concerned) are examined in Robert Green's *The 'Sissy' Boy Syndrome and Male Homosexuality* (New Haven, Conn.: Yale University Press, 1986).

7. Janice Raymond, in *A Passion for Friends* (Boston: Beacon Press, 1986), offers an insightful and clear analysis of why it is that female bonding and relationships, erotic or otherwise, so seldom figure in the crucial strands of Western culture.

8. Evelyn Fox Keller, "Feminism and Science," in *The Signs Reader: Women, Gender and Scholarship,* ed. Elizabeth Abel and Emily K. Abel (Chicago: University of Chicago Press, 1984), 112.

9. These chapters are pp. 139–149 and 150–157, respectively.

10. Quine, W. V. O., "Two Dogmas of Empiricism," reprinted in *From a Logical Point of View.*

11. Suppe, *The Structure, passim.*

12. These accounts are widely considered a response to rigid positivism because they emphasize the way in which scientists actually work, rather than the idealized model that would assume to prescribe the way in which they should work (the normative/descriptive distinction again). See Thomas Kuhn, *The Structure of Scientific Revolutions* (Chicago: University of Chicago Press, 1962).

13. Keller, *Reflections*, 126.

14. Keller, *Reflections*, 127.

15. Keller is very careful to avoid the trap of a too superficial, too easy "feminist philosophy of science." See her "Epilogue," pp. 177–79, in *Reflections*.

16. See Helen Longino's review of Harding in *Feminist Studies* 14, no. 3 (1988):92–109. This superb essay, which also looks at two other related works, is entitled "Science, Objectivity and Feminist Values."

17. Harding spells out what she means by these terms in a very important discussion in *The Science Question*, 24–29.

18. Harding, *The Science Question*, 25.

19. Ibid., 25.

20. Ibid.

21. The greater part of the work cited in Harding's lengthy bibliography falls into these two categories.

22. Ibid., 138.

23. Ibid., 147.

24. Ibid., 102.

25. Ibid., 150.

26. Ibid., 148.

27. Ibid., 151.

28. Ibid., 152.

29. Ibid., 153.

30. Ibid., 10.

31. Chodorow, *Reproduction*.

32. Bordo *Flight*, 94.

33. Ibid., 62–63.

34. This is the title of Bordo's second chapter.

35. Ibid., 4.

36. Bordo quoting Burtt, p. 35. The Burtt material is from his *The Meta physical Foundations of Modern Science* (Garden City, N.Y.: Doubleday, 1941), 16.

37. Ibid., 34 35; for commentary upon the Chinese, see p. 42.

38. Ruth Hubbard, "Science, Facts and Feminism," *Hypatia* 3, no. 1 (1988):5–18.

39. Ibid., 11.

40. Ibid., 12–13.

41. See Boston Women's Healthbook Collective, *The New Our Bodies, Ourselves* (Boston, Mass.: The Collective, 1984).

42. Evelyn Fox Keller, *A Feeling for the Organism* (San Francisco: John Wiley and Sons, 1983), *passim*.

43. Harding, *The Science Question*, 138.

44. Helen Longino, "Can There be a Feminist Science?", *Hypatia* 2, no. 3 (1987):52–53.

45. Elizabeth W. Prior and Robert Pargetter, "Against the Sexuality of Reason," *Australasian Journal of Philosophy*, Supplement to vol. 64 (1986):108.

46. Lorraine Code, "Second Persons," *Canadian Journal of Philosophy*, Supplementary vol., "Science, Morality and Feminist Theory," (1987):374, 376. The Baier quotes are from Annette Baier, ed., "Cartesian Persons," in *Postures of the Mind: Essays on Mind and Morals* (Minneapolis: University of Minnesota Press, 1985), 80, 86.

47. Code, "Second Persons," 376.

48. Alison Wylie, "The Philosophy of Ambivalence," *Canadian Journal of Philosophy*, Supplementary vol. (1987):71.

49. Ibid.

50. Dinnerstein, *Mermaid,* and Chodorow, *Reproduction.*

51. See Ruth Bleier, *Science and Gender* (New York: Pergamon, 1984).

52. Cf. fn. 49.

# Chapter Four

# Toward a Feminist Epistemology

In the previous chapters we have constructed more than one overview. Chapter one provided us with a large-scale view of analytic epistemology, from the early period of the twentieth century to analytic epistemology of the moment. In chapter two I sketched the project now dubbed "naturalized epistemology," and tried to make explicit how some of the strands of the more naturalistic work in theory of knowledge are best seen as offshoots of work originally in mainstream analytic epistemology. The overview provided in the last chapter, chapter three, was perhaps the most difficult of the three to design, and at the same time the most valuable broad view for the purposes of my project. An overview of what has come to be known as "feminist epistemology" inevitably omits or leaves out a great deal of material, since the scope of feminist epistemology is so large; nevertheless, it is feminist epistemology, as it has been constructed in approximately the last decade, that is of crucial importance for the intersection of naturalized and gynocentric strands that I hope to create here.

In chapter three we saw that a pressing question for the area of theorizing that Harding has labeled "feminist empiricism" has been the inconsistency between some of the claims of neutrality inherent in any empiricism and the claims of feminist scholars that the view itself is far from neutral. To recapitulate briefly, the debate had been characterized in the following terms: Empiricism purports or alleges to employ values and methods that are unbiased and untainted, so to

speak, by the personality or characteristics of the observer or investigator. But feminist analysis of the sciences and the theoretical structure of the sciences reveals them to be shot through with masculinist
or androcentric bias. How, then, could a feminist coherently argue for
the position called "feminist empiricism?" How could a feminist claim
that empiricism is the method of choice, while still claiming that the
facts that empiricists set out to investigate could be better investigated—more unbiasedly investigated, so to speak—if there were more
women investigators? Does not this very claim show that empiricism
is not the neutral tool it purports to be, thus demonstrating that
empiricism is not the tool of choice?

Harding's discussion of this question led inevitably to her thorough
analysis of the standpoint epistemologies. But in the opening sections
of the present chapter I want to continue an analogous discussion,
since it will prove central to my project.

The problem, cursorily sketched, is along the following lines. Analytic philosophy is a tool in and of itself, and during the twentieth
century the primary method of analytic philosophy has been what
philosophers have called the empirical point of view. This is not, of
course, identical to empiricism *simpliciter* as it functions in the sciences, since the areas of endeavor for the sciences and for philosophy
itself are not the same. Nevertheless, it is no accident that the sciences
declare themselves empirical and that analytic philosophy, influenced
by and to some extent (especially in this century) derivative of the
sciences, does the same and came to the fore at a time when the
sciences were becoming most prominent. So it seems apparent that to
employ analytic philosophy as a tool of investigation is to employ a
method that has traditionally been allied with empirical endeavor and
mimics its precision. Indeed, when we make the distinction between
analytic philosophy and the philosophy or philosophies of the Continent for our beginning students, we frequently focus on this distinction.
If they have one area in common, most of the Continental strands of
philosophy—whatever their origins—do not focus on the same sort of
empirically derived investigation that has been the hallmark of contemporary analytic philosophy.

So, of course, a question arises for the feminist philosopher that is
similar to, or more properly analogous to the question that arises for
the feminist scientist: Is it possible to employ a tool of analysis that
has already been shown to be androcentric in its origins and its goals
for feminist purposes? This question, seldom articulated so flatly, is, I
believe, at the heart of much of what constitutes feminist work in

philosophy today, for it is clear from a perusal of the major thinkers and the resulting publications that much of the work that has been done in philosophy and that is feminist is not within the framework of the analytic tradition. Indeed, in my portrayal of the major strands of thought in the feminist critique of science in the preceding chapter, it was clear that two of the three major thinkers I cited (Harding and Bordo) were not working primarily or largely within the analytic tradition, and that Evelyn Fox Keller may be said to be working within that tradition only insofar as her work refers to other strands of contemporary philosophy of science, such as positivism and the *weltanschauungen* responses to it, or to science itself (and even this assessment is, of course, up for grabs).

So it would appear to be controversial for a feminist philosopher to employ analytic philosophy to attempt to create a feminist epistemology. Indeed, the very critiques we have examined—particularly Bordo's, with its historical emphasis—have shown how the privileged access stances associated with epistemology and with the Received View or positivist work in philosophy of science are androcentric in their origins.[1]

## FEMINIST EMPIRICISM AND ANALYTIC PHILOSOPHY

In the opening sections of this chapter I have two major arguments to make. I propose to argue, first of all, that the mere fact that analytic epistemology has been, in its major constructions, an androcentric method should not mean that it cannot be reconstructed and used for feminist purposes. This argument, although not made explicitly with regard to epistemology, has been made by other feminist thinkers with regard to science itself. In fact, part of the debate between various schools engaged in the feminist critique of science has been on this very point. Some feminist thinkers seem to believe that the nature of science itself would have to be changed were it to become a less androcentric enterprise. Others feel that science as an enterprise must remain on the whole the same, but that it is the manner in which science is practiced (whether by feminists or not) that is the crucial point.[2] I propose to argue, analogously, that analytic philosophy is a tool that can be employed for feminist purposes. This particular line of argument, though perhaps somewhat controversial, should not be unfamiliar to those who have closely followed the debate over the science question in feminism.

My second argument, however, may be more controversial. It is not, after all, analytic theory of knowledge in its classic form that I propose to utilize to create a new and more fully articulated feminist epistemology. It would be difficult (although no doubt not impossible) to employ such theory of knowledge in its standard form, since it does not seem to lend itself readily to such a purpose. What I do propose to employ to create a feminist theory of knowledge is one or more of the strands of naturalized epistemology that I examined in chapter two. As I argued at the time, these strands of theory are already less distanced, less normative, and less idealized than many of the moves in analytic epistemology that preceded them, and they seem to lend themselves much more easily to the feminist project. My second argument—an argument not yet made in the literature, to my knowledge—will try to show that naturalized epistemology meshes with and can become a useful part of feminist theory, and will specifically point to the relevant portions of naturalized theory of knowledge that may be utilized.

Before proceeding on to the examination of naturalized epistemology in a feminist context, however, I want to elucidate some of the problems of feminist empiricism. It is important to argue that the baby need not be thrown out with the bathwater: Merely stating that we want to save the baby is not enough. We need to show why the project of saving the baby is a valuable one.

In trying to come to grips with the problem of feminist empiricism, it is helpful to note (as I have indicated earlier) that the problem is simply a more specialized version of a problem that affects most disciplines and, fortunately or unfortunately, most points of view from which a feminist might possibly theorize.[3] The problem, simply put, is that almost all theory—indeed, almost all articulation within the culture that has received any sort of official sanction—is done essentially in the masculine voice and with masculinist or androcentric aims. It is for these reasons that radical feminists writing and postulating in other domains frequently exhort us to create a new language so as to avoid the thought patterns associated with the patriarchal point of view.[4] Thus the problem of feminist empiricism is only the problem of feminist theory *simpliciter* writ small, so to speak.

Given, however, that some theoretical views seem to be more androcentric from the outset than others, how, one might inquire, could a feminist possibly employ them? Both standard science itself, as practiced in the various natural sciences, and theoretical overviews of science, such as history and philosophy of science, not to mention the philosophical parent of philosophy of science, epistemology, employ the thinking I have sketched in preceding chapters, and particularly in chapter one. Certain tenets of the thinking bear repetition, as they are broad and general enough to be relevant both to the practice of science and any intellectualized investigations of it, and also specific enough to bear weight in the charge of androcentrism. The sciences and their theoretical relatives accept the distinction between the empirical and the nonempirical (that is, the distinction between a world of facts reachable through the senses, and any speculation not confirmable by sensory evidence); between language that is theoretically confirmable/disconfirmable and language that does not employ statements susceptible of confirmation; and the distinction between what I might describe as the contents of my own mind, and the outer world knowable through the senses. These are crude formulations; any given body of theory has permutations that utilize elements far more sophisticated than the elements I have just described. Nevertheless, it is worth remarking on the fact that one of the feminist criticisms of masculinist thought has frequently been its tendency to think in dichotomies; the very setup of these theoretical dyads is already androcentric.

Perhaps more importantly, the sciences—at least according to some philosophers of science—long had as their foundation a sort of positivistic view of science that, however outmoded now, was once enormously influential. And as I have written here earlier, this positivistic view, with its emphasis on confirmation/disconfirmation and a logically idealized view of scientific confirmation, is a direct philosophical descendant of the sense-data views and the "incorrigibility" theses to which they gave rise.[5] These in turn are, of course, related to foundationalist epistemology and to the classic sorts of theories of knowledge examined in chapter one. And, lest the point be made too often, many commentators hold that the historical antecedents of all of this trace directly back to Descartes, if not further. Certainly it is not straining the matter at all to note the concern that Descartes had for the contents of his own mind, the peculiar epistemic status of a certain portion of those contents, and the later concern for the status of incorrigible mental images shown by twentieth-century analytic philosophers.

Bordo has Descartes as simultaneous victim of the cultural disruption of a Europe on edge and (although she does not spell this out) victim of the male rupture from the mother. But even if some elements of this rather poignant portrait of Descartes are not completely correct, one senses in the *Meditations* an author and thinker who is accustomed to cutting himself off from the senses with some regularity. One supposes that the chain of thought leading directly to the *Meditations* was far from the first such chain of thought he had ever had.

The charge of androcentrism is true then both of the sciences and epistemology/philosophy of science, and it may well be true that certain portions of contemporary epistemology and philosophy of science constitute almost a paradigmatically androcentric endeavor. (One contrasts, for example, even an area like analytic ethics, which does not have the same subject matter and consequently cannot have the same remoteness of style, try though it will.) Given all of the foregoing, then, the counterargument to the charge that the tools or methods of empiricism—or of empirically based philosophical work— are inappropriate for feminist endeavor must be spelled out.

My counterargument to this charge—and subargument along the previously stated lines of trying to show that portions of analytic philosophy can be reconstructed for feminist purposes—itself has two parts. I intend to reiterate more precisely my broad charge that virtually no area of theorizing is androcentricity-free; hence, we are speaking largely of degrees of androcentric bias. Second, and more importantly, I want to make the positive argument: Empiricism itself, its methods, and the analytic philosophy of recent times, derived from empiricist trends in previous centuries, is a tool of the utmost precision. Empiricism/analysis has the defects of its virtues and the virtues of its defects. It is distanced, dichotomizing, and "objective" precisely because it is neither metaphorical nor vague. Its precision may be bought at the expense of certain other qualities, but my argument will be that precision is a virtue that well-done feminist philosophy, and feminist epistemology in particular, badly needs.

For the first part of my argument I intend to reiterate what has already been stated, but I hope to state it more precisely. The feminist standpoint epistemologies and feminist postmodernism, as well as various strands of feminist theory that wear neither label but that deem themselves relatively immune to masculinist influence, all suffer from obvious androcentric tendencies. I am willing to concede that in style and content the bias may not be as blatant here as it is in standard empirical analysis; nevertheless, to fail to make this bias explicit is to do damage to feminist theory. The standpoint epistemologies, as exemplified mainly by Hartsock and Flax, rely almost entirely on theory developed by major male thinkers of the nineteenth and twentieth centuries. Hartsock's analysis is essentially Marxist and post-Marxist.[6] It may very well be a beneficial side effect of the work done by Marx and Engels that it at least took the status of nineteenth-century women into account, but the theory itself is related directly to the work of Hegel, Kant, and many others.[7] It is difficult to make the claim that this large body of Marxist-derived theory is significantly less androcentric than any other body of philosophical work. Flax's work (and Chodorow's, for that matter) is reliant on Freudian theory. Again the same sort of worry arises; again the response is the same. The fact that Freud was not a logician or semanticist and that his area of endeavor was different (one must not forget that he was originally a physician) does not make his theory any less masculinist. It is, of course, a staple of contemporary feminism that insofar as content is concerned, classical psychoanalytic theory is overtly masculinist, and in a very unrepentant sort of way.

Feminist postmodernism—with the possible exception of the strand relying mainly on Cixous—suffers from the same defects. Any theory borrowing largely from Lacan borrows from a thinker whose analysis of culture is that it is derivative of *la langue paternelle*. Cixous has attempted to describe a language of woman, and in this sense has gone against Lacanian theory in its boldest form. Nevertheless, her theory has been labeled incoherent by some for these very sorts of reasons.[8] The remainder of what is usually referred to as postmodernism has its sources in the thought of Jacques Derrida, Giles DeLeuze, and even the various members of the Frankfurt School. The reader can fill in the argument here for herself or himself.

Admittedly, none of this theory is as *rigorous* as empiricism and the theoretical work in philosophy derived from it. And if one associates this rigor with such characteristically rigid masculine endeavors as mathematics and the mathematically influenced sciences, it may be true that that body of theory is still more androcentric. But this can only be a matter of degree. There currently exists no well-articulated theory in the sciences that is not androcentric.

Having said so much, the positive argument remains to be formulated. It has been typical of analytic philosophy in the twentieth century to employ levels of analysis characterized by high degrees of precision. The antecedents of this carefully alembicated type of analysis are not difficult to discern; indeed, we have already examined them at some length in our look at the history of contemporary analytic epistemology in the first chapter. The moves in logic, Fregean and otherwise, which enabled Russell, Moore, and others to develop a style of analysis that employed logical rigor to approach problems of metaphysics and epistemology were moves that were to have a lasting effect on the philosophy of this century. However normative and intransigent to naturalized strains analytic philosophy may have become, it does not suffer from the defects of muddledness and poorly articulated conceptualizing that, according to Russell, typified much of the Anglo-American philosophy immediately preceding its development. Just as the rise in prestige and power of the sciences themselves during the twentieth century followed along lines established partially through nineteenth-century breakthroughs in physics and mathematics, work in formal logic allowed philosophers to address problems with a degree of specificity heretofore nonexistent.

It is a conundrum for feminist theory—particularly for a feminist trained as a philosopher—that the very methods that might be the most useful tools for developing new lines of theory are, at least in some instances, the methods that might also, in their extreme formulations, be dubbed the most androcentric. But failure to employ these methods does not guarantee that one will employ other methods that are somehow notably less androcentric. Indeed, phrased bluntly, part of the problem seems to revolve around which androcentrism one chooses. The insights of feminist postmodernism, and even of the standpoint epistemologies, are achieved at a price, that price being the loss of precision. I believe that newer, more powerful analyses, particularly in the rather narrowly focused endeavor of feminist epistemology, can be had simply by employing the tools of analytic philosophy in new and somewhat more creative ways. Feminist philosophy cannot afford to lose the hope of developing an analytically based conceptualization of some of its major problematic areas simply to avoid having to employ the politically incorrect tools of contemporary analytic philosophy.

## NATURALIZED EPISTEMOLOGY AND THE STANDPOINT EPISTEMOLOGIES

In this chapter I want to develop an outline of an analytically based feminist epistemology. Toward that end I need to introduce some helpful notions, partially derived from the work in preceding chapters, which lead to the realization of that goal. In the following section I want to expand upon some of the important points made by the standpoint epistemologies and then tie those points into work currently being done in naturalized epistemology, philosophy of mind, and even sociologuistics and discourse processing studies in psychology. The intersection of these areas of endeavor is a crucially important one for feminist theory.

The standpoint epistemologies, especially as articulated by Hartsock and Flax, remind us of the extent to which (as we saw earlier) female modes of functioning may be thought of as bodily aware, contextually sensitized, and interactionally sensitive. Hartsock has noticed that Marxist and quasi-Marxist analyses seem to posit an ontology that, in its emphasis on the individual seen in social relations, is uniquely suited to the needs of a feminist metaphysics and epistemology. But the bare bones of the Marxist ontology, even if viewed properly, is hardly sufficient to do all the work in the feminist project. Hartsock alludes to the fact that, in Marxist terms, "The focus on women's subsistence activity rather than men's leads to a model in which the capitalist (male) lives a life structured completely by commodity exchange and not at all by production, and at the furthest distance from contact with concrete material life." This allows her to define more fully what woman's contact with that material life amounts to, in terms of a division of labor.[9]

She writes:

> Her immersion in the world of use—in concrete, many-qualitied, changing material processes—is more complete than [a man's]. And if life itself consists of sensuous activity, the vantage point available to women on the basis of the contribution to subsistence represents an intensification and deepening of the materialist world view and consciousness available to the producers of commodities in capitalism, an intensification of class consciousness.[10]

Thus woman has the standpoint, so to speak, for a differing epistemology. Flax's analysis focuses on the "relational" aspects of experience; "dialectics" and the "multiplicity of experience" itself.[11] In an earlier passage on Harding's allusion to Flax's work, I mentioned the importance of object-relations theory for Flax's view. But as Harding puts it, more is involved insofar as styles of cognizing are related to styles of being-in-the-world.

> This small gap between the genders [the gap created, according to object-relations theory, by differing experiences of rupture from the mother] prefigures a larger gap between the defensive gendered selves produced in patriarchal modes of child rearing and the reciprocal, degendered selves that *could* exist were men as well as women primary caretakers of infants, and women as well as men responsible for public life.[12]

Again, there is certainly ample basis for the development of a theoretically based female standpoint, and hence a feminist epistemology. But a fuller articulation of such an epistemology is necessary.

The emphasis on the relational and concretely grounded aspects of women's experience discussed by Hartsock and Flax is intriguing from the overview of theory of knowledge because it is an emphasis that, despite the absence of naturalized views in earlier analytic epistemology, is now coming to the fore in analytic epistemology as a whole. That is not to say, of course, that new trends in analytic epistemology have utilized the feminist critique of science, or even that they have been largely aware of such critique. Nevertheless, it appears that in one of those odd cultural junctures that sometimes occurs in the histories of disparate disciplines, the feminist standpoint epistemologies are being brought to the fore just at the time when analytic epistemology itself is at least being made aware of the relational aspects of knowing for all knowers, so to speak, if not the "concretely grounded" aspects of knowing. In the following section I intend to argue that the newer, more naturalized trends in analytic epistemology are especially valuable to the feminist project, and to show how such trends might be used.

Insofar as contextual awareness is concerned, the development of the notion of female cognizer as more contextually aware and sensitive in the standpoint literature is a notion that can easily be ameliorated and developed in a precise fashion through the utilization of naturalized epistemology. Part of what is meant by "contextually sensitive" in the standpoint epistemologies has to do with, again, the notion of bodily awareness, but part of it has to do with notions of focus on interpersonal communication, awareness of nuance in interpersonal exchanges, and a focus on the texture or quality of interpersonal exchanges.

## NATURALIZING THE FEMINIST VIEWPOINT

These foci are directly tied into much of the work in naturalized epistemology that reminds us that current work in cognitive science emphasizes the fact that knowledge cannot be divorced from context. In other words, cognitive science stresses the fact that for all knowers—male or female, adult or child—the actual modes of cognizing and coming-to-knowledge are heavily reliant on context. Kornblith, in the work cited here earlier having to do with his analysis of the philosophical import of the Asch experiments, indicates that we are hardwired to pick up social cues that provide us with much of our knowledge. A great deal of data, and some nonempirical speculation, indicates that women might in fact be somewhat more adept at translating and noticing some of these cues than men.[13] But in any case, the important point is that everyone is contextually bound to some degree in his or her cognitive functioning. If women are more contextually sensitive, it merely highlights the theoretical uses to which a contextually sensitive epistemology or theory of epistemic justification could be put with regard to feminist thought.

In addition, the focus on contextual cues and interpersonal interaction also stresses some of what Annis, Kornblith, and others have cited as the interactional nature of epistemic justification.[14] The Cartesian doubt—the hyperbolic doubt characteristic of highly ramified androcentric theory, and marked by distancing and divorce from the body— is a doubt brought on largely, if not entirely, by pure speculation. But the vast majority of situations in which epistemic doubt actually occurs are brought on either by challenge from someone acting as a skeptical agent for the person in the position of making the knowledge claim, or initiated by the person himself or herself in a mundane context that actually puts the claim in doubt (not a context, like Descartes's, where ordinarily a claim to be in a dressing gown seated by the fire would not be in doubt). Thus there is an interactional, communicative edge to epistemic challenge, and if there is such an edge to the challenge, there is also such an edge to the justification. Justification is a process of answering the skeptic—the skeptic may be another person, or it may be that skeptical portion of oneself. Skeptical doubts are unlikely to be global (worries about Evil Demons) and unlikely to occur without mundane basis unless one is a professionally trained philosopher. It no doubt says much for the force of speculative androcentric theory that it can be used to train philosophers to attempt to doubt the sorts of situations that are seldom or rarely rendered dubitable in ordinary daily life.

The contextual nature of knowledge and the interactional pattern of knowledge acquisition are thus two areas that have been emphasized in feminist theory and that are ripe for expansion in a theoretically rigorous direction under the pull of naturalized analytic epistemology. A third area may be slightly less obvious but is just as important.

The emphasis on in-the-bodiness of feminist theory is also an emphasis on the senses. Whether it is female sensitivity to pain, to cyclical changes, or other hormonal capacities particular to females, it is clear that the feminine modes of knowing that have been described in the literature are related to bodily functioning in a way that the classic androcentric theory is not. Now here the fact that the pull is toward the senses rather than away from the senses provides fertile ground for further theorization. As Goldman has documented, recent work in cognitive theory emphasizes perception, visualization capacities, and even auditory and tactile discrimination.[15] It is, of course, completely true that the work cited by those interested in cognitive theory is intended to be applicable to all humans. But until the recent moves in naturalized epistemology, only feminist theory seemed to have any interest at all in trying to integrate an account of sensory awareness into an epistemology.

Now it may be objected here that what the feminist theorists have typically intended by contextualization, communication, and sensory awareness is all best described at a much more metaphorical level than naturalized epistemology would have it. But my claim, argued for here at an earlier point, is that to accept such a depiction is to accept a level of imprecision for feminist theory that is neither necessary nor desirable. It is not necessary simply because we do have the tools to describe more accurately some of the feminist claims. It is not desirable because to accept these claims as mere metaphor is, I argue, to seriously weaken them. Is what is meant by "bodily awareness" simply a poetic expression, of use because women have the capacity to give birth? Or is it in fact empirically true that women, taken as a whole, tend to be more bodily aware, less distanced from the body, and more fully integrated with the body and cognizant of its functioning? If the latter is the case—as evidence, both anecdotal and nonanecdotal, seems to show—then the claim may be filled out in a way that borrows the precision of analytic philosophy and even of the empirical sciences for feminist theory. It seems to be offering feminist theory much less than it should be offered to simply accept that its claims are largely or entirely metaphorical and that they lose something when attempts at more precise articulation of the claims are made.

I want for the time being to focus on the three notions I adduced above (contextualization, communicative awareness, and bodily awareness) to develop some relatively unrefined lines of theory with regard to epistemic justification. I intend now to begin to try to integrate feminist theory and naturalized epistemology in such a way that it is clear what the latter can do for the former. Inevitably the first attempts will be somewhat coarse, but I hope at a later point to be able to refine the theory.

With regard to the first two notions, contextualization and communicative awareness, standard analytic epistemology, even in its nonnaturalized guises, already has something to tell us about these notions. I have alluded to coherence theory previously, particularly in the first chapter, as being somewhat more intuitively palatable, even as a normative theory, than foundationalism, simply because the notion that cognizers deal with the formation of webs or networks of beliefs is an immediately appealing one. In previous work in epistemology, I have sketched some naturalized responses to the sorts of problems for classical epistemology that the standard androcentric theory proposes. In the first chapter we saw that the standard response to foundationalist theories that relied on notions such as "incorrigible" was a tight counterexampling, such as that proposed by Austin and others, which reminded us that no knowledge claim—even one that involves privileged access accounts of internal images—is safe from counters, from the possibility of refutation, or from the possibility of corrigibility. I did not go into detail with regard to the problems faced by classical coherentism in the first chapter, but a standard response to theories that tried to provide a cohering basis for knowledge claims (that is, which tried to establish that knowledge claims are justified by appeal to other claims or beliefs in a chain, with no claim or belief having special foundational status) has been that it is not possible to pinpoint a group or set of such claims that can serve as an epistemic basis for any possible claim and still be consistent.[16] Because the normative androcentric theories are concerned about any sort of epistemic challenge, no matter how far removed from the mundane, and because they are working within the Cartesian tradition of attempting certainty against versions of the Evil Demon hypothesis, it does not occur to normative theorists that the obvious way to reduce the size of a cohering network or set is to allude to context. That is, most cognizers make their claim within a context and attempt to justify it within that context. Appeals to esoteric topics such as theories of contemporary physics are rarely made, unless of course it is material from physics that is the topic of discussion.

Now these sorts of insights are already possessed by feminist theory, as we have seen. Because the emphasis in the standpoint epistemologies has been on context and communication, the style of theorizing that yields the sorts of problems familiar from criticisms of classical coherentism has not come to the fore.

## A FEMINIST EPISTEMICS

Preliminarily, then, I want to introduce the notions of contextualization and communication through work done previously in naturalized epistemology. Then I will be able to provide an analytic framework that integrates feminist theory and naturalized epistemology.

With regard to contextualization, it may prove instructive to look at a problem from classical coherentism formulated by James Cornman, and a naturalized response to it. The naturalized response relies heavily on the notion of contextualization as important for an adequate picture of the construction of a cognizer's justifying web or network.

Writing analytically, Cornman notices that even those who have attempted to construct coherence theories of justification based on the notion that explanation is the vehicle through which the coherence occurs have run across the difficulty that the justifying webs or sets are either too large or inconsistent, or that the existence of one set only is underdetermined. Cornman notes that "an EC-theorist [explanatory coherence theorist] who proposes principles . . . that rely solely on agreement has no non-arbitrary way to justify that some set from among the many conflicting maximally consistent sets of observation statements is to be explained [that is, is simultaneously to be explained and serve as 'explainers' for other statements]."[17] In other words, a justifying web or network that has explanatory power and wherein statements rely on explanation to justify each other is always underdetermined, since there will be too many such consistent sets. It is also, according to Cornman, difficult to restrict the sets by size. (The theorist struggles to find "a non-arbitrary way to restrict the statements that are to be explained."[18])

But if the notion that context usually provides the input that cognizers use for justification is fully retained, then it is clear that context vastly reduces the size of a potential justifying network or set. We have previously cited Kornblith's work on Asch in this regard, since it emphasizes the importance of social construction; we tend to rely not only on physical context, but on others and what they say.[19] David Annis is another philosopher who has written of the importance of context; he has noted that, socially speaking, "Meeting an objection does not require showing the objection is false. It only requires general agreement on the response.''[20] Therefore a technical problem like the Cornmanian problem for coherence theory can be resolved in a naturalized way, and a way that is in accord with feminist intuitions on the modes of functioning of female cognizers. I intend to argue at a later point that feminist intuitions may in some sense be applicable to a large part of the human race: It becomes clear that women, children, and males in tribal or preliterate societies probably all employ or did employ modes of reasoning that are more in accord with the principles cited by the standpoint epistemologists than one might at first be inclined to believe. The hypernormative androcentric style is probably a style that accrues mainly to extremely well educated males functioning in Western or Westernized societies. But, in any case, to make a first attempt to wed these two strands of theory—naturalized epistemology and feminist epistemics—one can provide a fair approximation of a naturalized, feminist overview of justification while employing the methods of analytic precision.

A statement $p$ is justified from the naturalized cohering standpoint if:

    (i) the statement is in a justifying network or set of statements, $J$, for cognizer $s$ at $t$;

and (ii) if it appears that the set $J$ is underdetermined, conflicting justifying sets or networks are discarded on contextual grounds, the grounds including

    (a) that the set $J$ that is picked out is most fully in accord with social norms and practices, and

    (b) that social communication itself helps to establish (a).''[21]

Now the normative theorists would object immediately that I have no provisions for assurance of truth here. A number of standard normative counterexamples come easily to mind: It might be the case, for example, that my justifying set in some context is determined by statements taken from a Ouija board, since I am in a context where I and others are believers in the efficacy of prognostication by Ouija boards and in the truth of the statements that are allegedly produced by the board. It is the case that a set of such statements does not meet standard normative conditions for knowledge; indeed, the literature is full of such examples, and the general tendency of theorists has been to argue that even where Ouija boards and gypsy fortune tellers seem to have unending reliability as prognosticators, their prognosticatory utterances cannot count as pieces of knowledge.[22] But normative standards do not drive us here, for normative androcentric standards are precisely what has created the theoretic dilemma in the first place, and also the theoretic divorce from the manner in which most cognizers acquire knowledge. Sophisticated normative counterexampling does us no good, since it is question-begging; the appropriate counterargument must be that knowledge is contextually bound and that what counts as knowledge is determined by context, communication, and social conditions. The androcentric theorist can argue that this does not meet conditions of preservation of Truth; this is *petitio principii*, and not up to the counter that what counts as truth-preserving is largely socially produced. It is by no means clear what one would do with extremely reliable Ouija boards, gypsies, or channelers. If they appeared with any great frequency, one is tempted to think other portions of our verities might also come up for reexamination.

Now let us refer to the preceding sketch of principles that might be employed to construct a naturalized set or network of justifiers as the Contextualist and Communicative Principles (CCP). Such a sketchy outline requires, of course, further work. At this point I want to introduce some notions from the work of Alvin Goldman, and also make a point about the importance of communication in a mode that further specifies the kind of communication and intentionality required by CCP.

In a paper entitled "The Internalist Conception of Justification," originally published in *Midwest Studies in Philosophy*, Goldman reminds us of why it is that the newer, less internalized theories of epistemology are unattractive to many.[23] We have already examined this line of thought with regard to the material in both chapters one and two, but Goldman's formulation is particularly appealing:

> [A previous articulation is] . . . "externalist" perspective: the perspective of a God-like observer who, knowing all truths and falsehoods, can select the [Doxastic Decision Principle] that optimally conduces to true belief and error avoidance. Traditional epistemology has not adopted this externalist perspective. It has been predominantly internalist, or egocentric.[24]

Now Goldman's goal, in this paper and in his work in general, is to try to construct a Doxastic Decision Principle that is in keeping with what we know about mental functioning from the cognitive sciences and that also retains the older, more normative desire to preserve truth. Since this is not part of our project here, this particular aspect of Goldman's work is not relevant to the lines of thought I am now constructing. Nevertheless, Goldman's insight that any Doxastic Decision Principle should be in accordance with the facts of mental operations is a powerful one, and combined with his categorization of the standard internalist, normative standpoint as "egocentric," it yields a new tool for analysis. Our CCP requires further modification to mesh well with some aspects of feminist theory, and Goldman's construction of some parts of traditional epistemology helps pave the way.

In addition, I want to reiterate a point I have made here previously: All epistemic justification, whatever the gender or background of the epistemic agent, occurs in a context and relies to some extent on contextualized principles. It has now been emphasized in the literature of naturalized epistemology that this is the case: Kornblith, Annis, Goldman, and others have reminded us of this fact. In a previous publication that drew on strands of new work in epistemology, I noted:

> . . . biologists, car mechanics and ballerinas all justify their claims. One justifies one's claims in response to a challenge—either a challenge from others or a challenge from oneself. . . . The ballerina may be challenged about whether a certain sort of *plié* is appropriate for a given *pas de deux*; a car mechanic may be questioned about a carburetor, a biologist about what purports to be ribonucleic acid. All then engage in a process which, I claim, can be modeled.[25]

Part of the modeling of the process involves CCP, as we have seen. But one needs to be more specific about what the communicative part of CCP amounts to, and it is here, I claim, that other trends in work in philosophy of mind and cognitive science (examined to some extent in the second chapter) come to the fore.

In my examination of the work of Lynne Rudder Baker, I noted that Baker sets out at the beginning of her work four possible positions that theorists might take with regard to the employment of folk-psychological concepts such as belief. It is probably the case that any position other than the position she refers to as (iii) could do the work here, but if one wants to retain utilization of folk-psychological notions such as belief—in a contemporary nonreduced theory—presumably one wants to retain them for a reason. The position she calls (iv), to reiterate, is as follows:

> (iv) The final, instrumentalistic approach deems the common-sense conception to be empirically false, yet worthy of retention. . . . Because of their convenience and practical value, they [the common-sense concepts] retain a kind of legitimacy.[26]

With (iv), one is still entitled to employ concepts such as "believes," "desires," "wishes," and so forth for purposes of theory-building, while acknowledging that there may be no extensional brain-state equivalent to these terms. Yet the appeal of the terms is, as Ruth Garrett Millikan acknowledges, to their predictive power on a mundane basis.[27] If I know the beliefs of the person next door, I may be able to predict some of her behavior. Therefore I want briefly to expand on some of the material used in CCP in connection with a communicative model that employs intentionalistic terminology for the purpose of getting clear on what communication, particularly communication in an epistemic context, amounts to.

CCP informs us that social norms and practices, and agreement on social norms and practices, can help delineate the set or network of justifiers. But what this means, in practice, is that if I am challenged epistemically, and if I am contextually aware of and sensitive to the nuances of interpersonal communication (as many women, and, indeed, many humans who are not female are), I will employ my utterances in a fashion so that you, the challenger, understand that I am responding to your challenge, and I will consider myself justified when you, or anyone else who may be present, agree with or acquiesce in my verbal defense. Thus intentionality—my desire to get you to believe what I believe—is at the heart of CCP in the sense that response to epistemically challenged claims calls for speech acts that may be analyzed along Gricean lines. It may very well be the case that at some future date a naturalizing gynocentric epistemologist would know enough about brain states to be able to perform the reductions that a theorist such as Patricia Smith Churchland would argue can and should be performed, and if that is the case then intentionalistic terms would no doubt drop out at that time. But in-principle reducibility of intentionality is not particularly germane to our line of argument here, since we are dealing with material that is more-or-less undeveloped along neurophysiological lines. (The same argument may be employed with regard to a connectionist model, although this model is currently somewhat more developed. It will allude to a connectionist model again at a later point.)

In other words, to flesh out CCP requires that I specify some conditions for acquiescence and communicative competence on the part of those involved in an epistemic interchange. Again, our model is in keeping with the insights of the standpoint epistemologists while utilizing the specific and precise tools of contemporary analytic epistcmology. Thus a newer, more fully developed version of CCP will look like:

A statement $p$ is justified from the naturalized cohering standpoint if:
  (i) the statement is in a justifying network or set of statements, $J$, for cognizer $s$ at $t$;
  (ii) if it appears that the set $J$ is underdetermined, conflicting justifying sets or networks are discarded on contextual grounds, the grounds including:
   (a) that the set $J$ that is picked out is most fully in accord with social norms and practices, *such practices reducing to*
    (1) specification of each justifier for statement-to-be-justified $x$ results from a process of epistemic intent on the part of the challenger and recognition of epistemic intent on the part of the epistemic agent. The utterances must be recognized by the epistemic agent as intended to produce a state of doubt
    (2) epistemic agent in a state of doubt responds to challenger with verbal output
    (3) challenger recognizes the output as justifiers and such recognition is manifested in output of acquiescence (or further challenge)
   and (b) that social communication itself is the norm by which (a) is judged.[28]

Thus far our naturalized female-centered model has focused on contextualization and interpersonal communication for most of its impact. To reiterate, I have employed lines of argument and strands of analysis borrowed at least in part from Kornblith, Goldman, and Baker to help establish a way of descriptively pinpointing the manner in which a justifying set might be concocted. Our model has, I hope, several virtues: It is not only more descriptively accurate that much of the material developed in preceding epistemological analyses (whatever their stated bias), it also makes use of the insights developed from the feminist standpoint epistemologies in a clear and straightforward way.

But thus far I have not focused on the notion of in-the-bodiness, nor have I attempted to articulate how the focus on interpersonal awareness might manifest itself in anything more than a superficial manner. Moreover, although I have alluded to the problem of reduction and to some of the newer models, such as connectionism, I have made no real attempt to tie any of this material into the model.

Now the focus on in-the-bodiness is one that is particularly challenging for an attempt to develop a feminist epistemology along analytic (however naturalized) lines, for it is clear that most of what has been done in this mode harkens more strongly to the Continental tradition. Although I will examine some portions of the Continental tradition in another chapter, I think it is true that something like a phenomenological account of in-the-bodiness cannot really be worked into the sort of model I am attempting here. However, this much may be said: Our model relies on interpersonal communication in its intentional aspect. That is, my account of epistemic justification that alludes to intentionality is already alluding to a speech act model that, because it focuses on speech patterns and even "body language" (that is, the kind of nonverbal communication in which we all engage, even when we are unconscious of it), is already significantly less distanced and significantly less normatively androcentric than the preceding models. So for the time being, my somewhat insufficient response to a request for a model that focuses on this important aspect of gynocentric theory is to allude to the aspects of the model already created that—however loosely—mesh with the concept of bodily awareness.

Still another problem, mentioned briefly above, is the emphasis on other aspects of interpersonal communication that occurs, for example, in the work of a theorist like Gilligan. The short answer to the problem of inclusion of notions such as "caring" and "interpersonal emotions" into a model of gynocentric knowledge acquisition is that these notions have much more to do with Gilligan's specific project, which deals with ethical decision-making rather than with decision-making or knowledge acquisition *simpliciter*. The long answer, however, is much more complicated. Although it is never addressed in Gilligan's book, there is an implicit undercurrent in her work to the effect that the sort of differentiation in reasoning styles that applies to males and females vis-à-vis moral questions may also apply to them in other spheres. The controversial work on grasp of spatial relations problem-solving, mathematics, and the relationship of these skills to hormonal influences may possibly have some bearing on these questions:[29] What bearing it could have is by no means clear, since even the bare bones work on spatial relations is still far from complete.[30] At any rate, it may very well be the case that this sort of question of style, which I alluded to in my brief discussion of Gilligan's work in the Introduction, ought to come up also in a general analysis of epistemological problems. If we look at this issue broadly, it turns out that a great deal of what Gilligan seems to be saying lends itself to the distinction between views and styles that are more cohering, and views and styles that are not—in other words, it fits in well with the lines of thought that I am articulating here.

Finally, the question of the possibility of reduction of our model along the lines of neurophysiological reduction, or even connectionist reduction, is an intriguing one, and here we may be able to posit more specific lines of theory that will go some way toward answering these questions. As we saw in our analysis of Baker's material, there is more than one way to deal with the question of reducibility. While one is tempted to say that the arguments for in-principle reducibility are overwhelmingly strong, one is also tempted to say (as I noted earlier) that there are powerful reasons for establishing, preliminarily, a non-reduced model, since this model incorporates the intentional aspects of behavior that, on an interpersonal level, we employ to regulate our daily lives, and since we cannot currently completely reduce. It is in fact this intentionalistic aspect of the model that lends it a much greater degree of applicability, and it is this emphasis within the model that makes it applicable not only to females but also to many persons, young and old, lettered and unlettered, who do not function in the more formal modes of reasoning characteristic of the androcentric and normative models. Nevertheless, the recent research on connectionist models, in particular, seems to provide us with food for thought.

As I indicated in my brief look at connectionism toward the close of the second chapter, connectionist processing models rely on weighted averagings of inhibitory and excitatory responses at the neural network level to mimic the way in which (at a reduced level) human beings actually perform some task such as typing.[31] Because our model is formulated at a relatively coarse-grained level of characterization, there is no question that it could be reduced now to some semi-connectionist account. Such an account would have the virtue that it would be still more naturalized than the account we already possess. On the other hand, it would cause us to lose the intentional aspect of the account, which might be deemed to be most fully gynocentric. Since I have, in another publication, provided an account of such a model (although not specifically intended as a gynocentric model), I will forego still more fully naturalized modification of this material for the moment.[32]

What is required now is a brief overview of the material presented so far in this chapter, with some room for still further modification, before turning to broader philosophical issues, such as the applicability of intentional and/or computational models in general.

## A COMPUTATIONAL FEMINIST EPISTEMICS

So far what has been accomplished is along the lines of creating a model of epistemic justification that is simultaneously naturalized and gynocentric. To this end I have employed material from some of those engaged both in the straightforward project of naturalizing epistemology and those engaged in areas of research that might be better categorized as philosophy of mind or philosophical psychology. The point has been to try to be specific (allowing for the fact that a view roughly called "coherentist" is already more naturalized than a view roughly called "foundationalist") about what could count as a justifying set or network, particularly taking into account three bases of feminist inquiry in the standpoint epistemologies: contextualization, interpersonal communication and its nuances, and in-the-bodiness. I have focused more on the first two than the third because the first two lend themselves more readily to work in naturalized epistemology and analytic philosophy in particular, as was explained above.

The fleshed-out version of the model with which we are already working, CCP, is inherently related to the computational model of mind, although this may not be immediately obvious. In the second chapter I commented on the primacy of the computational model or functionalist accounts in general for mental modeling, and use was made of computational terminology both in my discussion of Baker and my discussion of the work of Patricia Smith Churchland. To recapitulate briefly, the model takes as its analogue for mental functioning the functioning of computational devices such as computers.[33] These devices are characterized by internal relations that are a series of on- and off-switching mechanisms working at extremely high speed, and the portion of the brain, broadly speaking, which is supposed to mimic this sort of mechanism is the neuronal level with its on-and-off firing of neurons. To do the model justice, however, it rarely lets itself be subject to empirical confirmation by postulating entities at the "hardware" level; rather, the virtue of the model is supposed to be that these relationships can be instantiated in *any* sort of hardware, because the most straightforward characterization of the relations obtaining between the flip-flopping mechanisms is, of course, a logical one. Now the logical relations are the syntax, as it were, of the language of the brain, and representations (the semantic encodings, which translate into content) are the interpretations of these content areas. Thus the work of Patricia Smith Churchland is designed, at least partly, as an argument against those who would claim that the hardware in which the model is instantiated (for humans, the brain) never has to be specified simply because it is unnecessary (and maybe even impossible) to reduce the model any further.

The portion of CCP that most strongly partakes of the computational model is the portion that postulates justifications as output (utterances) resulting from a process of decoding and relying on the comprehension of verbal input by the agent and comprehension of intent on the part of the challenger. The intentional aspect of the model is at a level above the computational level, and hence is not strictly computational. But the model could be more fully specified (even without being reduced).[34] The conditions of the model that lend themselves most readily to this sort of analysis are (1) and (2), since it is clear what is going on for the cognizer is computation over strands of input that are interpreted (if they correlate with previous semantic interpretations) and then give rise to further output.[35]

Because of the importance of the computational model, and because it helps make still more precise our naturalized and gynocentric model, I want to rephrase the previously articulated conditions of CCP so that they can be thought of in computational terms. Then we can proceed to address some of the philosophical problems associated with this model, which must in any case be addressed if we are to think of our work in naturalized epistemology as being theoretically consonant with the work that has preceded it and from which we have borrowed.

Thus a rehash of our more fully structured model (see pp. 117–121 of this text) must make explicit the computational elements, since these elements derive from contemporary (although nonconnectionist and nonreduced) cognitive science. A still more fully developed version of the model, taking into account its computational specificity, would look like this:

A statement $p$ is justified from the naturalized cohering standpoint if:
  (i) the statement is in a justifying network or set of statements, $J$, for cognizer $s$ at $t$;
  (ii) if it appears that the set $J$ is underdetermined, conflicting justifying sets or networks are discarded on contextual grounds, the grounds including:
      (a) that the set $J$ that is picked out is most fully in accord with social norms and practices, *such practices reducing to:*

(1) specification of each justifier for statement-to-be-justified $x$
results from a process of epistemic intent on the part of the
challenger manifesting itself in a string of utterances, which
when heard by the epistemic agent result in a neurophysiological passage of the utterance into *symbolically encoded
information correlated with certain semantic interpretations*
if the utterance falls into a category of information that the
agent has processed before the utterances must be recognized by the epistemic agent as intended to produce a state
of doubt;

(2) epistemic agent in a state of doubt responds to challenger
with verbal output (processed along the specified lines);

etc.

Now the important point with regard to our new instantiation of the
model is that it makes still more specific the sorts of theoretical
ramifications that, as I have argued, feminist theory can employ to its
own ends, regardless of their conceptual history or antecedents. That
is, we now have the theoretical capacity to produce a highly specific
and sophisticated gynocentric, contextualized, communication-ori-
ented theory that possesses many of the characteristics tapped by the
standpoint theorists while simultaneously possessing the precision
and, to some extent, rigor of work in analytic philosophy and the
sciences as well.

I have felt free to utilize small portions of the computational model
of mind for our theory, despite the philosophical criticisms of it and
despite the newer work that some would argue is both more palatable
and still more precise[36] because it has until very recently been the most
acceptable model of mind and because it lends itself particularly well
to our work since it is construed at a level of theoretical modeling that
still allows for the notion of intentionality, in however basic a way.[37]
There are, however, many criticisms, both philosophical and even
psychological, which can be leveled at this model and with which we
must grapple if we are to achieve anything like the naturalized gynocentric model I originally aimed for. Consequently it will be the goal
of the next chapter to fill out some of the criticisms aimed at the model
while simultaneously presenting a defense of its use here, both for
straightforwardly philosophical reasons and for the reasons more
broadly feminist that were adduced in my defense of analytic philosophy at the opening of this chapter.

# REVIEWING THE NATURALIZED
# GYNOCENTRIC MODEL

An overview of this chapter helps us complete our sketch of naturalized gynocentric theory. The chapter opened with the debate to which I have just referred: I reminded us of the importance Harding places on what she refers to as "feminist empiricism" and the response to it. I took this theoretical problem to be paradigmatic of the problems facing feminist philosophers who wish to employ the admittedly androcentric methods of analytic philosophy while still pursuing lines of research that are wholeheartedly feminist in their formulation and aims. My argument had two main parts, one of which itself broke into two smaller divisions. The original two-pronged argument was both an argument that analytic philosophy could be transformed into a tool for feminist research and a specific argument with regard to epistemology—that it is naturalized analytic epistemology, in its contemporary form, which most naturally lends itself to this sort of research, rather than analytic epistemology as it has been practiced until recently. My first argument, that analytic philosophy can be retooled, then underwent mitosis into two strands: The first strand—the negative argument—reminded us (along the lines of a complicated *tu quoque*) that all lines of research available at the present time are more-or-less androcentric. My second argument within this argument—the positive line—emphasized the precision and rigor of analytic thinking and reminded us that much of what might be deemed to constitute an advance for philosophy within this century was conceptualized along analytic lines. I then returned to the second part of my major argument, the argument for naturalized analytic epistemology.

I began this more specific argument by detailing what I took to be some of the most important and fructifying material from the standpoint epistemologies, and then specifying their lines of intersection with naturalized epistemology. I mentioned the work of Hartsock and Flax, and Harding's analysis of it; I cited Hartsock's use of the notions of concrete material processes and subsistence labor and Flax's use of the notions of "multiplicity" and "dialectics." Both of these notions might also be related to contextuality; I then mentioned the philosophers working in naturalized epistemology whose own work has made extensive use of the notion of context—Annis and Kornblith were cited. I noted Goldman's work for its use of contemporary research on the senses (research undertaken by psychologists and physiologists) and I alluded to the focus on communication and interpersonal interaction and its nuances, which seems to occur throughout the work of the feminist theorists. Then I contrasted these notions with the work of one of the analytic coherence theorists of the prenaturalized period, James Cornman. In making the contrast, I argued (as I have in previous publications), that part of Cornman's problematic stems from insufficient attention to context and insufficient naturalization.[38]

After introducing notions borrowed partially from the naturalizing epistemologists that might be more helpful in the construction of a cohering-like justificatory set (and emphasizing that Gilligan, for example, seems to contend that females reason morally in a manner more closely modeled by coherence theory broadly construed), I developed an outline of a gynocentric, naturalized justifying set. I mentioned in passing that such a set probably pertains, descriptively, not only to females but to children and males who are not trained in the literate methods of sophisticated androcentric thinking characteristic of Western cultures.

Finally, I mentioned that this model could be reduced (following along the lines of argument formulated by Patricia Smith Churchland) or made connectionist, but that there were reasons for thinking—borrowed to some extent from the work of Lynne Rudder Baker—that the computational model afforded room for theorizing that might be more helpful at this stage. To close, I reconstructed the model along more overtly computational lines, with the promise that the criticisms of this model, ubiquitous in the literature, would be examined at a later point.

In this chapter I have sketched a model of epistemic justification that I contend is both gynocentric and naturalized. I have addressed at length the feminist concerns that an androcentric method cannot fully articulate a woman-centered epistemology. In another chapter, I hope to provide some details on alternative, nonanalytic feminist theories in use at the current time, particularly those derived from Continental thought. For now, however, my main task is to conclude a philosophical view of the theory offered that is in line with recent work in philosophy of mind and philosophy of psychology. Since my naturalized theory has relied heavily on advances in such fields all the way along, I must subject the theory to the sort of scrutiny that work in philosophy of psychology, for example, would demand. In the next chapter I put aside, for the moment, most of the debates in feminist theory itself with which we have been concerned to more fully portray what philosophy of mind and philosophy of psychology have to tell us about the use of the computational model of mind.

# NOTES

1. Suppe, *Structure of Scientific*.
2. Longino, "Can There Be?"
3. Hélene Cixous, working within a different tradition, articulates another version of this problem that I will examine at a later point. See Cixous, Hélene, "The Laugh of the Medusa," in *The Signs Reader: Women, Gender and Scholarship*, ed. Elizabeth Abel and Emily K. Abel (Chicago: University of Chicago Press, 1984).
4. Mary Daly is frequently cited in this regard. See especially *Gyn/Ecology: The Metaethics of Radical Feminism* (Boston: Beacon Press, 1978); and *Pure Lust* (Boston: Beacon Press, 1984).
5. Much of the classic work associated with positivism or the nomological-deductive hypothesis was done by Carl Hempel. See *Aspects of Scientific Explanation and Other Essays* (New York: Free Press, 1965).
6. Harding, *The Science Question*, 136–62.
7. See Friederich Engels, *On the Origin of Family, Private Property and the State*, notes by Eleanor Burke Leacock (New York: International Publishers, 1972).
8. This problem is addressed to some extent in an analysis of the work of Cixous and Derrida that occurs in Mark Krupnick, *Displacement: Derrida and After* (Bloomington: Indiana University Press, 1983).
9. Nancy Hartsock, "The Feminist Standpoint: Developing the Ground for a Specifically Feminist Historical Materialism," *Discovering Reality*, ed. Sandra Harding and Merrill Hintikka (Dordrecht, Netherlands: Reidel, 1983), 292.
10. Quoted in Harding, *The Science Question*, 147. Appears to be from Harding and Hintikka, *Discovering Reality*, 292.
11. These phrases occur in Jane Flax, "Political Philosophy and the Patriarchal Unconscious: A Psychoanalytic Perspective on Epistemology and Metaphysics," in Harding and Hintikka, *Discovering Reality, passim*.
12. Harding, *The Science Question*, 153.
13. This theme is found throughout Belenky, Clinchy, Goldberger, and Tarule, *Women's Ways*, and to some extent throughout Gilligan, *Different Voice*.
14. See my "Intentionality and Epistemology," *The Monist* 69, no. 4 (1986):620–26; see also Kornblith, "Psychological Turn," and David Annis, "A Contextualist Theory of Epistemic Justification," *American Philosophical Quarterly* 15, no. 3 (1978):213–19.
15. See Goldman, *Epistemology and Cognition, passim*.
16. Cornman, "Foundational."
17. Ibid., 246.
18. Ibid., 243.
19. Hilary Kornblith, "Some Social Features of Cognition," *Synthese* 73, no. 1 (1987):28.

20. Annis, "Contextualist," 217.

21. This is a partial adaptation of both material from Cornman, "Foundational," and from my response to Cornman's problem in "A Contextualist Modification of Cornman," *Philosophia* 16, nos. 3 and 4 (1986):377–88.

22. See, for example, Keith Lehrer and Thomas Paxson, "How Reasons Give Us Knowledge, or the Case of the Gypsy Lawyer," *Journal of Philosophy* 68, no. 10 (1971)311–13.

23. Goldman, "Internalist Conception."

24. Ibid., 32.

25. See my "Descriptive Epistemology," *Metaphilosophy* 15, nos. 3 and 4 (1984):187.

26. Baker, *Saving Belief,* 13–14.

27. Ruth Garrett Millikan, "Thoughts Without Laws: Cognitive Science Without Content," *The Philosophical Review* 95, no. 1 (1986):47–80, *passim.*

28. The above is a slightly modified version of the material appearing in my "Intentionality," 622.

29. This work is widely referred to in the literature, but to little avail, since so few conclusions can be drawn from the paucity of existing research. Some of the most discussed work appeared in an article in *Science* in the early 1980s. The piece is by C. P. Benbow and J. C. Stanley, "Sex Differences in Mathematical Ability: Fact or Artifact?", *Science* 210 (12 December 1980):1262–64. Replies to that piece and further discussion may be found in *Science* 211 (16 January 1981):231, and *Science* 212 (10 April 1981):114ff.

30. Since the *Science* piece, other work on the topic has appeared. Two books worth perusing are Susan F. Chipman, Lorelei R. Brush, and Donna M. Wilson, eds., *Women and Mathematics* (Hillsdale, N.J.: Lawrence Erlbaum and Associates, 1980), and *Women and the Mathematical Mystique: Proceedings of the Eighth Annual Hyman Blumberg Symposium on Research in Early Childhood Education* (Baltimore: Johns Hopkins University Press, 1980).

31. I alluded to this material more precisely in the last pages of chap. 2, specifically, pp. 64–67 of this manuscript.

32. The relevant publication is my "Reductionism and the Naturalization of Epistemology," *Dialectica* 42, no. 4 (1988):295–306.

33. The computer notion is stronger than a mere analogue, but I employ the terminology here simply to make a point. Several commentators have emphasized the extent to which the notion of a computer as model for the mind is stronger than analogue or metaphor.

34. This is an important point. To articulate the model more fully as a computational model does not, according to most of the computational theorists, in any way imply a further reduction. As I have stated, Patricia Smith Churchland's work is an argument against at least a portion of this claim.

35. One is sometimes tempted to forget that in many situations there is no interpretation. If I approach someone in Florence, believing the person to be British or American, and am met with a stream of Italian, there will be no

interpretation (unless, of course, I can glean some from my knowledge of Spanish and the appropriate cognates). Input from speakers of foreign languages is not the only situation that lends itself to this analysis. Input from some of the homeless wandering the streets of New York and our other large cities is, in many cases, almost impossible to interpret meaningfully even though the semantic strings are in English.

36. Stephen Stich, *Folk Psychology*.

37. I refer, again, to connectionism and neurophysiology itself, insofar as it constitutes a reduction of this model.

38. See my "Contextualist Modification."

# Chapter Five

# The Gynocentric Model Criticized

In the last chapter much attention was devoted to the argument that epistemological portions of analytic philosophy could be retooled and made useful for feminist theory. Part of the argument has been that this particular tack is itself related to the debate over what Harding calls "feminist empiricism"; the need to try to valorize a semi-empirical, or at least analytic approach was redoubled by the attacks on feminist empiricism and the seemingly established notion that analytic philosophy is itself an androcentric project.

This chapter is devoted to criticisms that might be made of the model, borrowed from naturalized epistemology and philosophy of mind, that was made explicit in the last section. But some lines of criticism carry more weight than others, and it is the technically oriented, computationally grounded criticisms to which I will make extensive reference in this chapter. Since the core issue of the relevance of analytic reasoning and its concomitant methods has already been covered, the sort of criticism that merely dismisses the model as inappropriate because of the androcentric nature of the material in which it is grounded will not be addressed at length here. It will be assumed that we have established a basis for the employment of analytic epistemology, especially its naturalized version, in feminist theory, and a corollary to that assumption will be that the most telling criticisms that can be made of the model spring from within a viewpoint that is already analytic and that utilizes contemporary philosophy of mind and philosophy of psychology as a given.

The model (CCP) relies on notions of coherence, context, and interpersonal communication, as has been stated. Coherence may be taken as primitive, since the point of using the notion is simply that it is an intuitively plausible one and certainly less fraught with the possibility of a cul-de-sac than any foundationalist view. Context, as a notion important to the project of epistemic justification, is borrowed partly from the work of Hilary Kornblith, David Annis, and other epistemologists who have emphasized the social nature of the process of epistemic justification (or of knowledge acquisition). The importance of interpersonal communication within this model is related to context, however, it the one conceptual apparatus of the three that speaks most directly to the heart of the theorizing constructed by the standpoint epistemologists. Lying at the core of the assertion that epistemic justification normally occurs in interpersonal communicative situations is the auxiliary notion that intentionality, *qua* predictive apparatus, is useful in developing a naturalized and female-centered view of epistemic justification.

The difficulty with intentionality is this: As we have seen at an earlier point (the second chapter), not all views that purport or allege to employ a computational or functionalist model will allow for the sorts of folk-psychological terms that intentionality seems to require.[1] Baker's four-part division of such views was examined earlier in the text. It is important to be clear about what, if anything, may be salvaged theoretically by adopting a model, like CCP, which encompasses a computational model and intentionalistic notions simultaneously.

Briefly, Baker's summation of the four sorts of views breaks down as follows:[2] the first view (i) sees little or no theoretical difficulty with the use of intentionalistic terms within an account of mental functioning amenable to the standards of science. This view is, if anything, too generous to such terms, as most of those engaged in the project of examining folk-psychological terms now seem to agree. What Baker refers to as (ii) holds that the standard terms are incorrect, but that other, extensionally equivalent terms are correct. (It remains to be seen, of course, precisely what these extensionally equivalent terms are.) Baker's (iii) holds that there is no extensional equivalence between the folk-psychological terms and terms that might be used nomologically, and this strongly reductionist view would have one discard such terms altogether. Her (iv) asserts that the terms are worthy of retention for their instrumental value, even if they are empirically false.[3]

The view that is most valuable for our project is (iv). Although it may very well be the case that (iii) is correct—and the arguments for it are quite strong—(iii) does little good currently for a project that wants to be able to employ certain sorts of common-sensical, experientially ratified concepts in such a way that they are useful for prediction on an everyday basis.[4] Here, then, a concession is made to the material developed from the standpoint epistemologies: The concrete ground-edness of women's everyday experience calls for a view that, while employing analytic precision, allows for the expansion of prediction along non-nomological lines, if such prediction is useful in a mundane context. So a preliminary criticism that might immediately be made of our model, namely that it employs the language of computation along-side the language of intentionality, is nullified from the outset when it is understood that the model is in no sense intended to be nomologi-cally correct.

Having said so much, however, a great deal more remains to be said. It is the relevance of the computational model itself, as a mental paradigm, that appears to be up for grabs. I do not here refer to the debate between, for example, the computational model and the con-nectionist model, or between functionalism and neurophysiological models. Those particular debates are only peripherally relevant to this project, since I have assumed from the outset that the model could be reformulated in connectionist terms, or even completely reduced (at some later point).[5] What is intriguing, since our model posits a level of intrapersonal interaction describable in terms of "symbolically en-coded information correlated with certain semantic interpretations," is the sort of criticism that might be addressed to this very level of theoretical entity-positing within the model itself.

The first theoretical material that recommends itself at this point is material that seems to pave the way toward our acceptance of a model containing elements simultaneously intentionalistic and computational. However crude our model may be from that standpoint, it does itself contain both of these elements. The first sort of criticism that might be made of the model (aside from the bare bones criticism of computation-alism) is the obvious argument that the model is defective or poorly wrought in containing the nonintentional and intentional simultane-ously. At this point I want to examine more closely the work of Daniel

Dennett, since he has been widely viewed as providing at least some sort of a way out of the theoretical slough just described.[6]

## DENNETT AND THE INTENTIONAL STANCE

Dennett has a number of books and articles devoted to an explication of how one can be a committed physicalist while still retaining room in one's overview for intentionality. Perhaps the most helpful work is *The Intentional Stance,* since by his own admission the essays contained in it were pulled together largely to articulate precisely this position. Briefly, Dennett's general position is that whether one speaks intentionally—in the language of folk psychology—or whether one speaks reductively (regardless of the level of reduction employed) depends more on the level at which one wants to achieve predictive and theoretical specificity than it does anything else. In other words, Dennett holds that there is an instrumental use to which our folk-psychological language can be put, and this use is an important one. It not only enables us to make predictions about our neighbor's behavior but also has the virtue that it is consonant with most of the important aspects of our culture as a whole.[7]

Baker appealingly quotes Dennett on this matter: "On the other hand, the validity of our conceptual scheme of moral agents having dignity, freedom and responsibility stands or falls on the question: can men ever be *truly* said to have beliefs, desires, intentions?"[8]

Dennett's long-term answer to this question, in one word, is "yes."[9] However, it is important to emphasize that what we are talking about here is, again, an instrumental view that does not wish to deny the primary validity of physicalism. It is important to be clear on this point since the natural move for many would be to attempt to deny primary physicalism at some level in order to try to save common-sense intentional concepts. Writing of Thomas Nagel's work, which argues strongly that certain aspects of experience cannot adequately be captured by physicalistic reduction, Dennett maintains:

> Perhaps those who mistrust the frankly materialistic assumptions and aspirations of the current scientific image are right to do so, but I doubt it. . . . [T]he best way to come to understand the situation is by starting here and letting whatever revolutions are in the offing foment from within. I propose to see, then, just what the mind looks like from the third-person, materialistic perspective of contemporary science.[10]

Dennett proceeds by distinguishing between the stance-dependent and the stance-independent. A stance-dependent feature is a feature "possessed only in relation to someone's strategies."[11] A belief is, of course, a paradigmatic item of the stance-dependent type, since attribution of belief is only made in relation to strategies that I or someone else may possess with regard to the alleged possessor of the belief.

As Dennett says in "Three Kinds of Intentional Psychology," reprinted in *The Intentional Stance,*

> Folk psychology is abstract in that the beliefs and desires it attributes are not—or need not be—presumed to be intervening distinguishable states of an internal behavior-causing system. . . . The role of the concept of belief is like the role of the concept of a center of gravity, and the calculations that yield the predictions are more like the calculations one performs with a parallelogram of forces than like the calculations one performs with a blueprint of internal levers and cogs.[12]

Thus our CCP model is at least partially vindicated by the Dennettian argument that the intentional stance is not wholly inconsistent with the computational model or with anything more physically reductionistic than the computational model. Before turning to other views that might be somewhat less sanguine than Dennett's about the possibility of using intentional constructs in a computational model, it seems worth taking the time to remind ourselves of what it is, specifically, that these intentional constructs can do. Clearly, communication is the issue, but one wants to be as precise as possible about the communicative virtues involved in employing intentional constructs.

Some of Dennett's position is echoed by Millikan's work and bears similarity to Searle's work. All three theorists have been concerned with intentionality in a way similar to that described here. Millikan argues that a virtue of the non nomological folk concepts is that they "enable us to do a great deal of explaining and a certain amount of fallible predicting of human behavior."[13] One is tempted to say flatly that Millikan's point is well taken; we are drawn to folk psychological concepts (and they recur in the computational model, albeit sometimes in another guise) because they are helpful on a general basis. But Millikan has several examples of this kind of folk-psychological aid and succor in her piece, many of which reinforce Dennett's contentions above and are more specific about the ways in which the concepts might be helpful.

Consider John, who wants to meet the girl next door:

The intentional characterization of John, "He wants to meet the . . ." where the blank space is filled in and read transparently, does give us a handle on what John might well do, and certainly a handle by which we might later be able to explain why John did what he did do, though not a handle that fits into a deductive or nomological scheme.[14]

Or consider the intentional status of my desire to visit China:

There is nothing wrong with me or my desire if I desire to visit China yet circumstances prevent my ever getting there or I decide I want to do something else more. But there is something wrong with me or my belief if I believe that China is west of Europe.[15]

Millikan also concludes that "folk psychology, embellished with something akin to the traditional notion that thoughts are like impressions or pictures, might be placed in the context of modern physiology to yield a theory of content for beliefs and desires—a naturalistic theory of intentionality."[16]

To add on to our citation of those who would employ the intentionalistic constructs, we must remember that cognitive science, broadly construed, comprises work in many disciplines and categories. Some of the cross-categorical work employs these constructs in interesting ways, without investigating their underpinnings. John Searle, in his "The Intentionality of Intention and Action," reminds us of the intentional patterns, of which we may be largely unaware, inherent in speech acts.[17] Since CCP is sensitive to context and the Gricean-descriptive effects of utterances on the listener, Searle's points are especially intriguing. Viewed from the standpoint of the speech act itself, the pattern of intentionality is a useful construct, however much a grosgrain, which aids us in the prediction of behavior at a broad-stroke level in much the same way that Millikan's example of John's beliefs about the girl next door does. Again, when one tries to be more precise about the intentionality (or the beliefs, *simpliciter*) one runs smack up against the very theoretical difficulties that Baker, for one, has delineated. Stopping short of that level, however, Searle provides us with a place for the intentional stance.

A useful exemplar here is Searle's description of what one intends to accomplish by certain sorts of speech acts: His example is of someone ordering someone else to leave the room. If the second person is gone after an interval of a few minutes, but later reports that she left to open a window, the first person has not accomplished her speech-act goal.

But what this illustrates is that the content of my order is not simply that you leave the room, but that you leave the room by way of obeying this order, that is: the logical form of the order is not simply that I order you (that you leave the room) but rather it is self-referential in the form "I order you (that you leave the room by way of obeying this order").[18]

Here Searlian intentionality, Millikan's beliefs, and Dennett's position hook up in a nice way to yield something that does give us a handle on behavior. Returning to Millikan's example, then, it is not only the case that John's desire to meet the girl next door helps us guess what John might well do, but also, at least in some situations, it helps us guess more specifically how John might go about it. To be precise, it helps us make the inference that not only will John engage in actions that might put him into proximity with the girl next door, but also that in his interactions (if any) with the girl next door he will intend that *she recognize his intentions* (at some point).

The previous example has been adduced merely to help us along with the contention that beliefs (and other intentional states) "give us a handle" by which we may be able to predict and/or explain action. Intentional states may give us handles that are somewhat precise. It is simply that they will not be precise in a nomological way.

The upshot of the foregoing for feminist theory is made quite a bit clearer when we remember that a great deal of the work cited, particularly in chapter three, focused on the importance of communication for female-centered epistemologies. Communication is itself a notion that may be broadly considered. Hartsock calls her feminist epistemology "relational" in part because she simply wants to make explicit the nonobjectifying tendencies she takes to be characteristic of women's thought.[19] Flux would emphasize the importance of communication at least partly because the greater identification with the mother that females possess allows for a greater identification with other persons on the whole, thus making the nuances of interpersonal conduct more accessible to conscious thought.[20] Hubbard reminds us that the androcentric style "implicitly denies . . . context,"[21] and Longino (while urging us to be careful) notes that the feminist critique of science "claim[s] that women have certain traits (dispositions to attend to particulars, interactive rather than individualist and controlling social attitudes and behaviors)."[22] In short, feminist theory posits special attention to communication as part of gynocentric style. We need to be especially aware of this in creating a model for female-grounded epistemic justification, or in any discussion of feminist epistemology. Hence the importance of intentionality.

But the material we have cited above (from Dennett, and also from Millikan and Searle) is, of course, only a small part of the picture with regard to the computational model and folk-psychological constructs. Dennett's instrumental view is, as I have stated, particularly helpful since it seems to provide a basis for CCP, but we need not be too self-congratulatory: There are many other commentators on both functionalism itself and the attempt to marry a computational model to an intentional stance who are somewhat less enthusiastic. It is to their work that I now turn.

Fodor's work is of paramount importance in philosophy of mind, and Baker cites Fodor as being an exponent of view (i), the most positive of the views regarding the use of intentional terminology and the computational model. This is not an entirely accurate characterization, however, as Baker herself more-or-less admits, for Fodor's views are complex. (It will be recalled that toward the end of chapter two I cited Baker's rebuttal of a significant portion of Fodor's position.) A better label for his views might be that they are, on the whole, weakly reductionist (the viewpoint that Baker labels (ii) in her own work). Fodor employs intentionalistic terminology and maintains that "Mental states . . . interact causally. . . . [I]nteractions constitute the mental processes that eventuate . . . in the behaviors of organisms."[23] This particular explication of the view does, in fact, seem to attribute more to mental states than many commentators associated with the computational model would be prepared to delegate.[24] Let us take a closer look.

## FODOR AND REPRESENTATIONALISM

Fodor's view, however—when it is more fully fleshed out—does not allow for the same sort of instrumentality with regard to intentionality as Dennett's. It is the formal operations (the syntactic aspect of the model, which, of course, is in theory instantiable in any hardware) that are more important, ultimately, than the representations themselves. He says that computational processes are formal because "they apply to representations, in virtue of (roughly) the *syntax* of the representations. It's the second of these conditions that makes the claim that mental processes are computational stronger than the representational theory of the mind.[25]

In other words, there is a real sense in which the most important part of the model for Fodor is the syntactical encoding. It is the emphasis he places on it that leads to his formulation of methodological solipsism as the research paradigm for cognitive fields. Since Baker's gloss on this term is perhaps the clearest brief summation available, I will cite Baker here on Fodor:

> Methodological solipsism is the assumption that mental processes, or at least those that explain behavior, are wholly·determined by properties of the individual whose processes they are. Developed from the plausible thought that whatever explains an individual's behavior must be "in the head" of the individual, methodological solipsism requires that mental processes than explain behavior must be considered in abstraction from the environment of the individual whose behavior is to be explained.[26]

But it is of course true that what is most fully "in the head" of an individual is the encoding, which presumably is reducible to the hardware (here the neuronal relationships) at some plausible point. Although there is a sense in which the representations are also in the individual, there is a genuine sense in which they are not, since what the representations are has never been specified within the computational model (most versions of the model leave the syntactical-semantic relationships vague, other than to specify that they exist). It is the latter lacuna, indeed, that prompts those who want to be completely eliminativist to move ahead, since to be an eliminativist at least gives one the theoretical strength of avoiding messy ontological commitments such as "representations."

In any case, it seems best, for our purposes, to label Fodor's overall position "weakly reductivist." He is willing to countenance the use of folk-psychological terminology, but he is not as sanguine about the use of such terminology as is Dennett, for example, nor does he expend a great deal of time on the explanation of what the relationships between representations and their syntactic correlates really are.

Finally, to utilize a further distinction, in *Modularity of Mind* Fodor argues for a vertical rather than horizontal approach to what psychologists have traditionally called "mental faculties." Although the question of vertical vs. horizontal faculties is not a particularly important one for our purposes, Fodor does provide some hints on how one ought to view, for example, the auditory input of utterances (utilized in CCP):

> Well, then, what precisely *is* the functional similarity between language mechanisms and perceptual mechanisms in virtue of which both count as

"input systems"? There is, of course, the obvious point that utterances
(e.g., sentence tokens) are themselves objects to be perceptually identified, just as mountains, teacups, and four alarm fires are. . . . Now about
language: Just as patterns of visual energy arriving at the retina are
correlated, in a complicated but regular way, with certain properties of
distal layouts . . . what underwrites the correlation between token
utterances and distal layouts is (roughly) a convention of truth-telling. In
the root case, that convention is that we say of $x$ that it is $F$ only if $x$ is $F$.
Because that convention holds, it is possible to infer from what one hears
said to the way the world is.[27]

In other words, in Fodor's view one can at least think of auditory
signals as information in the same way that percepts are information,
even if one doesn't want to speak in a laudatory fashion of the
instrumental or moral uses to which intentional language might be put.
Fodorian theory no doubt cannot accommodate a comparatively crude
model like CCP, which fails to be explicit about the syntactical encoding or the functioning on the syntactic level—which is, in this view,
the most crucial level. But insofar as utterances may be processed by
language mechanism *qua* "input system," there is still room on this
account for some level of intentionality.

## THE MENTALISTIC DILEMMA

To pause briefly for an historical gloss on the problem of intentionality and the computational model before proceeding, we must remember what it is, theoretically, that the computational model is supposed
to have replaced. The rise of the model came in the 1960s after a long
period of what can only be termed rampant behaviorism. Flanagan, in
his important and concisely written book *The Science of the Mind,* has
summed up the contrast between the two sorts of views as follows:

Surprisingly, cognitive psychologists start by sharing an assumption with
behaviorists to the effect that there are lawlike regularities between
stimuli and responses. They part company with behaviorists, however,
by claiming that any psychology which fails to talk about the intervening
mental processes that link these stimuli and responses will be unaccept-
ably incomplete.[28]

So the virtue of the computational model was that typically it
allowed for some sort of mentalism, even if the variety for which it

allowed was a far cry from previous mentalistic views. But that in itself is a virtue if it means that theoretically "messy" intentional terminology can more-or-less be done away with, which is precisely what has happened in the more eliminativist views, and even to some extent in a view like Fodor's where it is clear that one cannot push the intentionalistic terminology too far.

We will not be examining the strongly reductionist and eliminativist views in great detail here, since they go against the grain of the overall project. (Although they may, of course, be relevant for the future.) But the crux of the matter, insofar as folk-psychological terminology is concerned, is spelled out again by Flanagan when he writes of the eliminativist position:

> The eliminativist does raise an important point, however. To whatever extent theorizing in cognitive psychology is constrained by alleged truths of folk psychology from above, it is also constrained by known truths about the nervous system, from below. It would be dangerous for cognitive psychologists to entertain, even for a moment, the belief that research in brain science is irrelevant to their functional pronouncements, or to take metaphysical functionalism as proof that there are no interesting mappings of psychological processes onto brain processes. The amount of important work indicating all sorts of localization of function makes this view untenable. Furthermore, it would be a parallel error to think that neuroscience will never lead us to reconceptualize phenomena at the functional level.[29]

So one has to be prepared to abandon the computational model at some later point, even as one is prepared to accept it as a step forward—and to criticize it—now.

Moving from the past to the possibly eliminativist future, Stephen Stich, whose work I have alluded to here before, has as his main concern the demonstration that there is no one construction of the mind-brain identity thesis that really allows for the retention of the folk psychological. Again taking the computational model, in its various guises, as his target, he sums up his own view by stating: "A question I have often encountered in setting out my views is whether I think there are any such things as beliefs. . . . [I]f the question is construed as asking whether there are belief state tokens or belief state types (i.e., properties), then the answer is negative."[30] Baker provides a helpful summary of various sorts of versions of identity—token–token identity, type–token identity, and so forth. Stich finds strong counterarguments to all the variations on the identity position, and I will expand on his position at a later point. Finally, other theorists, such as Heil, have added on to Stich's criticisms by writing of incoherences in the model at the "down" end of the scale, that is, incoherences in the notion of the functional architecture to which such a model might be attached, regardless of the nature of the architecture. One of Heil's major points is that descriptions of the model seem to always be couched (necessarily, of course) in third-person language, but that it is a mistake to think that the third-person account, which the model necessarily invokes, has anything to do with what is actually taking place on a first-person level.[31]

We have briefly examined the work of Dennett and Fodor. Before proceeding on to two other theorists whose work has been extremely important in contemporary philosophy of mind, I want to reiterate some of the goals for a feminist epistemology reliant on naturalization and contemporary philosophy of mind. Although some of this will be in the nature of recapitulation, the scope and complexity of the project requires that we keep the theoretical overview and difficulties centrally in mind while sorting through the conceptually relevant material. In addition, I will articulate still another mode through which communicative intersubjectivity is important for feminist epistemology.

In chapter four I argued at length for the relevancy of work in analytic epistemology and analytic philosophy as a whole to feminist theory, and I will not rehash the argument here. However, there are elements of the feminist counter that are worth repeating, for they are perhaps more important to material in philosophy of mind than they are to material in epistemology. The reason for this lies in the reliance of philosophy of mind on material from contemporary cognitive science—a point made first in chapter two and repeated at several junctures. Until the past decade, much of the work in philosophy of mind had proceeded on a conceptual analysis level that seemed to owe much of its problem formulation to the later Wittgenstein. An important problem in philosophy of mind during the 1960s and early 1970s, for example, was the status of a pain, and whether pains could be accounted for in an identity theory.[32] This work was neither more nor less rigidly analytic than the concurrent work in epistemology, and both lines of theorizing were virtually completely nonnaturalized. Although great strides had already been made in what is now known as AI and cognitive science at that time (circa 1975), very little of this new work in the cognitive sciences had made its way into philosophy. Indeed, at the time of Dreyfus's *What Computers Can't Do,* almost no philosophers had published significantly in this area.[33]

So the move toward acceptance of the computational model of mind in philosophy and the very large amount of publishing that has been devoted to defending it, embellishing it, attacking it, or at the very least, taking notice of it, was a rather sudden one, and one that, again, went against the grain of the nonnaturalized theorizing that had preceded it. One wants to note, parenthetically, that work in functionalism or the computational model is not nearly as naturalized as it could be—and not as naturalized as the reductionists, whose work I have cited here before, might hope.[34] Nevertheless, the allusion to cognitive functioning that necessarily takes place when one employs (or notices) such a model is an intriguing one, theoretically, and one that cannot be ignored.

Now the difficulty for feminist theory here is on the same order as the difficulty for feminist empiricism, which I used in chapter four as an analogue for analytic theory as a whole. But contemporary philosophy of mind has this crucial component: Unlike the portions of epistemology that are labeled "naturalized," the relevant portions of philosophy of mind are still more empirically based, have greater intrinsic confirmability, and are still more susceptible to ultimate reduction. In other words, an epistemologist like Goldman can devote his time to utilizing work in the cognitive sciences to ameliorate epistemology while still maintaining an overall normative stance, and while still attempting to answer such questions as "What is epistemic justification?" or "When may an agent be said to be justified?" Since the import of these questions is still largely normative, one uses naturalized theory to embroider a normative project.[35]

## INTENTIONALITY AND FEMINIST THEORY

Current philosophy of mind has shaded into the sciences to such an extent that a good portion of the material being utilized may be said to fall within the scope of the sciences proper.[36] So the crux of the theoretical problem from a feminist viewpoint may be rendered as follows: To what extent does philosophy of mind buy into an account that, since it is essentially the result of the sciences (biological and otherwise; mathematics and contemporary logic figure heavily in computer simulation) is susceptible to all of the criticisms, political or of other sorts, which may be made of the sciences? To what extent would a model like CCP, derived from the computational model, be the result of politically incorrect theorizing that is, apart from being grossly androcentric, also the very sort of theorizing many feminists have labeled oppressive to minorities, Third World points of view, and, indeed, to anyone who is not white, male, and well-educated?

To the extent that this question may be identified with the questions of chapter four, it has already been at least partially answered here. I have cited Longino, among others, as being willing to countenance the claim that part of the meaning of feminist science or feminist philosophy of science is that feminists are doing it, rather than that the project in which they are engaged is not science or not recognizable as a scientific endeavor. But the thorniness of this problem may not be easily masked, nor is there any one mode of reply to the problem that is completely acceptable. Jane Braaten has written of the difficulty of trying to formulate a feminist philosophy of psychology that is aware of or makes use of current lines of research without imitating androcentric theory to the point that the original feminist commitment is lost:

> I believe that there are no *a priori* reasons for which a feminist philosophy of psychology should reject materialism, or even reductionism. Of course, there may be *a posteriori* reasons, such as the problems that Thomas Nagel raises for attempted reductions of the phenomenological features of experience. However, it seems to me that the more important issue here is the question of whose neurophysiological results would be of most interest to us.[37]

The danger of course is that any reducing theory—with its scientifically based underlying stratum and its commitment to a scientifically revealed ontology—will leave us with a structure so androcentric by its very nature as to preclude feminist usage. As Braaten also writes, "A complete reduction of folk psychology, then, would include not only the reducing theory itself but also a set of correspondence rules to match the mimicking entailments to our folk psychological terms and beliefs."[38] But the refinements and precision gained by such a reduction are benefits the advantages of which cannot be easily dismissed. Thus the conundrum of feminist empiricism reappears, albeit in somewhat different form, in philosophy of mind and philosophy of psychology. The conundrum does not completely disappear no matter what rostrum is applied to it, nor is it possible to attenuate its theoretical strength in a significant manner. Perhaps having made the commitment to the feminist usage of the tools of analytic philosophy of mind and analytic epistemology, we should focus on the benefits to be derived from the model. The pull of the model's precision is a powerful one and is not easily given up.

Part of the importance of philosophy of mind as a whole, both for our model and for feminist theory in general, lies in the notion of intersubjectivity. The level of intentionality posited by Searle is, as we have remarked before, an exemplar of the use of such a notion in the formulation of speech-act theory. The notion that a great deal of the intersubjective proceeds along the lines of conversational implicature within the framework of communicating individuals is a helpful one, both for feminist theory and for philosophy of mind as a whole, and Searlian intentionality is an aid in the elucidation of that notion.

But the realm of the intersubjective has still more to offer feminist theory, for it is a recurring theme in the work of the standpoint epistemologists that one's ontology is the partial creation of one's experiences, or one's mode of experiencing. Hartsock, for example, analyzes this in largely Marxist terms, as was stated in chapter three. But it is not merely the mode of production of a society, or its achievement of certain forces of production, that spells the manner in which individual communication is accomplished. For women, the notion of playing a crucial part in reproductive labor is important, and the notion that the interaction women typically have with small children, other women, and those generally in need of care helps develop constraints on a gynocentric worldview is also critical.

Now if women have a tendency to interpret the world relationally, or on an intercommunicative basis, they also play a part in the formation of the views of others that is, in this manner of theorizing, more crucial than the role played by most males, for example. So we may draw two brief conclusions here: (i) females have a tendency to construct personal ontologies, if you will, according both to their groundedness in the material life and according to the realm of intersubjectivity established by a mode and experience of communication that is peculiarly female; and (ii) females can play an important part in the development of intersubjectivity for others, at least partially because almost all of us are, in our earliest years, reared primarily by females. One need not agree entirely with the standpoint epistemologists to see the importance of these claims. Common sense informs us that our structure of reality is largely the result of communicative exchanges (see again Kornblith)—for those unfortunates who are either incapable of such exchanges, or who ignore them, realities are constructed that are not consonant with the prevailing point of view, all to their general detriment. Since the traditional female role in almost all Western societies, and even some non-Western societies, emphasizes the communicative exchange role of females, and the extent to which nurturing and care are developed from the standpoint of attentive listening and skill in interpersonal communication, common sense again vindicates a view that would make communication of the utmost importance both for a feminist epistemology and for a feminist philosophy of mind.[39]

So the construction of the problematic area of intentionality that I have given here is far from recondite, at least insofar as feminist theory is concerned: It is of the utmost importance for a gynocentric account of knowledge or epistemic justification that some attempt be made to expand on the importance of communication. The role of intentionality, then, given the place that communication plays in CCP, is crucial, and so the role of intentionality within the computational model that is part and parcel of CCP must be determined and sketched as fully as possible.

Moreover, to allude to a problem that will be examined more completely in a later chapter, one must note the importance for feminist theory of nonverbal communication. Nonverbal communication may be thought of either in homespun terms—the everyday gestures that make up a large part of our daily communication, especially between those who know each other well—or, in more dramatic terms, as the repertoire of intimate behavior that moves along the spectrum from demonstrations of friendship to erotic intimacy. One may, in fact, think of sexuality itself as an important form of communication, and here again intentionality is crucially important, as a number of theorists on matters sexual, including Nagel and Solomon, have concluded.[40] Although this aspect of intentionality does not come under scrutiny in the present chapter, I will have more to say about it at a later point.

## FOLK-PSYCHOLOGICAL TERMS:
## OTHER THEORETICAL VIEWS

To return to the examination of theorists with which we were proceeding, I want now to take another look at Stephen Stich's work, since it is less hopeful about the possibility of the utilization of intentionality than is either Dennett's view or Fodor's. Indeed, Baker alternately characterizes Stich as holding her (ii) or her (iii)—(iii) being the eliminativist view.[41] In any case, it is clear that even if Stich may be said to hold (ii) rather than (iii), he holds it in no strong sense. Stich sees no theoretical use for propositional attitudes or attributions of intentional states, and perhaps more importantly (insofar as the sciences are concerned), he sees no truth-value to the ascription of intentional content except in completely contextually defined terms.

Stich's book *From Folk Psychology to Cognitive Science* is a complex and elaborate look at the possibilities for various forms of intentional theorizing in philosophy of mind and their intersection with the computational model. Stich is remarkably clear in providing an overview of the positions for which he will argue at the beginning of the book, and it is here that we can glean some material useful to our own project.

Here is Stich on the overall project:

> The core of my argument is the claim that the theorist who seeks to couch the generalizations of cognitive science in the content-ascribing language of folk psychology will be plagued by problems that can be readily avoided. The fact that similarity assessments underlie the ascription of content entails that generalizations that attempt to detail the way beliefs interact with each other, and with other cognitive states in terms of the contents of these states, will be beset by the vagueness and context sensitivity which similarity assessments engender. The . . . parochialism of content ascription . . . makes it intractable to characterize in the language of folk psychology the cognitive states of relatively exotic subjects such as young children, "primitive" folk, and people suffering from various brain injuries and mental illnesses.[42]

Leaving aside for the moment Stich's characterization of exotic subjects, what he is attempting to state here is that intentionality will fail to exhibit strong nomic regularity on various interpretations of computational modeling, and thus will be unacceptable as the vehicle for a science of the mind. Tersely, Stich's argument will be that the various sorts of identity proposed between content states and the synaptically wired language of thought will break down, and that no one identity will be strong enough to exhibit the necessary nomic regularity. Although Stich thinks that token–token identity is the most plausible candidate for an identity view that would have the desirable outcome, he does not think that it really works either, except in a specifiable, contextually defined range of cases.[43]

The intriguing aspect of the foregoing is that it ties into our project in a very concrete sort of way. Since CCP is not intended as a model with nomological regularity, the usual sorts of riders that would be required for stringently scientific models do not apply. Rather, the point is, as I specified during the section on Dennett, whether it makes sense to refer to the intentional at all, in any sort of way, within the context of the computational model. The good news is that for all except the most stringent eliminativists, it does. Stich's own program has been referred to in alternating terms, so to speak, because Stich is concerned with the future of a science of the mind. If intentional terms do not work within a scientific framework—as he strongly argues—then for all practical purposes he is an eliminativist. But if Stich is prepared to say that there is some crude truth to intentional terms in pragmatic or socially defined contexts, then he has said enough to allow feminist theorists to purchase the sort of intentionality within a computational framework that might be useful for an amelioration of feminist epistemology.

Our overview of the computational model of mind and its applicability for a gynocentric epistemology will conclude with a look at some of the sketches of representationalism presented by Robert Van Gulick. Van Gulick's work is helpful in that it presents us with an adumbration of some of the terminological and other disputes within representationalist theory itself that are relevant to the problems addressed here. Although Van Gulick is not in general concerned with whether or not folk-psychological constructs are applicable within the context of functionalism in the piece cited here, he does point out another difficulty that the theorists are sometimes loath to explicate.

I have written so far as if it were a given that representations—the items in the conceptual apparatus that would allow us to posit intentionality in the first place—somehow hook up to or match the syntactical encoding that is supposed to be the hardware for the computational theory. But stating so much begs the question, at least when one inquires into what it is that does the representing. As Van Gulick points out, in a certain sense the encoding itself is representational; if it were not there, no semantic interpretations could be made. In another sense, it is as yet unrepresented, or uninterpreted. There must be something else in the system that correlates the appropriate semantics with the appropriate hardware, or functional architecture.

Van Gulick articulates this problem as follows:

> The term "mental representation" is ambiguous in a theoretically significant way. On one hand, it can be used to refer to the general capacity of minds for representing actual and potential states of affairs. . . . In other contexts mental representations are clearly to be understood as formal or

syntactic structures which function as internal symbols (as "formulae in the language of thought").[44]

In other words, if "representation" is understood in the second way, then part of the problem of intentionality is solved (only part, unfortunately). If "representation" refers to the syntactic encoding itself—the neuronal equivalents of the computer's 1's and 0's—then of course intentional constructs are encoded in some sense, and of course intentionality plays a role, possibly even a nomological role (although what it would look like to determine this or make it explicit is well nigh unimaginable). But this use of "representation" is the less common of the two and tends not to occur in the literature of those within cognitive science itself who have been concerned to provide some sort of basis or grounding for the computational model.[45] If "representation" means something like the meaning I have assigned to it in this text, then we are back, theoretically, to square one: It is by no means clear how one gets from the encoded material to the semantical correlates, by no means clear what the "transducers" are (to employ Pylyshyn's term), and by no means clear what role intentionality could play, since presumably the intentional has now been raised to a level that renders it non-nomological.

In his piece "Mental Representation—A Functionalist View," Van Gulick goes on to provide a version "of the accepted functionalist wisdom with a particularly naturalistic and biological slant."[46] His version, although not strongly different from the models we have examined here, does allow for a broader interpretation of the term "representation" than has characteristically been the case with other functionalist or computational accounts. Because he tends to define retrieval or decoding of a representation in terms of use ("a system's realizing a given informational state is a matter of the system's *possessing* and being able to comprehend and utilize whatever information specifies its content"[47]), Van Gulick's view allows for a certain amount of representation even among animals. This is particularly salient, for even the everyday use of folk-psychological terms tends to be hedged when confronted with nonhuman instances of apparent intentionality. Jovial disagreements about whether one's dog believes a bone to be hidden in a certain place, or whether one's mare knows that she is about to trot along her favorite trail, indicate that we are customarily uncertain as to how to apply intentional categories in cases involving animals. If intentionality is of dubious help in establishing a science of cognition for human beings, the argument would go, it would be of still less assistance in theorizing about animal cognition, since we know less about animal cognition to begin with and since animals do not possess language.[48] But Van Gulick is defining representations largely in terms of behavioral capacity to interact with the environment, and on this criterion animals, of course, do very well. As he writes,

> A chameleon acquires information about the color of its surroundings, even though its camouflage response exhausts the adaptive consequences of that information possession. And given their adaptiveness the genetically determined flight mechanisms of a swallow can be said nonmetaphorically to constitute the possession of phylogenetically acquired information about the air.[49]

In short, Van Gulick's account of functionalism is of interest here precisely because it is as naturalized as it is and precisely because it allows for a notion of representation that bridges the gap between the syntactic and the semantic by allowing representation to be largely behaviorally defined. From a behavioral standpoint, of course, our model is entitled to employ folk-psychological constructs—the behavior exhibited by speakers in most social situations is highly intentional. Debating the fine points about the nomological applicability of the constructs ignores the fact that, as Van Gulick has pointed out, there is a real sense in which birds and other animals utilize information and hence have representations, where "representation" is defined in terms of a being's interaction with its environment.

Thus we find ourselves with something of a mixed bag of responses to the theoretical difficulty posed by employing a model, like CCP, which is simultaneously computational and intentional. Dennett would tend to argue for the instrumental value of the retention of the intentional terminology; Van Gulick's account of functionalism does not preclude it. Fodor seems to want to retain some use of the terminology, but, as I have argued, it is not at all clear that the use retained is intentional in a clearly articulated and commonsensical way. Finally, Stich would find virtually no place for the language of intentionality or folk psychology in an account that pretended to be even sketchily scientific.

## PHILOSOPHY OF MIND AND FEMINIST EPISTEMOLOGY

I will conclude this chapter with a summary of the rather complex issues that have been raised here, and some additional comments. I have taken as exemplary for purposes of examination of the philosophy of mind and its relevance to gynocentric epistemology Baker's summation of four contemporary positions. Each of these positions has more than one exemplar, but the position that has caused perhaps the most debate in the literature—(iii), the strongly eliminativist position—is one that I have not examined here at any length because it has little or nothing to do with CCP. Thus we are left with the other three positions: Baker allies Fodor with (i), Dennett with (iv), and Stich alternately with (ii) and (iii). (Insofar as Stich is concerned, it is with (ii) that I am most concerned.)

Dennett, then, has a position most congenial with what we have tried to do in presenting CCP, since Dennett allows for the moral or instrumental use of intentional language even if it is understood to be nomologically weak or void. That, I take it, is the point of the preservation of folk-psychological terminology in semi-scientific contexts: One can still retain its weak predictive value while utilizing other sorts of terminology when strongly lawlike behavior needs to be described. Thus Dennett—and Searle, Millikan, and others who have employed speech-act theory to describe intersubjectivity—holds a view that is useful for our purposes and theoretically congenial at that.

Fodor and Stich, as I have argued earlier, maintain positions on the usage of intentional constructs that are theoretically difficult and that would also tend to undercut any relatively coarse model such as CCP, which purports to retain intentional terminology. Fodor's work is perhaps the most puzzling here. Although Fodor is identified by Baker and others as holding a positive position with regard to the usage of intentional terms, and although Fodor frequently takes as his target in the literature those who are ardently eliminativist, it is not clear precisely what Fodor's position on propositional attitudes boils down to for everyday purposes. Fodor also holds that what makes the computational model of mind nomological, and scientifically interesting, is its positing of the syntactical encoding in such a way that the computations reduce to actions over the syntactic encodings. But as we saw in the section taken from the work of Robert Van Gulick, it is not clear precisely what it means to hold a representational theory of mind and then focus on the encodings themselves, since presumably the encodings alone can only be correlated with propositional attitudes in the weakest sort of way. In other words, if propositional attitudes, folk-psychological terms, or the language of intentionality is important for Fodor, it is not important in the same useful way that it is for Dennett (for example), since Fodor does not focus on any theoretical position that would allow one to pull out the propositional attitudes in a clear and articulable way.

Stich's position is generally more along the lines of (iii), one feels compelled to say, rather than (ii). Nevertheless, as I indicated earlier, what is of interest about Stich's position for our purposes is that the only exceptions he allows for the use of folk-psychological terms are all context-bound and instance-dependent. That is, Stich sees no hope for the use of such terms in a genuine science of the mind, but he admits that at the level of individuals and particulars some usages of the terms may not be incoherent. It is this construction of the problem, no doubt, that leads Baker to claim that Stich is sometimes identified with her position (ii), and it is certainly this portion of Stich's position that makes aspects of CCP most tenable.

I have cited briefly the work of Ruth Garrett Millikan, John Searle, and John Heil for the light that it sheds on certain narrowly defined points of theory. Millikan's work is filled with illustrative examples of how prediction and intentionality can be preserved together without dissonance. Her mundane examples help to remind us of precisely what level of prediction we would be maintaining if we resorted to the language of folk psychology: Like Millikan's example of John and the woman next door, most of the examples that we can employ from our experience of the world have to do with a person's intending to do something, and what transpires after that. Admittedly, this is a crude level for prediction and prognostication, but more than that has seldom been required of folk-psychological terminology in any case. Searle's work is helpful in the same vein, while reminding us that much of our daily activity, insofar as speech is involved, is fraught with intentionality. Many of our remarks to others are along the lines of what Searle and other speech-act theorists label "indirect requests," or "indirect commands." If it is clear that some cultures employ these commands and requests more frequently than others, part of what it means to make an acquaintance from another background or to become friends with a person from a non-English-speaking area may include a heightened sensitivity to the indirectness of many speech acts. Thus, when Searle helps to fill in the blanks for us on this rather gray area of theory, he has hit on an area extremely important to human communication, especially cross-cultural communication.

In addition, this chapter examined once more, albeit somewhat cursorily, the problem of the alleged inconsistency of the usage of androcentric empiricism and its offshoots for feminist theory. We did not retread here the ground already covered in the previous chapter;

rather, I noted that the difficulty with material from philosophy of psychology or philosophy of mind is that this material is already somewhat more solidly within the framework of the sciences than is, for example, naturalized epistemology, much of which still retains a normative flavor. The consequence of the recasting of the problem of feminist empiricism, as it were, was that the adoption of the empiricist method and the acceptance of its ramifications is very much dependent on who employs the method and what use is to be made of its outcomes.

Finally, I noted an interesting problem for the notion of communication and intersubjectivity in general as it applies to feminist theory on the whole and feminist epistemology in particular. It is not only the case that a feminist account of knowledge acquisition wants to take into consideration the grounded, interpersonal, nuanced manner in which much knowledge is acquired, but also the case that females in general communicate with others in a sense that yields the construction of ontologies. The importance of communication for females, then, is not merely in its mode of epistemic justification, or knowledge acquisition, but also in its mode of world-making. I was unable to fill in on this material directly in this chapter, but the importance of this issue— as well as the importance of nonverbal communication and its off-shoots—makes it a relevant and worthwhile project for another chapter. Feminist epistemology leads, at least to some extent, to feminist ontology. In the androcentric mode, these lines of inquiry are sometimes sharply separated, but part of what it means to construct a feminist epistemology, I argue, is to note the interweaving of the two.

Gynocentric knowing, female voices, and gynesis are topics that have been covered by feminists working in a number of traditions. Although I will stay within the framework of analytic philosophy here, fairness requires that we acquaint ourselves, at least briefly, with other gyn-centered voices. In the next chapter we examine the work of some feminist theorists whose orientation and framework derive from another tradition.

## NOTES

1. The terms "computational" and "functional" will be used here more-or-less interchangeably. The literature has a tendency to run the two terms together, although presumably "computational" is the more broadly inclusive term, since it makes no allusion, even indirectly, to instantiation.

2. Cited on pp. 58–59, this text.

3. Baker, *Saving Belief,* 13–14.

4. Churchland, in *Neurophilosophy,* is, of course, most strongly associated with view (iii).

5. See my "Reductionism."

6. Baker, of course, very pointedly refers to his work in this way.

7. This same point is made by Ruth Garrett Millikan in a variety of pieces. (Cf. fn. 27, chap. 4.)

8. Baker, *Saving Belief,* 149–50. Quoting from Daniel Dennett, "Skinner Skinned," *Brainstorms.* Emphasis Dennett's.

9. Baker, *Saving Belief,* fn. 18, 153. Quoting from Daniel Dennett, "Intentional Systems in Cognitive Ethology: The 'Panglossian Paradigm' Defended," *Behavioral and Brain Sciences* 6, no. 3 (1983):380. Emphasis Dennett's.

10. Daniel Dennett, *The Intentional Stance* (Cambridge, Mass.: Bradford of MIT Press, 1987), 6–7.

11. Baker gives a particularly clear explication of this. She is here drawing on Dennett's *Brainstorms* essay, "Intentional Systems."

12. Dennett, *Intentional Stance,* 52.

13. Millikan, "Thoughts Without Laws," 50.

14. Ibid., 65.

15. Ibid., 68.

16. Ibid.

17. See John Searle, "The Intentionality of Intention and Action," in *Perspectives on Cognitive Science,* ed. Donald A. Norman (Norwood, N.J.: Ablex Publishing, 1981).

18. Ibid., 213–14.

19. Quoted in Harding, *The Science Question,* 148. Citation made in this manuscript on p. 96.

20. See Harding, *The Science Question,* 153.

21. Hubbard, "Science, Facts," 11.

22. Longino, "Can There Be?", 52–53.

23. Baker, *Saving Belief,* 24. Quoting from Jerry Fodor's "Propositional Attitudes," in his *Representations* (Cambridge, Mass.: Bradford of MIT Press, 1981), 182.

24. Many views deny that there can be causal interaction between mental states on a computational model. The relations are, rather, logical. This stance is taken by Patricia Smith Churchland, for example, to be paradigmatic of the computational account, and it also figures in Pylyshyn's work.

25. Baker, *Saving Belief,* 26.

26. Ibid.

27. Jerry A. Fodor, *The Modularity of Mind* (Cambridge, Mass.: Bradford of MIT Press, 1983), 44–45.

28. Flanagan, *Science of the Mind.*

29. Ibid., 221.

30. Stich, *Folk Psychology,* 226.

31. John Heil, "Does Cognitive Science Rest on a Mistake?", Mind 90, no. 359 (1981):328.

32. A theorist such as Putnam devotes a large part of his work in this area on this particular problem. See, for example, his *Reason, Truth and History: Philosophical Papers, Vol. II* (Cambridge, Mass.: Harvard University Press, 1975).

33. This book was published in 1972.

34. Churchland, *Neurophilosophy.*

35. Some of the naturalizing epistemologists retain the normative flavor of analytic epistemology to a greater extent than others. Goldman's direction seems to be more normative than, for example, Kornblith's.

36. Neurophilosophy *qua* area of endeavor is exemplary in this regard.

37. Jane Braaten, "Dizzy Dames and Loopy Ladies: Feminist Commitments in the Philosophy of Psychology" (Unpublished ms., University of Montana, 1987), 15–16.

38. Ibid., 15.

39. Hartsock, cf. fn. 19, this chapter.

40. See Thomas Nagel, "Sexual Perversion," in *Philosophy and Sex,* ed. Robert Baker and Frederick Elliston (Buffalo, N.Y.: Prometheus Books, 1983); Robert Solomon, "Love and Feminism," in Baker and Elliston.

41. Baker, *Saving Belief,* 113–16.

42. Stich, *Folk Psychology,* 8.

43. Stich, *Folk Psychology,* 226.

44. Robert Van Gulick, "Mental Representation—A Functionalist View," *Pacific Philosophical Quarterly* 63, no. 1 (1982):3.

45. Pylyshyn, for example, refers to his work as an "investigation into the foundations of cognitive science."

46. Van Gulick, "Mental Representation," 4.

47. I ignore, for purposes of this argument, the ongoing debate with regard to the great apes. (Koko, Washoe, etc.)

48. Van Gulick, "Mental Representation," 8.

*Part Three*

# OTHER FRAMEWORKS

## Chapter Six

# French Feminist Viewpoints

The critique of feminist empiricism articulated by Harding, which was presented in chapter three, turned out to be of the utmost importance for the model presented in the chapters that followed, since specification of the model involved extensive use of the categories of analytic philosophy and especially of analytic epistemology. But part of the difficulty for contemporary feminist theory has been the influence by sources so diverse as to be scarcely categorizable under related rubrics. The debate over feminist empiricism is only one part of a larger debate; Harding presents some of it in the guise of feminist postmodernism, but there are other categories to which allusion might be made.

Feminist work done in the United States, Great Britain, Australasia, and Canada is done largely by English speaking philosophers who have some training in the Anglo-American analytic philosophical tradition with which I have dealt extensively in this work. But feminist work done on the Continent necessarily derives from other traditions, and here one can, at least to some extent, specify nationalistic breakdowns (and possibly even regionalistic ones) as points of origin for various developments in feminist thought. French feminist thought has probably been paramount among those not of Anglo-analytic origin, but there have also been developments in Germany, Italy, Spain, Portugal, and Latin America, all of which are relevant to American feminist theory even if it is sometimes difficult to be precise about what the theoretical relevance or relationship is.

## THE RELEVANCE OF FRENCH THEORY

Before expanding upon CCP and developing some of its ramifactions, especially along the lines of sociology of knowledge and intra-American feminist debates, I want to depart briefly from the analytic tradition to examine, in particular, some examples of contemporary French feminist thinking. This chapter will make no claims to encyclopaedic inclusiveness or to pointed specification of various areas of French thought; the object of the chapter is, simply put, to examine some of the material that has appeared in translation and in leading anthologies so as to be able to gloss its relevance to feminist epistemology.[1] I will therefore dispense with the urge to provide the sort of overview of leading feminist thinkers in the French tradition that I provided for some theorists in analytic epistemology in the opening chapters. However tempting it might appear to be to focus on one or two thinkers, I will follow Toril Moi in attempting a more general overview, since the thought of the French feminists necessarily derives from and alludes to a large body of post-Kantian Continental thought to which I have so far made only passing reference.

The importance of French thought, in particular,[2] seems to lie partly in its virtually complete divorce from the categories employed by American and English-speaking feminists in general.[3] In other words, one might hypothesize that one is dealing partially with the appeal of the ''terrifying negative,'' as Moi has it, and also partly with the appeal of a theoretical stance that has its own sort of explanatory power, even if it is difficult to mesh this explanatory power with the more empirically based theories most English-speaking feminists are familiar with.[4]

It might be helpful, then, to remind ourselves that French feminist thought has as its background at least some theory to which I have already alluded here. In our overview of Harding, Flax and Hartsock were mentioned prominently, and the ties between Flax's psychoanalytic approach and Freudian/post-Freudian theory, as well as between Hartsock's variation on a Marxist account and Marxist theory itself was adumbrated. French feminist thought shares this general point of origin with the sorts of views we have associated with Flax and Hartsock, and is, of course, very prominently ensconced in the variety of stances that Harding labeled ''postmodernist.'' So the theoretical precursors of feminist theory in the French version are already apparent in other work, and have at least been referred to here. What I aim to do in this chapter is to be both more specific about what the theoretical developments entail and how certain varietals of the theory might be helpful in the further elucidation of feminist epistemology.

French feminism springs from the general Continental tradition in philosophy—all of the post-Kantian thought that was not originally written in English, with Hegel and Marx standing as the most prominent nineteenth-century thinkers, and Sartre, Heidegger, and Husserl serving as the most emergent of the twentieth century—and an interesting theoretical variation on traditional philosophy, to wit, psychoanalytic theory. It is the promulgation of the latter in place of what might appear to be more traditionally philosophical thought that has perhaps been the single greatest factor in the creation of lines of French theory that American and English thinkers find "incomprehensible." The immediate precursors to the work of feminist theorists such as Cixous and Kristeva, and others such as Annie Leclerc, Arlette Farge, and Michele Le Doeuff, are male French theoreticians whose work draws heavily on psychoanlytic theory, Marixsm, and post-Marxist structuralist trends. The trio of feminist theoreticians most frequently mentioned—Cixous, Kristeva, and Irigaray—has as its precursor still another trio, that of the best-known male French theorists, Lacan, Derrida, and Foucault. The peculiar difficulty for English-speaking feminists is that of grasping what it is that the feminist theorists have to say that is both important and new, and how it is that the material they present is related to the work of the preceding male thinkers.

Insofar as Derrida is concerned, the direct theoretical linkage is generally viewed as running most linearly from Derrida to Cixous. That is, Cixous is the feminist theoretician whose work most directly draws on the work of Derrida, rather than, for example, Lacan. Cixous's work has now received fairly extensive circulation within the United States, and certainly her notion of a "female voice" or "female writing" has been influential, even if it is not at all clear that the influence on British and American philosophers is anything like what was originally intended. I want now to sketch a bit of Cixous's work, as well as its Derridean underpinnings, before proceeding to do the same for other thinkers. The goal of the chapter will remain, however, as previously stated: an overview of French theory in general, and not merely that of the better-known or more prominent thinkers.

"Deconstruction" and the work of Derrida has now passed, however dilutedly, into the general and popular culture, so one is understandably a bit hesitant to attempt to provide a further gloss on it, particularly in the context of a work that does not have Continental underpinnings. But the core idea behind the notion of deconstruction, insofar as it applies to written texts, is not a particularly difficult one, and however, it has been caricatured, it is far from irrelevant to feminist theory, as French thinkers like Cixous have discovered. Derrida's central insight, promulgated in such works as *On Grammatology* and *Writing and Difference,* is that a given text is largely, if not entirely, the interpretation of the reader who reads it, and that just as the reader can construct a text in a certain way, it can be deconstructed. In other words, whatever might appear to be the "meaning" of a given word, phrase, or sentence is dispensable, and ambiguity, double or multiple meanings, and so forth are always available for further interpretation and permutation. Thus no text is really a text in the standard sense; every text is what the reader (or interpreter) makes it, and every text (including those not literary) may be deconstructed. One can always, as Kenneth Baynes remarks in his introduction to the chapter on Derrida in *After Philosophy,*[5]

> . . . look[] for the "tension between gesture and statement" in a text— that is, for the ways in which the text implicitly undercuts its own stated views—and . . . show[] how this tension contains a basic insight into the matter at hand. What is excluded by the manifest content of the text as inessential, what is separated off from it as a mere superaddition to what is central, will turn out to be essential, central after all.[6]

In other words, what the text doesn't say—on standard interpretation—is just as important as what it does say, and what is given only marginal importance or perceived as having peripheral impact is as important, perhaps more important, than what had been deemed to be central.

## CIXOUS AND WOMEN'S VOICE

The foregoing is the heart of Derridean deconstruction, and most of the critical work that has followed it is a set of epicycles on this rather basic and fundamental theme. The relevance of these notions to feminism is not obscure, nor is it particularly arcane or esoteric, especially given the metaphorical importance of the female and matters feminine in Western culture (an importance that we have already implicitly examined here during the course of the central argument on feminist empiricism in chapter four, where I mentioned that some credit most of what has been labeled feminist epistemology with largely metaphorical impact). Clearly, that which has been called "female" or "feminine" has always been marginal to Western culture and indeed marginal to most of the cultures of the world. The long list of citations regularly made by social scientists, and even literary critics, of the associations with the "feminine" (negativity, darkness, the moon, night, lack, deprivation, and so forth) reminds us that if culture is the text, then the standard interpretation of the text places the masculine in the role of signifier, message, or sign of central import, and the feminine in the role of the marginal. It is on the basis of these sorts of moves in theory, then, that Cixous and others among the French theorists have attempted to make a leap from deconstruction as promulgated by Derrida to the female voice.

Perhaps the best-known piece by Cixous is "The Laugh of the Medusa," originally published in *Signs* at a time when little French work had been disseminated in America.[7] This piece represents Cixous's thinking on the notion of female or feminine appropriation of the voice, that is, the voice of the text of Western culture in the vein of the analysis presented above. But Cixous's theorizing presents a problem for someone schooled in Derrida, for if the text of Western culture is essentially masculine, or "phallogocentric," to employ the term that feminist theorists borrow partly from Derrida, it is not clear that the female voice can appropriate this stance without itself constructing a text.

The metaphorical nature of French theorizing makes it difficult, if one has been trained in Anglo-American analytic philosophy, to make sense of the debate, and yet it is clear (once the initial hesitation to heavily utilize metaphor is bypassed) that the questions posed by the French theorists have their analogues in current English-language feminist debate, and, more importantly, that the less-than-literal nature of the discourse helps shed new light on the subject. For the problematic here is analogous to what I addressed in part in both chapters four and five: whether it is possible to employ the androcentric techniques of formulated and ensconced theory without rendering the new theory itself hopelessly androcentric. The crucial difference is that the French thinkers see this debate in somewhat larger terms: Since their overview is not empirical to begin with, it is the ground of literacy and culture itself with which they are concerned, rather than the smaller and narrower area of philosophical theorizing on a certain topic.

Here is Cixous on woman's voice and the seizure of the phallocentric space or text by the female:

[An act] that will be marked by woman's *seizing* the occasion to *speak,* hence her shattering entry into history, which has always been based on her *suppression*. To write and thus to forge for herself the *antilogos* weapon. To become *at will* the taker and the initiator, for her own right, in every symbolic system, in every political process.[8]

And:

Listen to a woman speak at a public gathering (if she hasn't painfully lost her wind). She doesn't "speak," she throws her trembling body forward; she lets go of herself, she flies; all of her passes into her voice, and it's with her body that she vitally supports the "logic" of her speech. Her flesh speaks true. She lays herself bare. In fact she physically materializes what she's thinking; she signifies it with her body. . . . In women's speech, as in their writing, [there is] that element which never stops resonating. . . .[9]

In other words, part of the female "voice" is the body, and part of what it means to signify in the female style is to utilize the body as part of the sign, rather than positing sign as independent of the body, in the male style. Again, it is not difficult to unpack these metaphors in terms at least moderately familiar to the Anglo-American context of feminist theory: In more than one chapter here, I have focused on the extent to which knowledge is divorced from context in the androcentric view, and in the presentation of an analytically oriented gynocentric theory, context was a major factor. In fact, in chapter four I presented the model as relying crucially on three emphases to be found in feminist epistemology and feminist theory as a whole—the emphases were on context, communicative relevance, and in-the-bodiness. The reader can see how Cixous's presentation of the female voice or female mode of signifying incorporates some of these same elements.

Part of the difficulty in writing about the French theorists lies in the fact that despite available book titles such as *The New French Feminisms* and *French Feminist Thought,* most of the theorists do not identify with feminism as a movement in the British or American sense.[10] This difficulty is ably articulated by the literary theorist Alice Jardine, whose *Gynesis* is a powerful exploration of the intersections of the various thinkers in the French postmodern tradition.

With regard to the awkwardness in the labeling, she writes:

The women theorists in France whose work has had or is beginning to have a major impact on theories of writing and reading, and who at one level or another are writing about women, at the very least do not call themselves feminist either privately or in their writing, and, at the most, posit themselves and their work as hostile to, or "beyond," feminism as a concept.[11]

That this may say more about French intellectual life than it does about feminism is no doubt true, but it does make difficult any easy translation (in any sense of the word) of French theory into Anglo-American feminism. Thus the theoretical difficulties that Cixous's appropriation of voice to woman encounters are obstacles only for a level of theory that already accepts Derridean deconstruction and is comfortable with its terminology. Nevertheless, I will spend some brief time setting out these difficulties, since they may be thought of as paradigmatic of the manner in which French theory has affected American thought.

To return to Cixous and her remarks on the female voice, I had indicated earlier that the theoretical problematic involved was one of whether or not it was possible to posit a female mode of signification without making the presumptuous sorts of errors inherent in the male mode. In other words, if the female voice becomes signifier within the text, it is no longer marginal but central. Krupnick, in his work *Displacement: Derrida and After*,[12] notes that Derrida's deconstruction "allies itself with the voiceless, the marginal, the repressed," but at the same time he notes that Derrida "has no conviction that the old, bad (metaphysical) order can be transcended."[13] Deconstruction "unsettles the idealisms that provide the ideological justifications for relations of power," but again it is not clear what one does with whatever has been deconstructed.[14]

So Cixous's work is paradoxical at best: As Cixous herself says, "It will usually be said . . . either that all writing . . . is feminine . . . or . . . that the act of writing is equivalent to masculine masturbation."[15] But in articulating the theory-driven and embellished problem of the masculine voice in Western culture—the signifier of Man's Truth, as Jardine has it—Cixous has brought to the fore a tension that already exists in the Anglo-American empiricist discourse, albeit in a different guise.[16]

## IRIGARAY AND LACANIAN THEORY

The work of Luce Irigaray presents us with similar concerns, seen from an American perspective, but at the same time these concerns, at least in small part, might more properly be said to be relevant to the overall projects of epistemology and philosophy of science. Irigaray draws on both Derrida and Lacan, but perhaps more strongly on Lacan, with his hypothesis that the childhood idiom writ large is *la langue paternelle*. In two pieces that have been translated into English and published in the United States (and here I largely exclude Irigaray's longer works, such as *Speculum of the Other Woman*, which are also now available in translation) Irigary is overtly reflecting on the sort of androcentric modes of thinking that have concerned us here, although in a less particularized fashion.[17] The first of these pieces is "Le Sujet de la Science: Est-il Sexué?" More than one passage bears directly on the notions of masculinst science and epistemology, and androcentric object-relations theory as well:

> If I tell you that two eggs can produce a new being, does this discovery seem to you possible, probable, true? Purely genetic? Or also of an order that is social, economic, cultural, political? Belonging to the exact sciences? Put a check there or in the appropriate boxes. Will this type of discovery be encouraged and subsidized? Will it be disseminated by the media? Yes? No? Why?[18]

And, on object-relations theory,

> Since psychoanalytic "science" is said to be a theory of the subject, *Freud's hypothesis concerning the constitution of the subject's relationship to discourse* deserves to be reconsidered, reinterpreted. Freud proposes the "bobbin game" as the scene that introduces the subject into language. The child—in this case a boy—would master the mother's absence by using an instrument that he throws far from him, brings back, moves away from or close to his place . . . while accompanying this gesture with the emission of alternating vowels. . . . This . . . would mark the child's entrance into the possibility of symbolic distantiation. . . . Does discourse remain at the level of partially theoretical exchanges between generations of men concerning mastery of the mother, of nature?[19]

These remarks by Irigaray on the subject of science and the language of science—or theoretical language in general, with its androcentricity—are relatively straightforward and fit well into many of the theses we have been exploring here. What gives these remarks their strength, however (particularly the second set of comments) is Irigaray's move from a somewhat direct look at the early language of infancy, hypothesized by Freud, with the infant male as subject, to her more oblique and embedded claim that language as a whole stems from the details of the male's relationship to his mother. Yet shorn of its somewhat literary air, Irigaray's point here is no more than has been made, for example, by Keller and others.[20] Other portions of Irigaray's work are, however, less direct and more in line with the sort of work I have just cited from Cixous. Here one must extrapolate from the somewhat precious style, albeit in translation, and make an effort to connect the general direction of the work to feminist work in the Anglo-American tradition.

Like Cixous, Irigaray borrows from Derrida and the deconstructionist influence in assigning woman a place in the text of Western culture that is at the margins, or even at the place of nothing. Moving from the asserted secondariness of female nature, as established in the ancient Western tradition by, for instance, Aristotle and the Church philosophers, Irigaray borrows the notion that woman does not possess a soul, hence has no center or core, and muses on the possibility that those without a center might place themselves and take center stage.

It is man who has been the subject of discourse, whether in the field of theory, morality or politics. And the gender of God, the guardian of every subject and discourse, is always paternal and masculine in the West. . . . [W]oman always tends *towards* something else, without ever turning toward herself as the site of a positive element. . . . In order to keep one's distance, does one have to know how to take? or speak? It comes down in the end to the same thing. Perhaps the ability to take requires a permanent space or container; a soul, maybe, or a mind? Mourning nothing is the hardest of all.[21]

Irigaray draws simultaneously from Lacanian theory and deconstruction here; the psychoanalytic moves are from Freud via Lacan, and the notion of a text of Western culture, which upon deconstruction reveals the spaces where woman has not been written, so to speak, is related of course to Derrida, Cixous, and to work by other French female thinkers. As Jardine remarks, Irigaray "[aims] her deconstructive strategies [at] . . . dissections of the 'male text,' interspersed with lyrical invitations to women to join with her in desacralizing male theory and liberating while valorizing the feminine repressed in male texts."[22]

## JULIA KRISTEVA AND THE NATURE OF OTHERNESS

Kristeva's work, like the work of Cixous and Irigaray, draws on Lacan, but Kristeva is perhaps a bit more concerned to delineate the difference that is paramount and chief among all the differences, that is sexual difference, rather than to elucidate the task of the female-appropriated voice itself. Jardine sees Kristeva in these terms:

> But . . . Kristeva . . . has suggested a more radical connection [between Other-ism and altruism as the peculiar virtue of women]. Beyond Freudian and Lacanian recognitions that the first significant Other is always the mother (to be replaced by "other women" in interminable succession for the male), Kristeva has repeatedly pointed out that the Other is always, in fact, the "other sex": "The difference between 'I' and 'you' turns out to be coextensive with the sexual difference, and every perturbation of the allocutionary polarity brings about or follows interferences between the two sexes. It is one way to show that the sexual difference is correlative to differences between discursive instances: that the 'other' is the 'other sex.' "[23]

Insofar as Kristeva retains a concern for the voice, she ties it to the notion of alterity in a manner that is reminiscent of Cixous but that predicates the crucial element of the female appropriation as a lack of positing of Otherness.

> If we confine ourselves to the *radical* nature of what is today called "writing" . . . there is nothing in either past or recent publications by women that permits us to claim that a specifically female writing exists. . . . I should say that writing ignores sex or gender and displaces its difference in the discreet workings of language and signification. . . . Knots of desire are created as a result. This is one way, among others, of reacting to the radical split that constitutes the speaking subject. This eternally premature baby, prematurely separated from the world of the mother and the world of things, remedies the situation by using an invincible weapon: linguistic symbolization. Such a method deals with this fundamental change characterizing the speaking subject not by positing the existence of an *other* (another person or sex, which would give us psychological humanism) or an *Other* (the absolute signifier, God) but by constructing a network where drives, signifiers and meanings join together and split asunder in a dynamic and enigmatic process.[24]

Here Kristeva treats language in a manner similar to that of Cixous and Irigaray, but with the difference that, as I indicated, the notion of alterity is more thoroughly worked into Kristeva's account. Whereas Cixous is concerned to articulate the in-the-bodiness of the female voice, and Irigaray the extent to which the male voice cuts off and displaces the concerns of the female, Kristeva moves along the lines of showing how the notion of alterity is primary for the masculine signifier but unimportant and irrelevant for the feminine signifier. Again, shearing away the trappings of literary theory, Kristeva's point with regard to the female signifier reinforces the theoretical points we have made here all the way along: When she says that one "construct[s] a network where drives, signifiers and meanings join together and split asunder in a dynamic and enigmatic process," she is describing a gynocentric interpretation of the move from male signifier to female signifier.[25]

At a later point, Kristeva is still more specific when she speaks of "the analysis of the work of language, not as something possessing an arbitrary but systematizable nature . . . [but possessing an] . . . ethical [preoccupation]. . . . [T]his ethics displays its own degree of *jouissance*. . . . Are women forever destined merely to be cast as witches . . . [o]r could they help conceive and construct a new comprehensive legitimacy for their jouissance? . . ."[26] Kristeva, then, closes the circle that we saw begun by Cixous. There is such a thing as a female appropriation. The chief difficulty is in providing an approximation of what a female appropriation would amount to. Kristeva defines it partially in negative terms: It does not rely on alterity, and (here she agrees with Cixous in *Laugh of the Medusa*) it has elements of looping, playfulness, and jouissance.[27]

## OTHER VOICES, OTHER CONCERNS: LE DOEUFF, FARGE, AND LECLERC

If Kristeva, Irigaray, and Cixous all have similar concerns, it may also be asserted that their concerns draw on strands of theory that are still relatively obscure for many British and American readers. There are, however, other French voices that are perhaps more straightforwardly feminist (rather than concerned with the notion of the "feminine") and also more accessible.

In an excerpt from the work of Michele Le Doeuff published in the Moi anthology, there is ample discussion of a problem that is much more on the level of practice and much less theoretical: the virtual exclusion of women from the discipline of philosophy itself. Le Doeuff treats this problem in terms comprehensible to those familiar with the problem-ridden humanities as they exist in virtually every cultural milieu and location. In noting both the treatment of women by the Great Thinkers and the exclusion of women from the list of great thinkers, Le Doeuff does little more than what has been done in a variety of other places.[28] What Le Doeuff does do, however, that is noteworthy from the perspective of what we have done here, is to tie the accession of women to philosophy—where and when it has occurred—to the female response to the male as it has traditionally been conditioned.

In the several glances at object-relations theory that have been provided here, I have been careful to try to delineate the male response to the female. But many feminist theorists have shied away from alluding to or extrapolating on the female response to the male, since it is a hallowed subject of male theory in any case and since to dwell on it does not seem to advance the cause of women. Nevertheless, as Le Doeuff points out, the female response to the male (both males as beings and that—like philosophy—deemed to be male), when set out, sheds light on philosophy itself, the sociology of philosophy, as it were, and male–female interaction.

Le Doeuff posits the entrance of females into the male-created and male-dominated realm of philosophy as essentially a movement wherein whatever is lacking for the female (whatever, in theoretical terms, would ordinarily constitute the grounds for positing an Other) comes in the form of a (male) Philosopher-who-is-Philosophy. In other words, the philosophical mentor for the few females admitted until recently has also been the embodiment of all that was Philosophical. Since males typically learn philosophy from other males, there can be no symmetricality in the manner in which males come into philosophy. In blunt terms, the male has as mentor for a while some other male, whose own theoretical views are then found to be lacking; the gap created by these lacks becomes a source of theory-building for the younger male.[29]

As Le Doeuff has it:

> On the other hand, if a woman has to have a philosophy of her tutor-lover, she is no longer within the philosophical enterprise, because she is spared (that is to say prohibited) a certain relationship with lack. . . .
>     Let us recall for example the *Phaedo* or the *Discourse on Method*. In both cases we are given the account of a disappointment and a frustration in teaching: "I imagined I had found the man who would teach me, but he disappointed me." (97c-99d). The disappointment begins the story . . . in trying to fill the lack.[30]

What Le Doeuff explicates here is in some sense the intellectual analogue and mirror image of the kind of response of the male to the female that we have engendered from object-relations theory. Le Doeuff is not primarily concerned here with how the female comes to heterosexual relationships. She is primarily concerned with how female thinkers have encountered the male discourse. Nevertheless, as is crucial to the point she is trying to make, it is precisely in viewing the modes in which female thinkers have encountered male discourse that one gains some insight into how females move to heterosexual relationships and to male erotic objects. If the male is afraid of the overwhelming power of the female—power that, as has been indicated, is largely connected to the mother and the infant's need for mothering—the female is drawn to the power of the male, and not simply in a fashion that reminds us of small children encountering their fathers. Rather it is also that the male is simultaneously giver of knowledge and the embodiment of knowledge itself. Once the male knower has spoken, no further elaborations are needed, and knowledge becomes eroticized and the erotic intellectualized in a peculiar sort of intricate movement.

Toward the end of her essay, Le Doeuff offers a straightforward analysis of the results of what were (at the time) the recent *aggregations,* and the comparative standing of males and females. But she also remarks, not surprisingly, that what is necessary in philosophy is a transformation of the "relationship of the subject to the philosophical enterprise."[31]

Arlette Farge is still another thinker whose work, at least as excerpted in American texts, is more accessible than Cixous's or Kristeva's but who still has a point to make with regard to the intersection between our interpretation of deeply structured feminist theory and the French version of such theory. In a rather short piece on women's history and the notion of constructing a feminine voice for the writing of history, Farge starts out with a compilation of the number of citations of women's history and its projects in the leading French journals such as *Annales.*[32] But then Farge reminds us of a difficulty related to the construction of a gynocentric voice in historical theorizing, which is relevant to the difficulty already articulated here in the work of Cixous. It is not, of course, merely that one requires a gynocentric voice in order to do women's history justice, nor is it the case that mountains of citations of the failure to incorporate women into accounts of events can actually make up for their absence. The difficulty, precisely put, is in trying to construct a gynocentric voice for women's theory without having that voice assume the dominating, magisterial tone that we associate with patriarchal theory and that, in any case, is offensive and biased with regard to certain sorts of events, interpretations, and views.

In the case of Cixous and the sophisticated theoretical dilemma to which she alluded, we articulated the problematic area for her theory as being whether or not women could appropriate voice without that voice acquiring its own kind of phallocentricity. In the language of Cixous and the Cixous-influenced deconstructionists, if woman's filling in the marginal space she has been assigned with her own voice results in a phallocentricity, it is as if woman has picked up the phallus herself.[33] Farge is not concerned to phrase the problematic in deconstructionist language, however; phrased differently, the difficulty is "Under the guise of exposing the misogyny of certain texts, we can perceive a strange alliance (not to say complicity) with them." She expands on this theme as follows:

> The vocabulary becomes gourmand and jubilant; and the reader is left wondering whether the author is condemning or condoning the effects of the texts as he surreptitiously falls into line with the very misogyny which he had denounced at the outset. . . .[34]

This difficulty is not only related to Cixous's theoretical question, but is, of course, the French version (at least to some extent) of the problem broached here in chapters four and five. We can construct a theoretical model for the gynocentric voice that utilizes precise and closely articulated theory, theory that is already in its origins androcentric. But to do this is, naturally, to create as a gynocentric voice a theoretical view that is less gynocentric than it could have been, particularly because it borrows from androcentric theory. There is no obvious path out of this dilemma, and the French versions of the dilemma merely remind us of this grave problem for feminist theory.

Farge notes that so far, in the French journals, the tendency by mainstream historians has been to ignore the problem and to use the standard modes of historical theorizing to write of women's history. Thus, she explains, "The focus of the works concerned with the eighteenth and nineteenth centuries reveals the existence of a predilection for normative texts and discourses, which is natural enough, given the difficulty of locating sources. . . . There is no shortage of normative discourses, and women certainly occupy a central place in them." But she also concludes her view of feminist attempts at defining the history of women in a French context with a pertinent remark on what it is that males and females can hope to gain from the new women's history.

As she phrases it,

> It is important to write at last a history of the tensions existing between
> male and female roles, and to articulate their conflicts and their comple-
> mentary functions in a way capable of spanning the whole of our historical
> narrative. The aim would then be not to construct a separate enclosure of
> knowledge, but on the contrary to revitalize the agenda of all historians
> by introducing the notion of sexual difference. . . .[35]

It has been a staple of feminist theory, even including some versions
of post-Freudian theory, that what women do—whether reproduc-
tively, within the work force, or otherwise—is something genuinely
valued, respected, and feared by men, and that part of their aim is to
keep such knowledge from consciousness. Whereas both Michele Le
Doeuff and Arlette Farge had specific points to make about the role of
women in philosophy and history, respectively, Annie Leclerc, another voice widely cited among the French theorists, addresses the
question of what it is that women do and what men make of this in
*Parole de femme*.[36] Although Toril Moi is quick to note that *Parole de
femme* means both "words spoken by a woman" and "[I give] my
word as a woman," and then that "English expressions such as
'womanspeech' and similar phrases would seem quite out of place in
this context," there does seem to be a case for thinking of the title as
meaning something like "womanspeech," especially when one remembers that forms of signification can include verbal utterances accom-
panied by gestures, or gestures alone.[37]

In any case, Leclerc's point in many of the passages of *Parole de
femme* is that the work of woman, reproductive or otherwise, is a work
of joy, and that males have conspired to degrade and demean work
that is the work of life. Thus the emphasis that Cixous, for example,
had placed on woman's signification as a thing of laughter and of the
body is redoubled by Leclerc, who sees the work of women as
inherently life-affirming, mirthful, and pleasurable. By contrast, she
sees the androcentric view and its accompanying tasks as desolating,
apocalyptic, and "prefigur[ing] . . . death."[38] Although Leclerc does
not go into any theoretical overview of what it would mean to make
such claims in the published and translated excerpts supplied by Moi,
there is again a hint that the origin of this desolation is the distancing
from females that is a necessary part of male being. Leclerc is not
nearly so straightforward about this as is, for example, Kristeva, but
she follows the other theorists whose work we have examined in having

object-relations theory as an implicit thematic element of her view.[39] With regard to the relationship betwen women's labor employment in the home (the sort of labor that Hartsock, for example, sees as the basis for her standpoint epistemology) and women's reproductive power, Leclerc writes:

> How can work that produces immediate results, results which are carried forward in the very task itself, be thankless? The house takes on a festive air, the meal smells good, the child burbles contentedly while showing off its silky little bottom, and an hour's dreamy efforts grant the trousers another year's wear. . . .
>
> But alas, you have seen fit to make of all that a chore, a trial, a duty, a painful affair. . . . It was a rare delight, a form of work akin to ecstasy, of supreme value, as valuable as life itself, totally in tune with life. . . .
>
> But you invented the terrible value of power, in order to attack life, women, their fertile wombs, their fruitful hands. . . .[40]

This quotation, especially in its sparkling translation, is powerfully evocative of what women's work can be when seen from a certain point of view, that is, a gynocentric point of view. When the investment of time and energy is thought of in terms of relationships connected and refastened rather than as a mere category of objects dealt with and discarded, the actual work accomplished takes on a specific meaning that is tied to the various strains of epistemology we have examined here. Even work performed by women alone can take on a connectedness to others in their absence; it is not necessary for one to interact with a physically present other in order to feel this connectedness, according to most of the gynocentric theorists. One might add the obvious here: From the androcentric point of view, one could indeed have others present and still fail to connect (one might almost feel required not to connect), so the differences between the two viewpoints, two worldviews, two sorts of ontology construction, and two epistemologies become quite explicit.

Toward the end of the Moi excerpt, Leclerc writes that "Man has always decided what can be talked about, and what cannot."[41] Like the other French theorists (and this is a point emphasized by Cixous, Irigaray, Kristeva, Le Doeuff, and Farge, all to varying degrees), Leclerc asserts that there is a need for woman's voice and woman's thought. She finds it a "terrifying undertaking," but cannot imagine the continuance of a world without it.[42]

# FEMINIST EPISTEMICS AND FRENCH THEORY:
## THE TIE-IN

In this chapter I have focused on French theory with an eye to articulating how it intersects with Anglo-American theory, and with trying to make clear the nature of the intersection. Part of the difficulty has been, as I elaborated at an earlier point, that many of the French thinkers do not regard themselves as "feminist." (As we have seen, Jardine even refers to them as being "beyond" feminism as a doctrine.) But if the thinkers are not feminist, their theorizing on the notions of female and the feminine is certainly of the utmost use for contemporary feminist theory, and insofar as it derives most of its impetus from a different set of concerns, affords us a brief scherzo that meshes well with the rest of our theorizing.

The tendency within printed work published in English-speaking countries has been to focus on Cixous, Irigaray, and Kristeva almost to the exclusion of other thinkers, but the truth of the matter is that until approximately 1985 very little of their work had been translated into English, and they were known more by reputation than by actual familiarity. As we have seen, several other thinkers have written on a number of topics that are both less arcane from the point of view of theory and more accessible, since they deal with everyday practices of exclusion of women.

If the chief difficulty is to find and make explicit the area of intersection between the French writers and American feminist theorists and their British cousins, the obvious point of departure is object-relations theory. The Anglo-American theorists tend to approach it empirically, as one would expect; data (taken largely from psychoanalytic therapy and interviews) tend to support the validity of the theory, and everything we know about male functioning is consonant with it, even if it is in a sense question-begging to pose elements of the theory as explanatory. The French theorists approach the theory less literally and less empirically, but the greatest area of intersection between these two orientations seems to come with hypotheses about language use and language acquisition. The French thinkers posit discourse as a male construction that stems from the need to connect with the mother; the first sounds (I follow Irigaray here) are made to gain the mother's attention, or to signal that it is not needed. Although the empirical version of this is not quite as dramatic, Chodorow, for example, posits the mother as first object, and the development of a sense of self, including acquisition of language, is clearly related to being able to move, manipulate, and master the external world—the mother.[43] Thus the acquisition of language is central to the work of both groups of theorists.

Following a linguistic theme, the other issue that seems to cut across both Continental and Anglo-American theorizing is the development of a woman's voice. Again, the more empirically oriented English-language theory hypothesizes the development of a gynocentric view, employing different sorts of theoretical underpinnings for different sorts of disciplines. The metaphorical and literary French views, working within the tradition of literary criticism and the notion of a text, write of the voice of Western culture as a whole (by which they seem to mean everything in Western culture—science and the humanities both—taken as an amalgam) and of its appropriation by women. Here is one of the larger areas of divergence, for the appropriation of the voice by women causes theoretical difficulties for the French that are entirely unrelated to practice and not empirically confirmable, whereas the difficulties caused for the English-language theorists were clearly set out here in earlier chapters where the elements of precision contrasted with the elements of "relatedness," "connectedness," and so forth.

We return now, at the close of our look at the French thinkers, to the model introduced in chapters four and five. The model has been subjected both to the sorts of criticism that would be aimed at it from analytic philosophers familiar with the tradition from which it derives, and from feminist critics who, at least in some cases, would attempt to undermine the case for constructing a gynocentric model from analytic origins. But the model emphasizes communication in the form of both verbal and nonverbal nuance, and the ramifications of this emphasis on linguistic pragmatics lead us in some interesting directions. The work of the sociolinguists reminds us of the difficulties of intercultural communication, second-language acquisition, and communication between a native speaker and someone whose native language is not English.[44] As feminists, we desire a gynocentric model of epistemic justification that is applicable cross-culturally and that, perhaps more importantly, enlightens our view of the multifarious ways in which women live, work, and communicate. In addition, we need a fleshing out of the role of nonverbal communication, since it is crucially important from a gynocentric point of view. The next chapter addresses these areas of concern.

## NOTES

1. The two anthologies most frequently cited are Elaine Marks and Isabelle de Courtivron, eds., *New French Feminisms* (Amherst: University of Massachusetts Press, 1980), and Toril Moi, ed., *French Feminist Thought:* A Reader (Oxford, U.K.: Basil Blackwell, Ltd., 1987).

2. Other Continental feminist thought seems to have been imported much less widely. There is the intriguing (and, for aesthetics, very important) German reader, Gisela Ecker, ed., *Feminist Aesthetics,* (Boston, Mass.: Beacon Press, 1986).

3. Moi, for one, is very specific about this. She cites the "spectacular development of the new theories of sexual difference . . . which gave rise to the myth of the radical difference of French feminism itself." Moi, *French Feminist Thought,* 4.

4. Ibid., 5.

5. Kenneth Baynes, James Bohman, and Thomas McCarthy, eds., *After Philosophy,* (Cambridge, Mass.: The MIT Press, 1987). The chapter on Derrida is pp. 119–58.

6. Baynes, Bohman, and McCarthy, eds., *After Philosophy,* 120.

7. This piece is also available in Abel and Abel, eds., *The Signs Reader.* Keith Cohen and Paula Cohen translated Hélène Cixous's work.

8. Ibid., 284.

9. Ibid., 285.

10. The reference for the former is Marks and de Courtivron, eds., *New French Feminisms* and for the latter it is Moi, ed., *French Feminist Thought.*

11. Alice Jardine, *Gynesis* (Ithaca: Cornell University Press, 1985), 20.

12. Krupnick, *Displacement; Derrida and After.*

13. Ibid., 2.

14. Ibid., 3.

15. Cixous, "The Laugh of the Medusa," in Abel and Abel, *Signs Reader,* 287.

16. Jardine, *Gynesis,* 27.

17. See Luce Irigaray, *The Speculum of the Other Woman,* trans. Gillian C. Gill (Ithaca: Cornell University Press, 1985).

18. Irigaray, "Le Sujet de la Science: Est-il Sexué?"

19. Ibid., 85, 87.

20. Cf. my quotation from Keller on stylized aggression in chap. 3, p. 76.

21. Luce Irigaray, "Sexual Difference," in *French Feminist Thought,* ed. Toril Moi (Oxford, U.K.: Basil Blackwell, Ltd., 1987). Translated from portions of *Ethique de la Différence Sexuelle* (Paris: Editions Minuit, 1984), 13–15, Sean Hand, trans.

22. Jardine, *Gynesis,* 262.

23. Jardine, *Gynesis,* 114. (Quoting from Julia Kristeva, *La révolution du langage poétique* [Paris: Editions du Seuil, 1974], 326.)

24. Julia Kristeva, in interview with Francoise van Rossum-Guyon, "Talking About *Polylogue*." *French Feminist Thought,* ed. Toril Moi (Oxford, U.K.: Basil Blackwell, Ltd., 1987), 110–117.

25. To be fair, in this particular quotation what Kristeva actually says is "As a result, a strange body comes into being, one that is neither man nor woman, young nor old." One may assume, however, that the quoted passage certainly describes a move away from the exclusively male signifier.

26. Kristeva, interview with Kossum-Guyon, in Moi, ed., *French Feminist Thought,* 115–16.

27. At the close of "The Laugh of the Medusa," Cixous notes (of women) that "laughs exude from all our mouths."

28. This sort of topic has been treated by many women philosophers in a variety of locales. Jean Grimshaw's *Philosophy and Feminist Thinking* (Minneapolis: University of Minnesota Press, 1986) is a recent work that deals with this problem extensively. See especially chap. 2, "The 'Maleness' of Philosophy."

29. Michele Le Doeuff, "Women and Philosophy," in *French Feminist Thought,* ed. Toril Moi (Oxford, U.K.: Basil Blackwell, Ltd., 1987), 181–209. Perhaps this one sentence taken from Le Doeuff is the single best summation: "these women . . . all experienced great passions, and their relationship with philosophy existed only through their love for a man" (pp. 184–85).

30. Ibid., 188.

31. Ibid., 207.

32. The material from this section is taken directly from Arlette Farge, "Women's History: An Overview" in Moi, ed., *French Feminist Thought,* 133–49.

33. With regard to another text that was viewed as exemplifying, to some extent, the same sort of problematic, Gayatri Spivak had written that the textual personage in question, Jean Genet's mother, "ha[d] stolen a march on the false price of the phallocentric idea. . . . She has taken the phallus out of the circuit of castration. . . . With her it is not a question of having or not having a phallus. She can change it, as if she had a collection of dildos or transvestite underwear." Spivak, in Krupnick, *Displacement,* 177.

34. Arlette Farge, "Women's History" in Moi, ed., *French Feminist Thought,* 146.

35. Ibid., 147.

36. Excerpted in Annie LeClerc, "Parole de Fame" in Moi, ed., *French Feminist Thought,* 73–79.

37. Ibid., 73.

38. Ibid., 78.

39. In the Moi excerpt, this is especially obvious on p. 77.

40. Ibid., 76. Translated by Roisin Mallaghan.

41. Ibid., 78.

42. Ibid., 79.

43. Chodorow, *Reproduction*.

44. Among these I count such theorists as Dell Hymes, Deborah Tannen, and John Gumperz. See Dell Hymes, ed., *Language in Culture and Society* (New York: Harper and Row, 1964); Deborah Tannen, *Conversational Style: Analyzing Talk Among Friends* (Norwood, N.J.: Albex, 1984); John J. Gumperz, *Discourse Strategies* (Cambridge, U.K.: Cambridge University Press, 1982).

# Chapter Seven

# The Gynocentric Model Expanded

Our digression into French theory has helped to emphasize a point that has become a bone of contention for feminist thought and a recurring problematic area: the multiplicity of women's voices. Up to now I have been concerned with the more technical aspects of the development of a gynocentric model of epistemic justification, with the aim of making clear some of the notions and conceptualizations inherent in a feminist epistemology. But the work of the standpoint theorists alone, developed and expanded upon in chapters three and four, suggests that part of what is meant by "feminist epistemology" or "feminist epistemics" is a model that is not only grounded in inherently female practice or pragma but that is also applicable to women cross- and intra-culturally.

The development of a model that has such applicability is no small task, but I want to suggest that CCP, as formulated here, already contains elements that lend themselves to just such application. If part of the difficulty for contemporary feminist theory has been the development of a "view from everywhere," it is also the case that feminist theory is at least aware of the pluralism of our society, and indeed the pluralistic nature of human society on the planet as a whole.[1] Feminist critics have also frequently conflated the white power structure within the United States and the Western countries with a phallocratic or androcentric power structure; in other words, the standard phrasing has been "white male . . . ," rather than merely "white" or merely "male." Part and parcel of the argument has been that it is no accident

183

that a social structure as deeply patriarchal as that of the Western nations is also deeply racist; indeed, following along the lines of thought developed here, the androcentric view is simultaneously divorced, distanced, and cut off from others, which according to many theorists accounts for the fact that androcentric power yields a race-conscious social structure.[2]

If I claim, then, that a feminist epistemology, or model of epistemic justification, is applicable to the various voices in which women have been and are being heard, I must be able to show what specifically in the model lends itself to such an interpretation, and I must also be able to say something about what Harding terms the "fragmented" nature of women's voices.[3] In this chapter I plan to tackle both of those tasks, and to provide some small description of the hypothesized (and very real) multiplicity. Because CCP is reliant on intentionality and communication—aspects of the model that were addressed from the standpoint of standard analytic theory in chapter five—I hope to show without much difficulty that the model is applicable to a number of ethnicities, cultural backgrounds, and orientations.

But I have also emphasized in this text the importance of nonverbal means of communication and the sensitivity of the female to such communication in general. Thus my model has allowed for acquisition of knowledge, or justification of knowledge claims, to be accomplished on the basis of informational input that is both verbal and nonverbal, straightforward and nuanced, articulable and only somewhat expressed. We need to investigate further what this reliance on forms of communication other than the verbal (or its offshoot, the written) may amount to, and one area that must come under scrutiny in this chapter is the importance of sexuality both as a mode of expression of the personality and as a vehicle for interpersonal communication. That venture can be postponed, however, until the two tasks I mentioned earlier are developed and set out.

At an earlier point in this text I was at pains to emphasize the normative nature of the analytic epistemology that has constituted the bulk of the work in epistemology done in this century. In chapter one I provided a brief overview of the tradition and pointed out that, historically speaking, the emergence of views that might be considered more naturalized is a very recent phenomenon, not dating back more than a couple of decades at most. While emphasizing the history of Anglo-American epistemology and the set of problems that led up to the current pronounced emphasis on naturalized views, I also mentioned (in some detail, in chapter three) some of the feminist work itself that sheds light on the historical origin of the traditional problems of epistemology. Specifically, the work of Susan Bordo was cited, and her account of Descartes's epistemological panic was alluded to.[4]

A panic like Descartes's—if indeed we may think in terms of other such panics—is the result, I speculated, of the intersection of two or three separate areas of anxiety. I cited Bordo's account of the cultural dislocation of the seventeenth century and Descartes's personal battle with his Jesuit training and general upbringing. I then allowed myself to hazard the guess that the distancing from the mother that psycho-analytic thinkers theorize as characteristic of male development merged, in Descartes's case, with these other problematic areas to create a personality especially prone to the kind of psychic removal required to author a work such as the *Meditations*. In other words, Bordo's phrase is most apt. Descartes was, no doubt, the victim of some sort of panic, and the epistemological nature of it stems partly, one supposes, from Descartes's situation vis-à-vis his milieu and background, from his sense of his own intellectual superiority, and from the fact that he was male.

## THE GYNOCENTRIC MODEL AND CULTURAL CONTEXT

Part of what I have hypothesized here as the gynocentric view is, one might say, antithetically related to the sort of personality portrait that emerges from an examination of the life and work of Descartes. The gynocentric outlook is not distanced, not divorced from ground-ing, and not hampered by a severe and irretrievable rupture from the mother. So the emphasis on, as the standpoint theorists had it, "im-mersion," "grounding," and "reciprocity," shows up in the construc-tion of our model, derived as it is from naturalized epistemology, current trends in philosophy of mind, and the work of standpoint epistemology itself.[5] Our model is reliant upon the notion of intention-ality, and communication is at the heart of the epistemic justificatory process, according to the gynocentric stance that undergirds our analytically structured model.

Thus it is an upshot of our model that knowledge acquisition—epistemic justification—is a context- and culture-related process. And because it is such a process, it is applicable to all contexts and cultures. This gives the model a fluidity not found in nonnaturalized models, and also makes it profoundly relevant to that particular critical area of contemporary feminist theory that deals with the pluralistic nature of women's voices.

As part of the immediate task of trying to come to grips with the nature of women's voices simply within the United States alone, I plan to cite some material from feminists working in several of the traditions that are usually considered to deviate strongly from the white, middle-class, and Anglo-rooted norm. At the risk of omitting some voices (and this account cannot, of course, be encyclopaedic), I will cite material that is both feminist and exemplary of the cultural background with which it is associated. Although many Third World and minority group women within the United States have little interest in what they take to be white-dominated feminist concerns, a number of black, Asian, and Hispanic scholars have tried to articulate gynocentric or female-centered views, and at least one Native American, Paula Gunn Allen, has written in a similar vein.[6] After describing some of the work of these women, I plan to show how CCP allows for a view of thinking, epistemic justification, and knowledge acquisition that is culturally sensitive and sufficiently non-normative as to be adaptable to a variety of backgrounds, viewpoints, and outlooks. In line with the work done in chapter five, I will retain the emphasis on folk-psychological constructs important for the sort of everyday epistemic work that we associate with, as Dennett had it, an instrumental account and an account that can be used for predictive purposes over a wide range of behavior.

## CONTEXT, CULTURE, AND GYNOCENTRISM: FOUR VIEWS

A catalytic beginning for our analysis can be provided by the work of Maxine Hong Kingston. I will draw here primarily from *The Woman Warrior,* although any one of a number of works by Kingston is useful in this regard. *The Woman Warrior* constitutes a paradigm of work that is both feminist in its orientation and particularly lucid in its presentation of another cultural viewpoint. The work has the added virtue of being one that implicitly contains several philosophical themes, since part of the narrator's difficulties seem to lie along the lines of ontology construction.[7]

In my discussion of the work I will assume some familiarity on the reader's part and I will not attempt to recount the plot. Rather, I want to draw out here several lines of thought that present themselves as difficulties in the articulation of feminist theory, and I want to do so in a way that indicates the epistemic relevance of the material and the importance for a gynocentrically structured model of epistemic justification to have flexibility with regard to cultural viewpoints.

In *The Woman Warrior* many of the narrator's difficulties are only partially related to the crucial fact of being an American child of Chinese ancestry in a small town in California in the 1950s and 1960s. The shame that the narrator sometimes feels about her background derives to some extent from the image of herself and her ethnicity that she sees in the eyes of the surrounding white (and even non-white, to the extent that it is also non-Asian) culture. A large part of the discomfort and confusion felt by the narrator, however, derives from a sense of not knowing how to construct a consistent and coherent personal ontology, and not being able to employ consistent epistemic standards about what counts as true and what as false. The narrator not only receives one impression of reality from her Han relatives, but she finds splits even within the Chinese culture itself as she is forced to grapple with what the Western world perceives as Chinese mythology along with the pickled pig's feet and rice that are part of the mundane Asian culture.

The narrator perceives her dilemma, then, as partially a difficulty of not knowing what is real. Which should she value more highly—the American world with its hierarchical rules and regulations, or the somewhat (to Americanized eyes) jumbled Chinese world, with its ghosts and warriors, its dragons and harmonies? And within the Chinese world itself, which is more real—the dragon and the woman warrior, or her mother's medical college diploma? And how does one distinguish?

Thus Kingston lets the non-Asian reader know that in other cultural spheres the cut-and-dried quality of daily life disappears, or is devalued. It is part of the appeal of her writing that the novel mirrors and mimics the in-and-out style of the narrator's childhood experiences:

> When we Chinese girls listened to the adults talk-story, we learned that we failed if we grew up to be but wives or slaves. We could be heroines, swordswomen. . . . Perhaps women were once so dangerous that they had to have their feet bound. . . . Night after night my mother would talk story until we fell asleep. I couldn't tell where the stories left off and the dreams began, her voice the voice of the heroines in my sleep. . . . She said I would grow up a wife and slave, but she taught me the song of the Warrior Woman, Fa Mu Lan. I would have to grow up a warrior woman.
> The call would come from a bird that flew over our roof.[8]

As the woman warrior, the narrator not only is able to construct an ontology that makes some sense to her, but perhaps more importantly is able to utilize aspects of the culture, which simultaneously pleases and repels her, to ward off the misogyny implicit in the culture itself. A good deal of Kingston's artistry is employed in depicting the deadly woman-hatred of the traditional village-bound Han culture; several instances in the narrative illustrate this, including a well-known passage in which the narrator says " 'I'm not a bad girl,' I would scream. 'I'm not a bad girl.' I might as well have said, 'I'm not a girl.' ' "9

So Kingston shows how a culture completely foreign to the dominant Anglo-centered American culture infuses the past and present of a female of Asian descent. Interestingly enough, the author is also able to capture some of the knots and inconsistencies inherent in any brief attempt to present another culture or worldview. Although the misogyny to which the author was exposed may seem, at first glance, to be more virulent than any Western variety, this is a too-simpleminded analysis. For an awareness of both male and female principles is part of the ancient and traditional Chinese worldview—the same principles that contemporary American popularizations refer to as Yin and Yang—and this awareness, too, suffuses the author's narrative.

Kingston has given voice to American women of Chinese descent, and many others have given and will continue to add voices.10 But one of the primary areas of importance addressed by the novel is, as I claimed earlier, the notion of reality-construction. Fa Mu Lan is important for the young narrator precisely because she figures prominently in the stories told by the narrator's mother and other adults. Webs of conversation about Fa Mu Lan constitute, however briefly, the justification for belief in her existence (at the naive level), and at a later point in the author's life, conversation about and reference to Chinese "mythology" and Chinese "folk culture" provide epistemic justification for a new set of beliefs about Fa Mu Lan and similar figures that interprets them somewhat differently. The narrator's childhood world of cooked raccoons and garden snails, preserved "bear claws" and weeds from behind the house, is justified in the cultural context of Chinese life and of recognized intentionality on the level of verbal and nonverbal interaction.11

Black voices may have been heard more frequently than Asian voices in the contemporary feminist writings, but given the importance of black culture in American life and the lengthy history of blacks on the American continent, they have not been heard nearly enough. Because the popularized body of work by black women authors is perhaps somewhat greater than it is for many other non-white groups, we have more than one area of theorizing or literature to which we can allude. The rise in prominence of black women novelists in the past twenty years is too patent and too large a part of the popular culture to need recapitulation, so although I may cite some such work, I will for the moment cite black feminist work from a different source.

The black experience is not only great in longevity but also rich in documentation. In *When and Where I Enter,* the historian Paula Giddings provides a superbly detailed look at the role of black women in both black history and the history of the culture at large since the Civil War era. Giddings is especially sensitive to the textured intersection of black and feminist issues. She notes repeatedly that the situation of women in general provided an unusually fruitful base for movement for black women, since black females were not found to be as threatening as black males by the society at large and hence were accorded, perhaps, some greater social freedoms.[12] This fact was acknowledged, at least to some extent, by whites and blacks alike, and among the most intriguing documents cited by Giddings are those that are exemplary of the general black awareness of the special position of black women:

In 1892, Anna Julia Cooper commented that uneducated Black women in the South "have actually left their husbands and homes and repudiated [their husbands'] support [for] . . . race disloyalty in 'voting away' the privileges of herself and little ones.' . . ." Underlying these attitudes was the conviction that unlike the masses of Black men, women would never betray the race if they had the power of the vote. Their exalted sense of themselves as a group extended to their feelings about the suffrage issue. . . . Black women weren't the only ones to hold this attitude. W.E.B. DuBois applauded the greater tenacity of Black women as a group: "You can bribe some pauperized Negro leaders with a few dollars at elections time," he said, "but you cannot bribe a Negro woman."[13]

Black women were prominent in the teaching profession in the earlier part of this century, and in many parts of the country black women entered the professions in numbers very much out of proportion to their pro rata share based on population alone. The black woman was viewed as a vehicle through which she could "uplift the masses," and Giddings notes that the "great desire for education, combined with the status of teaching, provided an escape from the limitations that the society imposed on women.''[14]

From the standpoint of feminist theory, then, the black woman has a doubly privileged epistemic position, and not simply in the perhaps somewhat trivial sense that she has suffered from both sexual and racial discrimination. More importantly, the upshot of this massive burden of devaluation and discounting was a sort of social blindness that allowed the black female a freedom to explore that may have been denied the black male. In any case, black women were frequent contributors to the burgeoning literature of the post-Reconstruction era, and writers such as Ida B. Wells and Mary Church Terrell left a lasting mark on the journalism of their day at a time when few women could write and publish.[15]

Again, the importance of connections, both verbalized and nonverbalized emerges for women and the history of black women is illustrative of this. The obvious connections of the written work left by these early writers and teachers are only one part of the story: The importance of the oral tradition is gargantuan here, and it is, of course, the oral tradition that was paramount in keeping much of black history alive. Since Giddings uses largely written sources, her work can emphasize the oral tradition only in part, but the work of contemporary novelists (as well, of course, as the Harlem Renaissance novelists such as Zora Neale Hurston) focuses in detail on this crucially imporant aspect of black life.[16] The impact of Alice Walker's *The Color Purple* stems not only from its epistolary form: The conversations between Celie and Shug help to create a reality—including speculations about the nature and origin of things of beauty in the world—that transcends and is ontologically firmer than the ugly everyday reality they are surrounded by. In *The Temple of My Familiar,* the male protagonist Arveyda lives in a present informed by the memory of his deceased mother. Like Celie and Shug, his mother had the ability to transform the mundane and create a vision of something larger:

> His mother, whose name was Katherine Degos, was one of the most intrusive people he knew. She did not recognize limits, whether of body or of mind. . . . She was a woman of such high energy she always seemed to him to be whirling, and the first time Arveyda heard the expression ''whirling dervish'' he thought of it as a description of his mother.[17]

Thus the privileged position of black women, from the standpoint of feminist epistemics, is a position that evolves not only from thoroughgoing oppression but from richly articulated oral networks. Any model of gynocentric epistemic justification that captures the importance of the oral tradition and relies largely on a notion of orality or oral-mimicking thought for its concept of that which justifies, is a model deeply appropriate to the history of black women, as well as to the history of women at large.

The oral tradition is also of the utmost importance for the Native American or American Indian culture. If it is the case that the voices of American Indians—whether male or female—have not been heard by the white culture at large in anything like the numbers that should be relevant, it is true that that tradition is now being heard with more and more frequency, and with greater clarity. Although there are a number of black women authors and theorists whose views have become prominent—and certainly more than one Asian female thinker to whom one can turn, as the paragraphs above suggest—among female American Indian thinkers only Paula Gunn Allen appears to be known on a general basis, and it is her work that is most frequently cited in this context.[18]

Allen draws often in her work on what she takes to be the general matriarchal culture of the pre-Columbian Native Americans and the mythological and oral nature of their worldview. Indeed, the views cited by Allen in *The Sacred Hoop* and other works seem almost paradigmatic of many of the themes we have been examining here: What Allen terms the Indian outlook is matrilineal and gynocentric, contextually aware and consistent and justified within its purview.[19] Because of the importance of the oral tradition in Indian cultures, Allen presents us with a view that embodies a feminist epistemics and a mode of justification about the world that is much in accord with the principles underlying CCP, with its context-centered, grounded, and nondistanced standards for the construction of an epistemology.

Here is Allen on the importance of the matrilineal for American Indian culture:

> Traditional tribal lifestyles are more often gynocratic than not, and they are never patriarchal. . . . Some distinguishing features of a woman-centered social system include free and easy sexuality and wide latitude in personal style. . . . Also likely to be prominent in such systems are nurturing, pacifist and passive males (as defined by western minds) and self-defining, assertive, decisive women.
>
> Structural and thematic elements from the oral tradition, usually from the writer's own tribe, always show up in contemporary works by

American Indians, and elements from contemporary, non-Indian works sometimes show up in contemporaneous tribal social literature.[20]

Allen is especially eloquent about two major points with regard to American Indian culture: the extent to which the greater white colonizing culture feared the gynocratic elements of the Indians, and so attempted to write them out of existence, and the extent to which that same culture today can and must (and indeed does, at least in small portions) draw on these matriarchal and feminist elements for the healing of the androcentric culture and its rigidly industrialized detritus.

Allen finds the motivation for some of the most vicious crimes against the Native Americans to have been a pervasive fear of the nature of the feminine in Indian culture, and for this she provides extensive documentation.[21] But she also finds an Indian influence throughout contemporary American culture, and not only in the most obvious sort of places (for example, the current emphasis on ecology and the importance of natural resources). Rather, Allen notes that "Americans find themselves more and more likely to adopt a 'live and let live' attitude in matters of personal sexual and social styles. Two-thirds of their diet and a large share of their medications and medical treatments mirror or are directly derived from Native American sources."[22] Furthermore, Allen even goes so far as to acknowledge that the co-opting of the figure of Sacagawea—even if reprehensible in many respects—can have and has had a beneficial effect on the national American consciousness. Allen reminds us that Sacagawea was mentioned by Dr. Anna Howard Shaw at a women's suffrage conference in 1905, and she quotes Shaw as saying "May we the daughters of an alien race . . . learn the lessons of calm endurance . . . May 'the eternal womanly' ever lead us on!"[23]

Although there is still comparatively little written about the Native American culture that backs up Allen's overtly feminist work in tone and tenor, it is interesting to note that most of the other available literature—whether blatantly anthropological, critical in a literary vein, or sociological—confirms the gynocentric and context-centered mythological nature of the Indian worldview. Gretchen Bataille, in an article on the autobiographical work of Indian women, quotes Ruth Underhill on the Papago:

Indian narrative style involves a repetition and a dwelling on unimportant details which confuse the white reader and make it hard for him to follow the story. Motives are never explained and the writer has found even Indians at a loss to interpret them in older myths. Emotional states are summed up in such colorless phrases as 'I liked it,' 'I did not like it.' For one not deeply immersed in the cultures the real significance escapes.[24]

Few quotations could better sum up the difficulties that an androcentric and normative view of the universe has with the Indian outlook than this particular accidentally salient paragraph from Underhill. The collision of the normative and idealizing concern for motive with the rich and particularized world of Indian existence leaves the statistically average non-Indian investigator puzzled and slightly derisive.

If American Indian culture is an isomorphic exemplar of what I have termed the gynocentric view, there are still other cultures with which the dominant Anglo culture comes into constant contact that require mention. In the next section I turn to still another view, and then I hope to show why the naturalized lines of justification that provide the base for CCP are particularly relevant to the bringing together of what Harding has termed the "fragmented" voices of women.

I want now to turn to the voice of Latina or Hispana women. Their voices, too, have seldom been heard, although Sor Juana Inés de la Cruz was one of the first prolific writers on either of the American continents (and has been recognized as such for a lengthy period of time). I want to examine briefly some of the destructive stereotypes with which Latina (and particularly Chicana) women have had to contend, through the eyes of a Chicana scholar, and then refer to some work by Latina philosopher Maria Lugones.

As Maria Nieto Senour notes, "literature relating directly to the Chicana . . . is extremely limited."[25] Senour sees this as being the result of the double denigration that we have noted here before: the general invisibility of women combined with the invisibility of persons of color, specifically. But Senour also contends data that do exist on Chicanas (and, perforce, to some extent on other Latinas as well—although the failure to distinguish between different sorts of Latin cultures is an example of the stereotyping here under examination) indicate that the Chicana or woman of Mexican ancestry lives under the burden of extreme and intricate stereotypes. Senour states that—according to the literature—"The Mexican family is purportedly founded on the supremacy of the father and the corresponding total self-sacrifice of the mother," and there is a belief that "the wife must devote her-self to everyone else's needs by the complete denial of her own."[26]

Senour is largely paraphrasing others here, but I take it that part of her point is that sociological investigators, mental health professionals, and others engaged in work in the social sciences are blinded by these widely held typologies before they begin their investigations. Senour goes on to present more data and to appeal for more research on Chicana women, preferably performed by Chicanas. But just as Maxine Hong Kingston's narrator was faced with the Anglo mirroring of her culture in its views of the Chinese, the Latina or Chicana is faced with these same obstacles; Senour's reporting simply serves to underline how common and deeply rooted these views of Latina and Chicana women are.

Within the United States itself, comparatively few Latinas have achieved prominence in literature, so Latina voices have tended to be heard in other modes of expression. Partially, no doubt, because of the very proximity of the United States to Mexico and other Latin American countries (a proximity for which there is no parallel in the case of persons of African or Asian descent, and which is irrelevant to persons of American Indian ancestry, where more than mere proximity is at stake), a variety of cultural ties has been maintained that allows for the expression of misogyny and certain forms of female submission within the culture. Fortunately, however, some Latina academics have been able to make their voices heard, and their work is enlightening with regard to modes of personal expression available to Latinas.

Maria Lugones's "Playfulness, 'World'-Travelling and Loving Perception" is a work by a Latina philosopher that is relevant to the project here in more than one way: Maria Lugones not only writes about the power of rigidly maintained typing against women of color, but she also writes about modes of expression that might allow us to enter another cultural/contextual "world" and break out, to some extent, of our own.[27] She notes that "women of color in the U.S. practice 'world'-travelling, mostly out of necessity, and that "A 'world' need not be a construction of a whole society. It may be a construction of a tiny portion of a particular society. It may be inhabited by just a few people. Some 'worlds' are bigger than others."[28]

So a world can be a cultural context, a nation or an ethnic group, or simply a way of looking at things. Like Paula Gunn Allen, Lugones here spells out a view of reality construction that is particularly sensitive to context. But it is part of Lugones's point that many in the dominant Anglo culture lack this sensitivity to context, so that the ability to "travel" (to immerse oneself in another's viewpoint) is either nonexistent or nonfunctional. With regard to Latinos and Latinas specifically, and cultural variety, Lugones notes that

> What it is to be "hispanic" in the varied so-called hispanic communities in the U.S. is also still up in the air. . . . Thus one cannot really answer questions of the sort "What is a Hispanic?", "Who counts as a Hispanic?", "Are Latinos, Chicanos, Hispanos, black dominicans, white cubans, korean-colombians, italian-argentinians hispanic?"[29]

Lugones mentions this partly to make a point about world-construction, but her point reminds us of what I mentioned a few paragraphs earlier—the wide variety of backgrounds that, within the United States, count as Latino. Lugones lauds the notion of playfulness— receptivity, spontaneity, openness to surprise, and openness to self-construction—as a palliative to the cultural arrogance and insensitivity that the white Anglo mainstream frequently exhibits.[30] But in doing so she makes two important points for feminist ontology and epistemology: that women can construct ontologies (that is, the "worlds" that are created, entered, and re-created) through their communicative, open, and spontaneous interaction, and that the gynocentric mode of knowing is exemplified by this nuanced style of interaction that understands the other at least partially because the intentionality of the other is heard, understood, and integrated at a deep level. In fact, insofar as Lugones's theorizing relies on the integration of the other's view—achieved partially through the world-traveling—I have not dealt with any epistemic of comparable complexity here. One notes, however, that Lugones terms this "loving perception," and it is perhaps in the most intimate sort of relationship that this world-traveling reaches its highest pitch and achieves its greatest degree of integration. In that sense, then, I am inclined to think that some of what Lugones has written is more applicable to a discussion of the erotic and sexuality, since the erotic is informed by, and to some extent informs, its own variety of communication. I hope to expand upon this notion at a later point. In any case, Lugones's essay simultaneously reminds us of the stereotypes faced by Latinas and valorizes the notion of a certain form of communication that is gynocentric, nuanced, and highly interactive.[31]

## THE MODEL AND RELATIVISM

In the preceding paragraphs I have focused on trying to articulate some points of view that all too frequently are ignored in American society, and I have also tried to indicate that I think the contextualized model of naturalistic epistemic justification presented earlier here is appropriate for the specification of some of the knowledge-acquisition processes pertinent to those views. But I need to be still more precise about what I have in mind: CCP can work as a model only if certain basic assumptions about the nature of justification, of knowledge acquisition, and of the relevance of analytic philosophical models are accepted. The latter point, I believe, has been addressed here in terms full enough to do it justice; hence, for the moment, I will say no more about the value of analytic philosophy or of models derived from it.

Another area of concern has only been hinted at in preceding chapters, however. A descriptive model of the process of epistemic justification might well utilize some of the components with which I have endowed CCP, given the full-blown presentation of it made in chapter four. But isn't it relativistic to assume that a model should be all things to all knowers? Aren't we once again faced, at least on some level, with the concerns central to what I have called the androcentric view? Isn't the picture of medicine and medical treatment that I obtain from visiting the Sloan-Kettering Center a truer and more accurate picture than that which I might obtain from one of the tribal views referred to in Allen's *Sacred Hoop*? And if that is the case, how does an inherently descriptive model like CCP make these sorts of distinctions?

Some of the foregoing is along the lines of the sorts of analyses usually given of problems in the sociology of knowledge, and unlike the normative theorists, I do not hold that sociology of knowledge is irrelevant to epistemic concerns—far from it. I plan to address some recent feminist work in sociology of knowledge in the coming chapter. More importantly, however, the sort of attack that an androcentric normative theorist would make on a model like CCP (or on any of the oral and folk modes of knowledge dissemination that are predominant in the work of Kingston and Allen, in particular) seems to assume that there is an epistemic dichotomy around which one cannot get. One either attempts to develop a normatively constrained, noncounterable epistemology within the framework of the Cartesian tradition and its descendants, or one settles for a hopelessly relativistic view that assigns the same values to differing knowledge claims, made in different communities, regardless of such empirically confirmable factors such as the statistical likelihood of their "truth." I have addressed this issue to some extent before, but it is of central importance and must be addressed again.

I believe that there is a middle ground. It is not only the case that one could normativize over a descriptively accurate justificatory set—anyone who feels called upon to try her or his hand at this task is welcome to it.[32] More importantly, one can be contextually sensitive (aware of and responsive to relativistic concerns) without being a relativist. One can delineate epistemic conditions that are descriptively accurate in most situations (in addition to being, à la theory construction, gynocentric) without claiming that no one will ever be in a position to choose between such conditions or the situations that give rise to them. The normative theorists frequently write as if they believe that there is an inherent contradiction in my claiming that Kiowa medicine is justified in a Kiowa context and that Western medicine is justified in a Western context. I may decide, under a certain set of conditions (which, again, will be context bound and therefore capturable under CCP) that I prefer Western medicine to the Kiowa variety, or vice versa. Nothing in the formulation of a model such as CCP means that I may never make a choice. Rather, the whole point of the model is that any choice I do make is determined largely, if not entirely, by context.

That this works both ways, so to speak, is not a point of debate if one bears in mind the long human history of contact between groups of radically differing backgrounds. When the Cherokee or Kiowa were first faced with Western medicine, disbelief and resistance were rampant. Change came, however, when it became clear that—at least for certain sorts of treatments—some parts of Western medicine had superior efficacy. The ubiquitousness of Western medicine for treatment across the globe of, say, dysentery or small pox, is simply an illustration of the fact that the pragmatic value of certain treatments was noted by members of the non-Western groups in question and that arguments, of whatever sort, were made for Western treatments within these groups. That Ethiopians and Bangladeshis allowed themselves to be vaccinated for small pox and cholera indicates that, within the Ethiopian or Bengali frame, such inoculations—however bizarre they may initially have seemed—were deemed to be justified.

Thus CCP by no means implies a thoroughgoing relativism. As Larry Laudan has written about a somewhat different controversy (realism vs. antirealism in science, although realism is clearly related to normative epistemology),

We have overwhelmingly good reasons to suspect that our theories about the world, even our best-tested ones, are not true *simpliciter*. Yet the realist still wants to cash in on the hunch that the "truthlikeness" of our theories is responsible for their success. . . . The core idea here is that an approximately true theory will have consequences most of which are true, or at least which are close to the truth.

As I have shown elsewhere in detail, this argument is fundamentally flawed.[33]

Laudan goes on to make the point that some of our best-confirmed theories will have portions that are "truthlike," and portions that exhibit no such relation to the world, and that these relationships themselves may change over time. What is required to beat one's way past the realism/antirealism dispute (or the normatively justified/descriptively justified dispute) is the recognition that these dichotomies are far from demarcating the entire range of positions, and that appearing to buy into one position—at least for awhile, and at least at one point—does not mean that one has bought into the position for all time and for everywhere. Perhaps the virtue of CCP is that it helps to model our intuitions that, as I find more and more contexts (numerically) wherein certain beliefs are justified, I will tend to retain those beliefs and discard any others that are obviously conflicting. The reverse also holds, of course—as I find fewer and fewer contexts where my beliefs are justified, I may very well abandon those beliefs.

Sometimes those from fundamentalist backgrounds find that as they make their way in the world they find fewer and fewer contexts where their beliefs are justified. They may well find themselves acquiescing to someone else's argument rather than having others acquiesce to their own. Thus are beliefs about the age of the earth, for example, discarded. CCP allows for these sorts of moves and indeed is an accurate model of the manner in which these sorts of moves are made.

I have claimed that CCP allows for the sort of justification of beliefs that is contextually bound and that frequently accrues to those who hold minority viewpoints or positions, whether derivative from differing ethnicities or arrived at in other fashions. Indeed, I just claimed that the numerically unpopular (at least in the United States) view that the earth is only a few thousand years old, derived from the Old Testament, is the sort of belief that one could hold up to CCP. Living within a community of believers, one would tend to find this belief justified, but greater and greater contact with nonbelievers would leave one exposed to more and more occasions when the outcome of the input–output process left one on the losing side of justification. What I want to do now, however, is to provide a brief look at a hypothetical position derived partly from the literature we have examined in this chapter that is important for CCP not only because the view is itself gynocentric but also because it is part of a strongly oral tradition—a tradition where justification, *a fortiori*, would proceed along the lines modeled here. I will use the work of Paula Gunn Allen to construct my hypothetical position, but any of the work examined here could be used as a point of departure.

Let us suppose that I hold any one of a number of beliefs common to Native American cultures but somewhat statistically unusual in the Anglo-American culture in which many or most Native Americans currently find themselves enmeshed. It should go without saying, but probably needs to be said, that these beliefs are held on a deep and profound level, and thus the superficiality of the style of exampling common to many writing in the analytic tradition is somewhat inappropriate. I will assume, however, that although the beliefs are deeply held and form part of the backdrop of life, they can be articulated if necessary (in time of danger, perhaps). Let us take just one belief, the belief that "Everything is spirit." Allen has an extremely moving chapter in *The Sacred Hoop* that makes this fundamental point, which is articulated at several places in the chapter.[34]

Now if I grow up in a Native American culture, presumably the belief is inculcated in me from an early age. Nevertheless, like all children, I may have some questions about it. Perhaps, if I am small, it is easier for me to understand and believe this fundamentality of my world if I am looking at a plant, or even a moss. But perhaps I become somewhat confused if I look at the rock on which the moss grows, and perhaps I ask—or challenge—some nearby adult on the matter. I would then be functioning in the role of epistemic challenger, along the lines of our CCP model, specifically as developed in chapter four of this text (pp. 117–21).

Let us suppose, for the sake of hypothesis, that my adult friend, although secure in her beliefs and understanding, is mildly moved because she remembers having asked the same sort of question herself at an earlier age. At that point, conditions (ii) (a) (1) and (ii) (a) (2) of the model have been run through. Then my older friend reminds me of the story of the origin of all, according to the set of beliefs surrounding the existence of Maheo, the creator, and after several explanatory sentences—strings of output—I am satisfied. Thus my initially somewhat weak belief is contextually justified, and if my context remains the same throughout other portions of my life, my belief about the ontological status of spirit may remain justified for me and unchallenged for a lifetime. This would correspond to conditions (ii) (a) (3) and (ii) (b) of our model.

I do not need to run through the manner in which, possibly, I might come to lose some of my Native American beliefs if, for example, through much formal education, I come to believe that there is no such thing as "spirit" and that a rock consists of matter. This example is similar to the example above of the fundamentalist coming to an alteration in her beliefs, and in any case could easily be modeled (again) by CCP.[35] Perhaps more importantly, it should be obvious by now that CCP is not only gynocentric, in all the senses explicated in earlier chapters, but also as I asserted at an earlier point, CCP is applicable to the modes of justification for most humans (male or female, adult or child) most of the time. It is, in fact, the way in which most philosophers receive justification for epistemically doubtful points during the course of the average day. The published epistemologist at Harvard probably looks no further than the printed schedule to see what trains are going from the Square to Roxbury during a given interval. The sort of normatively tight justification for this piece of empirical information, which he is fond of requiring in his articles, is an acquired taste, and one which is easily abandoned at the slightest provocation since, statistically speaking, he is under the influence of reliable cognitive processes most of the time and the chances that fake train schedules are being printed up to deceive him are virtually nil.

So the model on which we have been relying here gives us insight not only into how the fragmented voices of women might make themselves heard, but also reminds us of the general utility of descriptive epistemology, a point first made in chapters one and two. But the model relies largely on verbal communication and does not take into account the nonverbal, the gestural, or the language of the body. Our common experience of life informs us that this sort of mode of communication is of greater importance in more intimate experiences, and it is to these experiences that I now turn.


## CCP, THE NONVERBAL, AND SEXUALITY

Since our work has focused on intentionality, it is appropriate to note that a number of contemporary philosophers have addressed problems of sexuality and the erotic in terms of heightened intentionality. Thomas Nagel's widely reprinted piece "Sexual Perversion" has been cited in this regard, and he posits as paradigmatic of nonperverted sexuality a degree of ramification of intentionality that, one supposes, is in actuality rarely achieved.[36] I will in this section be concerned largely with heterosexual nonverbal expression and with some of the dynamics of intentionality exhibited on the level of the erotic. Since an explication of intentionality on this level draws on some material that I have utilized several times up to this point, we will need to bear in mind some of the theoretical importance of the work on object-relations theory and related material, much of which was first examined here in chapter three. The larger point here will be to show how CCP models even our nonverbal and gestural communication (insofar as any epistemic import is concerned), and how the erotic is connected to our accounts of knowledge.

Given what we have said about the relevant theorizing at an earlier point, we may remind ourselves that the male's rupture from the mother signifies the leave-taking, for him, of the world of cozy intimacy. The reward, if this task is accomplished successfully, is male identity and an entrée into the world of masculine activity.

But the upshot of all this for male female intimacy is that males experience intimacy with females as a powerful, nonverbal form of merging and, to some extent, regression. This strongly releasing experience seems to be one that, for the male, is beyond words and one that not only does not require verbal expression, but is actually interrupted by it. The female experience of male–female intimacy is rather different. The female is not, in heterosexual relations, experiencing (as is the male) close contact with a female body, so the experience is not as evocative of early intimacy for the female, in any case. In addition, the female has never had to make the rupture with the mother figure in the same sort of way, so the female has learned, over a period of time, to associate intimacy—with mothers, other adult figures, and persons in general—with a gradual process of verbalization and the expression, both verbal and nonverbal, of feelings and emotions. The female is unlikely, in heterosexual experience, to find physical intimacy nonverbalizable or so overwhelming that it constitutes a regression to a level of more infantile needs.

The foregoing reminds us that almost all our accounts of sexual relations (male–female relations) are essentially androcentric, including many accounts authored by women. The simultaneous distancing from the object and intentionality of erotic desire so characteristic of androcentric accounts of heterosexual relations is a hallmark not only of constructions of sexuality in Western culture, but also of coming-to-know and knowledge acquisition. Now, it seems, the tie between the erotic and knowing is clearer: The desire to objectify the other, while still achieving bodily release in the other, has its epistemological analogue in the history of androcentric attempts to divorce the senses of the knower from accounts of what it would take to "know" the object.

Just as one can summarize the connection between knowledge and the erotic in androcentric terms, so one can attempt to qualify it in gynocentric terms. Although the experience of bodily immersion may be a cause for some regression, it seems that this regression is seldom at a level so profound as to be inarticulable. Just as this intimate connection with an object—with the outside world—can be expressed and verbalized by the female, the feminist standpoint epistemologists hypothesize knowing or the process of coming-to-know in general as "dialectical" or "relational" (as we have seen at an earlier point).

Now the relationship between the sort of intentionality employed by some previous writers on the topic of sexuality and the knowledge/erotic connection becomes much more apparent. For the layers of intentionality posited by Nagel, for example, make sense only when one objectifies as fully as possible the object and its relation to other things. But this androcentric view (which also, not so incidentally, focuses on physical arousal) misses the point of the sort of connectedness that is important, typically, to females.

One might think of this gynocentric connectedness as heavily reliant upon intentionality, but in a different sort of way. Here it is not ramifications of intentionality that are crucial, but the type or sort of intentionality. And the wishes, hopes, and desires one maintains as propositional attitudes, to emply the relevant phrase, take as their object other sorts of things that are related to the knower in a grounded, contextualized, or connected sort of way. Thus it is inconceivable that the hallmark of a gynocentric epistemology could be knowledge divorced from the senses, and it is also inconceivable that the hallmark of an erotic intentionality could be the desire to objectify the other so completely that the other becomes a mere reflection, as it were, of one's desires.[37] Gynocentric eroticism is typically characterized by an intentionality directed toward the other but coupled with a desire to know the other as a true other, that is, as another person.

All of this is related to CCP in more than one way. Since CCP is intended to model what is constitutive of epistemic justification, genuine instances of questioning and skeptical doubt are unlikely to occur in sexual contexts, although they could certainly, of course, occur in nonverbal contexts.[38] But more loosely—and more appropriately—one might think of the erotic and sexuality as themselves modes of communication designed to furnish reassurance of a sort. The reassurance is not, of course, bluntly speaking epistemic (unless one chooses to place a rather strained interpretation upon it). But much of the gesture, nuance, glance, and caress of sexuality is intended to communicate feeling, and in the more powerful instances deep feeling. This feeling may or may not have been understood, doubted, hoped for, or guessed at by the recipient of an individual caress or gesture beforehand, but it cannot help but have the intent of communicating simultaneously with the desire that this intent be understood and recognized by the other, and this sort of intentionality (although much less ramified than, say, Nagel's) is also at the heart of CCP.

I ignore for the moment the obvious sorts of cases where sexuality is employed solely for purposes of bodily sensation and where some who have a purely physiological view of sexuality will claim no communicative intentionality is involved. Although I believe that instances of the pure form of this are much less frequent than many seem to believe, this sort of sexuality certainly exists.[39] But that need not concern us here, since the desire to construe sexuality in terms purely physiological is itself consistent with the androcentric point of view. The sort of sexuality that desires to experience the other as another person, however, rather than as an other-objectified-as-fully-as-possible, will, perforce, mimic some of the conditions listed under (ii) (a) in our model, without the doubt clause but with the crucial components of intentionality and recognition of intentionality intact.

The androcentric theorists mention the possibility that one might be moved by the "softness" and "diffidence" of one's would-be lover.[40] In Nagel's model, once one is so moved, one might begin the ramified process of intentionality that would lead to some sort of sexual culmination. But it is possible during the course of making love to communicate to one's lover that it is these very sorts of qualities one finds moving and/or appealing, and although this communication can be done to some extent verbally, it can also be done by gesture. Now in communicating these intentional states one is doing a great deal more than communicating intended sexual desire. At another level, one communicates one's feeling of similarity to one's lover, one's sense of existential aloneness, one's joy in the blurring of the boundaries that are ordinarily constitutive of this separateness, and so forth. And although these attitudes may in some sense be constitutive of certain kinds of sexual desire, they can certainly be separated from sexual desire, and in the realms of literature have frequently been completely divorced from conscious sexual desire. Yet the gynocentric view seems to push our view of complete sexuality in this direction.

It is perhaps for these sorts of reasons that lesbian literature and the description of lesbian sexuality so frequently mention states that might be thought of as transcending, or transcendental, in the sense that the ordinary self-conscious awareness concomitant to certain kinds of sexuality has been surpassed.[41] One might hypothesize that once neither partner demonstrates the androcentric distancing and divorce from awareness of the other-as-person so characteristic of masculinist views of sexuality, heightened intentionality, awareness, and the ability to move through levels of immersion without fear of immersion could lead to radically altered erotic states. Although it is, of course, possible that similar states could result from heterosexual eroticism with certain partners, what we know about the development of the genders and the different modes of communication characteristic of males and females would tend to make this, in such a view, probabilistically infrequent.

Thus much that is important to gynocentric views of communication and knowledge acquisition carries over into nonverbal communication and even into that most gestural area of communication, sexuality. A model for epistemics that posits intentionality and the recognition of intentionality by another as crucially important is relevant to all the sorts of human communication.

## CONTEXTUALIZED EPISTEMOLOGY: DESCRIPTIVE EPISTEMOLOGY FOR HUMAN BEINGS

In this chapter I have tried to focus on issues crucial to work in feminist theory, particularly as such work cuts across disciplines and orientations. The first theme relevant to cross-disciplinary investigation is the fragmentation of women's voices, and, as was noted in an earlier chapter, it is because of this fragmentation that Harding, for one, ends her work with a plea for tolerance of a divergence of views and with an allusion to the recognition of texts that springs from postmodernism. Within the United States alone the many-strandedness of feminist theory has frequently not received the notice that it should, particularly when the assumption is made that there is little or no literature relevant to a given voice or point of view. For this reason I have tried to set out interpretations of woman's standpoint from four groups that might be thought to be representative of the diversity of women's thought within the United States. I asserted at the outset that these four groups—black, Native American, Asian American, and Latina women—were not to be taken as representing anything more than a smattering of what was available, but I assert simultaneously that to fail to take notice of these voices is to make a serious mistake.

In setting out the exemplary material, I relied heavily on work by women who were not academic theorists, and only one of the women whose work was cited is a trained philosopher. But all of the work cited lends credence to the contention for which I have argued here: that the gynocentric view is a view that relies on communicative and contextualist principles and is aware of the nuances of interpersonal communication. The work of Alice Walker, Paula Gunn Allen, Maxine Hong Kingston, and Maria Lugones helps us to understand the importance of context in ways that may not be immediately evident simply from a perusal of the more standard feminist theory. In particular, the work of Allen, citing as it does a matrilocal and matrilineal tradition that was originally pre-industrial, helps us to focus on that which is more purely gynocentric in its standpoint and grounding, since Allen is able to articulate precisely the degree to which American Indian culture depended on the feminine for its development and growth.

The point has been, then, that any set of principles, such as CCP, which helps to remind us of the nature of women's knowing, is applicable, by virtue of its contextuality, both cross- and intra-culturally. More importantly, CCP is also applicable to most sorts of situations that do not call for the extremely normative and distanced view of the androcentric theorists. CCP is applicable to children and also to adults in non-Western cultures. It is only within the context of the Western, industrial culture, and particularly with regard to educated adult males, that the modes of thinking associated with normative androcentric epistemology are operant.

Finally, I tried to show the relevance of views roughly analogous to CCP—that is, views that model communication on the basis of intentionality, recognized intent, and response to recognized intent—for the nonverbal, gestural part of communication that, again, is associated most completely with the gynocentric view. At the heart of this sort of communication is the erotic, and instances of erotic communication and knowing may be thought of as the most profound of all.

If the divorced view of the males, which according to the object-relations theorists arises from crises in male development, may be construed as a view that objectifies and distances the female in heterosexual relations, then heterosexual relations when seen from the standpoint of the female are attempts to communicate with persons who profoundly fear the immersion of heterosexual experience. The desire to create constraints that cannot be abridged in theory mirrors itself in male heterosexual relations by the desire to objectify the female as fully as possible, thus rendering her increasingly more a body and increasingly less a person. To the extent that this distancing is overcome, and to the extent that the male is able to move past his inarticulate fear of drowning in the body, the more positive potential for communication in heterosexual relations is realized.

I want now to turn briefly to issues in the sociology of knowledge, before closing the development of our feminist epistemology. To the extent that sociology of knowledge has always stood apart from—and indeed been critical of—standard epistemology, this area of endeavor is also relevant to our project. Recent work by feminist theorists in sociology of knowledge underscores the extent to which what passes for knowledge (even in the sciences, as we saw in chapter three) is a product of social conditions and social communication. The androcentric view has frequently failed to deal squarely with the ramifications of sociological accounts of knowledge growth and knowledge acquisition.

# NOTES

1. I owe this phrase to Susan Bordo, in a talk given at the Eastern Division of the American Philosophical Association, December, 1988, in Washington D.C. The talk is entitled "Feminist Skepticism and the 'Maleness' of Philosophy", and a somewhat different version of it appears in *Journal of Philosophy* 85, no. 11 (1988):619–29.

2. One of the best accounts of the relationship between racism and androcentric authority available is the work of Susan Griffin, which addresses itself to these problems. Specifically relevant is her work *Pornography and Silence* (New York: Harper and Row, 1981).

3. See Harding, *The Science Question*, chap. 7, "Other 'Others' and Fractured Identities: Issues for Epistemologists," 163–97.

4. See Bordo, *Flight, passim.*

5. Some of these terms occur in the work of Hartsock and Flax, especially as cited in Harding. See *The Science Question*, particularly 147–49 and 151–55.

6. Paula Gunn Allen, *The Sacred Hoop* (Boston, Mass.: Beacon Press, 1986).

7. Maxine Hong Kingston, *The Woman Warrior* (New York: Vintage Books, 1977).

8. Ibid., 23–24.

9. Ibid., 55.

10. As this is written Amy Tan's *The Joy Luck Club* (New York: G. P. Putnam & Sons, 1989) constitutes still another such voice.

11. Kingston, *Woman Warrior*, 106–07.

12. Paula Giddings, *When and Where I Enter: The Impact of Black Women on Race and Sex in America* (New York: Bantam, 1985). The chapter most illustrative of this theme is perhaps "The Quest for Women's Suffrage," pp. 119–31.

13. Ibid., 122–23.

14. Ibid., 101.

15. See chap. 1 of Giddings, *When and Where,* "To Sell My Life as Dearly as Possible: Ida B. Wells and the First Antilynching Campaign," 17–33.

16. In fact, Giddings begins Part III of her work with the following quotation from Hurston: "Now, women forget all those things they don't want to remember, and remember everything they don't want to forget. The dream is the truth. Then they act and do things accordingly."

17. Alice Walker, *The Temple of My Familiar* (New York: Harcourt Brace Jovanovich, 1988), 12.

18. I will draw largely from Allen's work *The Sacred Hoop,* but Allen herself cites a number of female Native American authors.

19. See Paula Gunn Allen, *Shadow Country* (Los Angeles, Calif.: American Indian Studies Center of UCLA, 1982), and Paula Gunn Allen, ed., *Studies in*

*American Indian Literature* (New York: The Modern Language Association of America, 1983).

20. Allen, *Hoop,* 2, 4.

21. See in particular the chapter in *Hoop* entitled "Who Is Your Mother? Red Roots of White Feminism," pp. 209–21.

22. Ibid., 217.

23. Ibid., 221.

24. Gretchen Bataille, "Transformation of Tradition: Autobiographical Works by American Indian Women", in Paula Gunn Allen, ed., *Studies in American Indian Literature* (New York: The Modern Language Association of America, 1983), 89.

25. See Maria Nieto Senour, "Psychology of the Chicana," in *Chicano Psychology,* ed. Joe L. Martinez, Jr. (New York: Academic Press, 1977).

26. Senour, "Psychology of the Chicana," 233.

27. Maria Lugones, "Playfulness, 'World'-Traveling, and Loving Perception," *Hypatia* 2, no. 2 (1987):3–19.

28. Ibid., 3.

29. Ibid., 10.

30. Ibid., 16.

31. Lugones writes, for example, of "intensity" as being a stereotype of Latinos and Latinas.

32. What this would require is the construction of a set of riders, like the riders employed by Swain and cited in chap. 1, to try to preserve truth. This is a difficult but presumably not impossible project. I am inclined to say that the real question is whether this is a worthwhile project, given what we are now in a position to say about the normative tradition.

33. Larry Laudan, "Explaining the Success of Science: Beyond Epistemic Realism and Relativism," in *Science and Reality: Recent Work in the Philosophy of Science,* ed. James T. Cushing, C. F. Delaney, and Gary M. Gutting (Notre Dame, Ind.: University of Notre Dame Press, 1984), 90.

34. Allen, *Hoop.* The relevant chapter is "The Sacred Hoop: A Contemporary Perspective," pp. 54–75, and the requisite point is made, at least, on p. 59 and again on p. 70.

35. These alterations could also be modeled by the full-blown computational version of CCP presented on pp. 117–121, although I have not done so here, since it would seem that the important points with regard to the model are covered, for the purposes of our example, with the beginning version of the model.

36. See Nagel, "Sexual Perversion."

37. An interesting passage in Kierkegaard's *Diary of the Seducer* talks about Johannes's desire that Cordelia mirror or reflect his desire, and in such a way that the reflections become indistinguishable from that which they originally reflected. Soren Kierkegaard, *Either/Or,* vol. 1, trans. David G. Swenson and Lillian Marvin Swenson (Princeton: Princeton University Press, 1971), 410.

38. One imagines, for example, questioning or doubt signified solely by gesture, as in a situation where one did not know the language or one was speaking by sign language. Then, I claim, the set of conditions (ii) (a) (1)–(2) through (ii) (a) (3) and (ii) (b), which I alluded to in my development of the Native American example, would be utilized again, but this time completely nonverbally.

39. In his article on infidelity, Richard Wasserstrom refers to this view as the view that sex is an act with no more moral worth or import than the sharing of a good meal together. ("Is Adultery Immoral?", ed. Richard Wasserstrom in *Today's Moral Problems,* [New York: Macmillan and Co., 1985], 213–14.)

40. Nagel, "Sexual Perversion," 273.

41. See, for example, the work of Adrienne Rich, *The Dream of a Common Language* (New York: Norton, 1978); or Judy Grahn, *The Queen of Wands* (Trumansburg, N.Y.: Crossing Press, 1982).

# Chapter Eight

# Feminist Sociology of Knowledge

Since sociology as a discipline owes so much to the post-Kantian theorizing of the nineteenth century, it begins from a standpoint that is at once philosophical and outside the Anglo-American tradition. The categories of sociology and of sociophilosophical thought, if one may employ such a phrase, already manifest an awareness of certain sorts of distinctions that have been crucial in our theorizing here: subject/object, inner/outer, noumenal/phenomenal. If it is possible to think of the social conditions that give rise to the categories of knowledge acquisition, particularly in the sciences, as themselves subject to explanation along similar sorts of lines, then a sort of circularity—an enlightening one, at that—lies at the heart of sociology of knowledge, since it admits from the outset that no set of categories can have a privileged position. Thus this particular line of work, with its Continental origin, bears a resemblance to the work of the French theorists, since that work, too, is admitted by the theorists not to be free from self-criticism along the lines employed to criticize other sorts of theories.

Sociology of knowledge asks us to employ the reasoning that we use in the social sciences to investigate human behavior in the marketplace, for example, to construct a similar sort of investigation of human behavior in the theoryplace. Just as Marxist lines of analysis can inform us of the female standpoint with regard to what might be labeled "reproductive labor," other lines of analysis, in some cases borrowed from theorists such as Durkheim and Gurvitch, can inform us of the extent to which "knowledge" is shaped by a variety of social factors, including gender-related factors.[1] It is part of the modus operandi of sociology of knowledge that any set of principles that would purport or allege to constitute an epistemology is not itself free from criticism, and thus no stance can be considered immune.[2] The upshot of this, of course, for the androcentric mode of theorizing, which we examined here in the first two chapters and that has been so prevalent in English-speaking countries throughout the twentieth century, is that it may be criticized along the same lines as any other theory, and thus can serve as no foundation or bedrock. Sociology of knowledge might invite us to consider the historical, cultural, and social factors that gave rise to the pretense that it is possible to develop an epistemology *de novo* and with impunity.

Interestingly enough, some of the theoretical underpinnings of contemporary sociology, at least from the standpoint of its historical antecedents, seem to imply an awareness of various modes of thinking and conceptualization that themselves are reliant on androcentric/gynocentric distinctions and that hold across cultures and epochs. Durkheim's original inquiry into the nature of "moral life" and his distinction between organic and mechanical solidarity—the former being characteristic of societies before the Industrial Revolution—reveals his awareness of the extent to which what counts as a moral concept is a result both of the prevailing form of solidarity and the intellectualizations that spring from it. In *Division du Travail Social,* he notes

> . . . but rather man is a moral being only because he lives in society, since morality consists in being solidary with a group and varying with this solidarity. Let social life disappear, and moral life will disappear with it, since it would no longer have any objective.[3]

If human moral categories are the result of social conditions and the various sorts of social solidarity, then so are epistemic categories. It is the task of the sociologist of knowledge, then, to try to relate these categories to regnant norms and to interpret the norms with the help of the categories. Here arable gound for the feminist theorist presents itself, since it is clear that the force of patriarchal hegemony will be a powerful determinant of many or most of the epistemic categories in all societies that demonstrate patrilocal and patrilineal structure.

Several women sociologists have begun the process of critique of sociology of knowledge—and indeed critique of the discipline of soci-

ology itself—from the feminist point of view. Dorothy Smith is prominent among these, although the British theorists Sheila Rowbotham
and Anne Oakley have also worked in this area. I want to examine
some of Smith's claims, in particular, but with an eye toward the
development of lines of thought taken from gynocentric sociology of
knowledge that will mesh specifically with the work here. Fortunately,
this will not be difficult: The reader will notice immediately that much
of what has been articulated in feminist sociology of knowledge is
directly relevant to the gynocentric epistemology developed in this
text. Perhaps most strikingly, the feminist sociologists have not been
content to create a critical theory with regard to sociology that focuses
on the timeworn areas of exclusion and domination of theory by sheer
number of males. (Even Arlette Farge, writing about history as a
discipline, focused to a great extent on these issues, as we saw in
chapter six.)

## FEMINIST SOCIOLOGY OF KNOWLEDGE: SMITH, STEHELIN, AND COOK AND FONOW

Smith and others have argued that sociology (and, implicitly, other
disciplines as well) is dominated by a point of view that is taken for
granted—taken as ground—and that prevents the theorists from seeing
what framework they employ. Thus sociology of sociology, which is
part of what Smith does, requires that we see that the canons of
sociology are androcentric in their structure and reflective of a male
point of view. It is a point of view that assumes women cannot be the
articulators of its peculiarities and ramifications; it is for this reason
that the overt question of whether or not the female voice could ever
develop theory along the given lines does not arise. The question does
not arise simply because it is assumed that the question would never
be asked. Smith is a forceful exponent of the details of this critique,
and she explicates her stance with a sense for the meticulous that all
theorists would do well to emulate. Perhaps her greatest asset is her
ability to force the reader to pull away from the taken-for-grantedness
of the male point of view, while still being able to conceptualize (as
the situation requires) in its terminology. She writes:

> The first difficulty is that how sociology is thought—its methods, concep-
> tual schemes and theories—has been based on and built up within the
> male social universe (even when women have participated in its doing). It

has taken for granted not just that scheme of relevances as an itemized
inventory of issues or subject matters (industrial sociology, political
sociology, social stratification, etc.) but the fundamental social and political structures under which these become relevant and are ordered. . . .
An important set of procedures which serve to constitute the body of
knowledge of the discipline as something which is separated from its
practitioners are those known as "objectivity. . . ." Entering the governing mode of our kind of society lifts the actor out of the immediate local
and particular place in which he is in the body. . . . This mode of action
creates then a bifurcation of consciousness, a bifurcation of course which
is there for all those who participate in this mode of action. . . . The more
successful women are in mediating the world of concrete particulars so
that men do not have to become engaged with (and therefore conscious
of) that world . . . the more complete the dichotomy between the two
worlds, and the estrangement between them.[4]

In other words, the practice of sociology as a discipline—or any
other mode of theorizing open to the intelligentsia—requires the use
both of male categories and the peculiarly male mode of thought (called
"objectivity") that requires one to rid oneself of awareness of particulars to as great an extent as possible in order that one may adopt that
universalizable and normativized view that Bordo has called (following
Nagel) the "view from nowhere" and that we have examined at length
here in preceding chapters. Now males are able to do this not simply
because they may come somewhat more naturally to this mode of
thinking, but also because the social framework is supportive of their
efforts precisely to the extent that it keeps women in the concrete
mode, thus enabling women to take on a burden of awareness-of-
particularity that permits the male to theorize. Part of the upshot of
this is that for those few women who are able to attain a position such
that the method of distancing is open to them as a regular intellectual
option, the gap of the bifurcation can be experienced with unrivaled
intensity, and the knowledge of the world of particulars can be brought
to bear on theory in a new and powerful way.

If this extraordinary cognition or sort of awareness that stems from
having crossed, as Smith has it, "a daily chasm . . . on the one side of
which is this special conceptual activity of thought, . . . and on the
other the world of concrete practical activities in keeping things
clean," is allowed full expression theoretically, then a wide range of
moves is available to the theorist who utilizes the cognitive apparatus
peculiar to theory simultaneously with the mundane cognitive methods
from which theory so frequently divorces itself.[5] The luster gained

from this new sort of theorizing is not so much, Smith claims, the result of "a junking of everything that has gone before . . . [as] a reorganization which changes the relation of the sociologist to the object of her knowledge and changes also her problematic."[6]

In other words, what Smith is suggesting is not so much an alternate sociology (although it may be thought of in those terms) as an alternate sociological method or stance. We label this stance "gynocentric" for the obvious sorts of reasons—the methods available to it are more commonly associated with the worlds of women and with the contextualization of thought processes peculiar to those who experience in-the-bodiness. The methods could, however (no doubt with some difficulty), be employed by males. In general, it is the stance itself that is important, for as Smith suggests, the recognition of one's theoretical distancing at the same time that one experiences, on some level, the call of the particular in place and frame of reference, gives one a special sensitivity—perhaps a special insight—into the locus of others. Smith provides a poignant example of this: She writes of riding a train through Ontario while watching a family of Indians standing on a nearby spur observing the train. As she says: "There was (for me) that moment—the train, those five people seen on the other side of the glass. I saw first that I could tell that incident as it was, but that telling as a description built in my position and my interpretations."[7]

For Smith, a theory that is not aware of its limitations *qua theoria* is no theory at all, for it lacks the self-consciousness that would allow it to reflect all the facets of a given situation.

Writing from a standpoint that encompasses both sociology of knowledge and sociology of science, the theorist Liliane Stehelin has expressed some of the points made so evocatively by Dorothy Smith while underscoring points examined earlier here in the summation of the work of Harding and her examination of Flax and Hartsock. Stehelin, insofar as she does feminist sociology of science (and hence of scientific knowledge), does not simply confine herself to a repetition of the relevant points regarding exclusion or the androcentric nature of theorizing. Rather, Stehelin employs some of the Marxist terminology utilized by other critics in a new and dynamic way. Stehelin reminds us of the use of the term "ideology" in standard Marxist theory: An ideology is not merely a set of beliefs. Rather, it is a set of beliefs explicitly related to the modes of production of a class, usually the dominant class. Thus the ideology of the bourgeoisie in Marxist theory is the dominant rationale for a society based on relationships between capitalists and proletariat, forces of production and modes of production. This ideology manifests itself in two important ways, so far as women-knowers (especially those who would aspire to be scientific knowers) are concerned: There is both a sexist ideology and an ideology of science itself, and the two become linked in ways that make it peculiarly difficult for women to achieve the status of knowers within the sciences.

> Sexist ideology itself, even if it cannot argue from a basis founded on the true idea, has not on that account been less effective over the centuries, and a woman in science (women practitioners of science) seems to be situated at the crossroads of these two ideologies: on the one hand the ideology of science to which she adheres (or not) as an *individual,* on the other the sexist ideology which governs our patriarchal society; and which she confronts as a *woman.*[8]

Part of Stehelin's argument is the specific claim that science as presently constituted will actually, in a hypocritical mode, pretend to be in the vanguard of the pursuit of woman's freedom and development while actually remaining (in its androcentric formulation) one of the chief obstacles to her development, and certainly one of the last bastions of complete male privilege. Thus science, Stehelin claims, will tell woman that more scientific research is needed to put to rest the shibboleths that keep women from full entry into the professions and the public workplace at large, while the rigidly masculinist mode of theorizing employed in the sciences simultaneously ensures that women's needs and values will be overlooked and that they will not themselves be permitted to participate in any of this valuable research, at least not in large numbers. What makes these observations of Stehelin's particularly valuable from the point of view of our task here is that Stehelin is one of the few to interpret the androcentricity of science both partly in its own terms (as, for example, Keller and Harding have done) and partly in terms of the role played by science in society according to a Marxist analysis of modes of production. Stehelin is not only concerned with the place of the intelligentsia as social class; she is also concerned with the notion that intellectual theorizing itself constitutes a mode of production that can be analyzed along neo-Marxist lines and the analysis of which is fruitful for feminist theory. She says specifically, insofar as the notion of production is concerned:

> Let us return to the thesis that every mode of production is of masculine origin. . . . It is thus necessary, in order to avoid ideological subversion,

that the production code should raise this negation of the differentiation of the sexes to a postulate; but a negation defined with reference to the characteristics of those who themselves established this production code: men.[9]

In other words, Stehelin tells us, science purports or alleges to assert that women may participate in all the socially valuable spheres of endeavor, including those having to do with the production and acquisition of knowledge, because they are, after all, persons. There is no doubt that they are the equivalent of men. And it is precisely in this positioning of male as the norm, a norm to which women must conform to be considered "persons," that the greatest level of androcentricity lies.

A brief digression through some of the work of Karl Mannheim, usually referred to as the founder of sociology of knowledge as a subdiscipline, may be useful here before proceeding. A few paragraphs back I drew attention to the natural outgrowth of sociology of knowledge from the portions of Durkheim's work that emphasize the social construction of value. Although Mannheim is best known for his *Ideology and Utopia,* shorter pieces, analyzed recently by John Harms, seem to provide fertile soil for feminist analysis, and are certainly helpful in coming to understand Smith's or Stehelin's work.

Harms reminds us of three salient forms of knowledge, seen from a social perspective, which spring from Mannheim's work. Mannheim refers to these forms as "objective meaning," "expressive meaning," and "documentary meaning," respectively. The distinctions between these three aid us in comprehending how classical sociology of knowledge ties into feminist sociology of knowledge; it may very well be the case that because the groundwork is already sensitive to social distinctions the feminist version of the theory springs forth more readily than it does in some other disciplines.

In any case, Harms gives us the example of a person giving money to a beggar. The objective meaning of the act is assistance; this construction arises from a relatively uninterpreted construction of the empirical material at hand. The expressive meaning of the act arises from a construction of what is taken to be the intentionality of the actor or agent—in the case of an alms-giver, one would (without other evidence) assume it to be the desire to help an individual or to improve a given lot. The third account, the documentary meaning, "involves fitting one event into a larger pattern of events which establish integral meaning."[10] If one had still more evidence about the person assisting the beggar, one might come to see the act as an example of hypocrisy (when construed along lines greater than those afforded by mere access to intentionality, as Harms suggests). All of these notions are, of course, related to the long-familiar notion of *weltanschauung,* which has perhaps a more honored history in sociology than in some other disciplines. According to Harms, Mannheim takes a *weltanschauung* to be an "organizing lens that orders experience by arranging events into a web or 'coordinate system' where these events and experiences become interrelated and thus meaningful."[11]

What is remarkable from the foregoing material is the extent to which it meshes and intersects with feminist theory. Given an androcentric *weltanschauung,* such as informs not only the sciences and intellectual life in general but all of Western culture, certain sorts of "objective meaning," in particular, become inevitable. The crux of the matter, of course, is the paradoxical nature of this objective meaning. The antinomy with which we are faced is similar to that found in feminist empiricism: There is a sense in which the theoretical stance, when taken self-reflectively, yields an inconsistency. The "objective meaning" for most social acts is not a bare account derived from an uninterpreted series of raw phenomena, but rather is an account already seen through the lens of a masculinist *weltanschauung* and hence susceptible to the charge that it is far from objective. The same applies, of course, to the expressive meaning of the act and to its documentary meaning. Thus the taken-for-grantedness of the androcentric point of view is obscured and veiled by the pretense of objectivity that is thrown up by it, and by its promulgation of the notion that it is the ultimate standard. The paradox revolves around whether the objective meaning, as formulated by sociologists, can indeed be objective, and it is scarcely less a paradox than the classical Liar puzzle.

Harms's distillation of some parts of Mannheimian theory intersects with the work of Dorothy Smith and also provides an interpretive apparatus for the work of other feminist sociologists whose concerns may be more overtly methodological.[12] Smith had noted that

> . . . the relevances of sociology are organized in terms of a perspective on the world which is a view from the top and which takes for granted the pragmatic procedures of governing as those which frame and identify its subject matter. . . . The kinds of facts and events which are facts for us have already been shaped up and given their character and substance as facts, as relations, etc., by the method and practice of governing.[13]

Smith and Harms (via the notions of *weltanschauung* and the triad of meanings) provide us with a powerful array of devices for discerning the androcentric core of social theory and of social accounts of knowledge and knowledge-and-power relations, but the focus on issues somewhat more oriented toward research practices opens still another door.

In my account so far I have tended not to focus on the obvious power relationships that prevent the furtherance of feminist concerns. In one sense, one is inclined to say that these imbalances come directly from the deeply rooted sources that the more psychoanalytically oriented theory has pointed out to us; in another sense, however, to fail to mention the tilts and biases is to do an injustice to everyday, non-theoretical life—the plane on which, after all, we both exist and theorize. Sociologists and social scientists on the whole are perhaps most sensitive to the prevalence of these imbalances since their work reveals them, even when the work itself is cast in a masculinist mode. A male theorist doing sociology of the workplace or labor force cannot fail to notice male/female inequities, even if there is nothing in his mode of theorizing or *weltanschauung* that would allow him to interpret the material in a profoundly feminist or gynocentric way.

Cook and Fonow, in a piece entitled "Knowledge and Women's Interests: Issues of Epistemology and Methodology in Feminist Research," have focused both on the sort of underlying androcentricity that Smith examines and brings to light, and on the more overt—and perhaps more obvious—androcentricity that reveals itself in methodology, practices of research, and the sheer ubiquitousness of male power. One of the basic epistemological principles that Cook and Fonow cite is similar to the view provided for us by Smith:

> From a review of the literature we have identified . . . basic epistemological principles . . . [one of these is] the need to challenge the norm of objectivity that assumes that the subject and object of research can be separated from one another and that personal and/or grounded experiences are unscientific.[11]

But Cook and Fonow are not, perhaps, as concerned as Smith with a theoretical overview of the androcentricity inherent in sociology as a discipline. What they take to be the most forceful brand of feminism involves not merely the uncovering of male-oriented bias, but the move to challenge, dissect, and disrupt male power. And, fortunately for those who would prefer to think of male dominance as stemming more from socialization than from neonatal experiences, they assert that the sociologist can make power-giving moves right within the framework of professional sociology, if she is careful enough.

As a starting point, Cook and Fonow recommend that the feminist sociologist challenge male "objectivity" not only by unccovering what they call its "old way" theoretic, but by altering its old-vision methodology and practice. Within the scope of sociological research, Cook and Fonow recommend:

> [that feminist investigators reject] the assumption that maintaining a strict separation between researcher and research subject produces a more valid, objective account. One way in which feminists avoid treating their subjects as mere objects of knowledge is to allow the respondents to "talk back" to the investigator.[15]

Thus Cook and Fonow recommend that sociologists engaged in feminist inquiry join in an active dialogue with those whom they interview; the norm of failing to respond to the subject's questions (long a staple of interview training), or treating the subject's questions with a putatively objective and neutral "Mmm" is countered with the mode of active participation. It goes without saying, of course, that when the sociologist interacts verbally with the participant, new networks of meaning and reality are created, some of which are inevitably revelatory of underlying currents not available for viewing by the investigator who insists on a terse "Mmm." Thus Cook and Fonow not only do feminist sociology of knowledge in the sense that they lay bare the androcentric structure of the old stated problematic, but they become actual knowers and epistemic agents in a process of knowledge creation that serendipitously mimics in its theoretical structure the view we have created here and that, moreover, has the added benefit of chipping away at the prevailing masculine power base.[16] Their theory, too, is self-reflective—but the happy difference is that when their view of knowledge-creation and acquisition is put to the theoretical test, no paradox results. They would interpret their methodology and epistemology as validated by the interactive nature of their feminist worldview.

## GYNOCENTRIC SOCIOLOGY: OAKLEY AND ADLER, ADLER AND FONTANA

I have concentrated thus far on feminist sociology of knowledge, with an overview of some feminist amelioration of sociological methodology. But feminist sociology itself—that is, sociology done with an eye to feminist concerns (in whatever area or branch of sociology)—cannot help but reflect some of the material that we have already examined. Ann Oakley, the British theorist, is a feminist sociologist whose work has been widely cited, even among feminist philosophers.[17] Oakley's well-known *The Sociology of Housework* might at first appear to be only marginally relevant to our concerns, but it will come as no surprise to those who have understood the points Smith makes about sociological constructions that a feminist sociology of housework is intimately tied not only to feminist methodology but feminist sociology of knowledge.

Oakley is concerned to begin her work with an analysis of how little traditional sociology has responded to the world of women; in this she echoes many other social scientists, including some males.[18] But the interweaving of the strands of analysis stemming directly from the sociological aspects of housework itself and the perhaps more overt strands of the theoretic of female socialization creates a texture that responds almost directly to Cook and Fonow's concern about the "taken-for-granted problematic,"[19] or to Smith's concern that "facts . . . have already been shaped . . . by the method and practice of governing."[20] Oakley begins by noting that "The more sociology is concerned with such areas [the male-dominated areas] the less it is, by definition, likely to include women within its frame of reference. The appropriate analogy for the structural weakness of sociology in this respect is the social reality sociologists study. . . ."[21]

So Oakley will make two major points: (1) housework, *qua* labor category, has never been given proper sociological attention because of the male domination of category construction; and (2) insofar as housework is given proper attention, a feminist sociology of housework will reveal that attitudes toward housework are deeply related to female socialization as a whole, and hence are inextricably entwined with the very same processes of socialization that give rise to the masculinist bias in the first place. The apparent circularity here is deliberate: One cannot properly get at a sociology of housework without uncovering other aspects of child-rearing, gender-creation, self-perception, and so forth, which are, in their full ramifications, related to sociology of knowledge, and of course, problems of methodology.

Much of Oakley's work is provocative in that it implicitly provides us with the following conditional: If a woman defines herself as a housewife (this term, rather than "homemaker," was deliberately employed in the study, which took place in Great Britain in the late 1960s and early 1970s), then she does so largely because of a social process, beginning in childhood, that taught her not only to identify with her mother as a female but also as a housewife. Surprisingly, as Oakley found, this set of conditions seemed to hold across social classes and regardless of whether or not the mother was deemed to be a good, or even acceptable, housewife.[22] In other words, to be a female—to identify with one's mother—was to be a housewife in some sense, even if one felt that one's mother had somehow failed in her primary task.

One might at first be inclined to think that sociological studies would reveal parallel orientations for males along certain occupation- and class-lines. The difference is that it seems unlikely that the concept of maleness itself would so closely follow the concept of occupational or vocational role. Oakley writes that the notions of femininity and housewifery–motherhood are so closely linked that it is difficult to make any theoretical separation of them:

> But a female's induction into the domestic role—unlike these other schemes—lacks a formal structure, and consequently is rarely seen as an occupational apprenticeship. A main reason for this is that preparation for housewifery is intermingled with socialization for the feminine gender role in the wider sense. Neither in theory nor in practice is one process distinguishable from the other.[23]

Now the tie-in here with sociology of knowledge probably becomes somewhat more obvious. Almost all women, theorists or not, sociologists or not, have been socialized along these same lines. Consequently, the female theorist has already, by training, known what it is like to be immersed in the world of particulars (as the housewife is) and may in fact be immersed in that world a great deal of the time when she is not functioning in her professional role. Because this world of particulars is so closely allied with what it means to be female, it is an invisible world from the standpoint of the standard categories of knowledge. But by the same token, it is a world that allows the theorist, when she actually works in the intellectual realm, to inhabit the "bifurcated consciousness" that Smith claims is responsible for the best sort of feminist sociological theorizing.

At this point, it might be good to return to one of the founders of sociology for some illumination of the underlying principles of sociology of knowledge. Durkheim wrote, in *Les Formes Elementaires de la Vie Religieuse,*

Since the world expressed by the system of concepts as a whole is that represented by society, society alone can furnish the most general notions in terms of which it can be conceived. . . . Since the universe does not exist except in so far as it is conceived in thought, and since it is not thought of as a whole except by society, it is comprised within the latter. . . .[24]

Durkheim is essentially writing of religious concepts here, but the male–female dichotomy is certainly one of the categories of which he is thinking, since it appears as fundamental cross-culturally and in many religious views. Just as Aristotle provided us with the categories of space and time, number and substance, Durkheim seems to be saying our social organization provides us with the conceptual schemes and logical categories that we employ to divide up the world. As he also says, "Far from it being the case . . . that the social relations of men are based on logical relations between things, in reality it is the former which have provided the prototype for the latter."[25]

Thus the very concepts of male and female themselves, so important for categorization, arise from the social organization of male–female interaction, which for the past several thousand years has been rampantly patriarchal in most parts of the world. This gives rise to the conceptual scheme in which anything associated with the female is deemed to be inferior, and this valorization of maleness and the masculine, combined with the devaluation of femaleness and the feminine, means that knowledge—in whatever sense—becomes connected to that which is masculine. The categories of knowledge acquisition are constructed in male terms and male interests decide what would count as a worthy object of investigation along the lines of inquiry in the androcentric and male-dominated sciences.

Oakley's *Housework*, then, leads us full circle: Housework has never really been investigated by the social sciences because it is an occupation consigned to the female realm and hence not worthy of inspection. Empirical investigation into housework, following feminist methodology, reveals that those who become full-time housewives have been socialized to believe that part of being female is doing housework. This belief is itself a product of androcentric ways of conceptualizing and cutting up the world, which in turn spring from the very androcentric social relations that created the problem of female housewifery in the first place. A Durkheimian account of the origins of knowledge categories, an overview of sociology of knowledge as it were, is quite consistent and consonant with the results of work by a contemporary feminist sociologist.

One last area of investigation for both sociology as a discipline and sociology of knowledge as its offshoot is the area that those in the profession have come to term "everyday life sociology." Oakley's analysis of housework is, in fact, part of this sort of investigation, but the analysis of this area provided recently by professional sociologists is valuable because of the insights it gives us into the nature of some of the microperspectives of everyday theorizing.

I intend to refer here to the work of Patricia and Peter Adler and Andrea Fontana, as encapsulated in a brief overview of this sort of theoretic appearing in *The Annual Review of Sociology*. Their work is not overtly feminist; in fact, the article in question does not make use of feminist categories. But if Smith is correct (not to mention Cook and Fonow, and Oakley), and if the ground of sociology more-or-less prohibits the examination of certain areas because they fail to fall into the given problematic, then the insightful analysis of "everyday sociology" provided by Adler and Adler will help us to understand why the notions of female and the everyday seem so deeply intertwined.

Adler, Adler, and Fontana begin their overview of this subarea by noting that the term "everyday life sociology" is not completely acceptable among those in the field.[26] As they phrase it, a standard objection from the field asks "Is there anything that characterizes the everyday life perspective as a distinctive body of theory?" But, they go on to assert, one only asks this question if one is enamored of some of the older sociological orientations that, not surprisingly, focus on semi-positivistic and "absolutistic" attempts to capture phenomena.[27] As the authors characterize it, the move toward a sociology of everyday life is a move away from the predominantly androcentric aspirations of that part of the social sciences that wants strictly to separate the object of knowledge from the knower.

> Everyday life sociologists critiqued traditional sociology epistemologically for its "absolutist" stance toward underlying phenomena. . . . They rejected the premise of *subject-object dualism*: the belief that the subject (knower) and the object (known) can be effectively separated through scientific principles. Procedures such as the objectification, detachment, control and manipulation of abstracted concepts and variables violate the integrity of the phenomena under study.[28]

In other words, as the authors argue, it is a mistake to assume that a replicatable and valid approach to the study of phenomena involves only objectification. Phenomena in their everydayness are not experienced in this manner; part of what constitutes the manner in which they are experienced must surely count in any study of phenomena, since it is an inseparable part of the overall view.

Such a view not only posits the dynamic of object-in-relation-to-knower as crucial, but also takes into consideration the multiplicity of interpersonal relationships that constitute part of the woof and warp of everyday life. Again, it is assumed that these relationships are not only available for analysis but also that they help to create *part of that which is analyzed*. My very attempt to analyze a given interpersonal or social situation creates a certain type of interaction that in turn creates another, and so forth, and my analysis of interpersonal interaction cannot, theoretically, be divorced from such considerations. Such a view includes, as the authors are at pains to point out, "an interactionist view of the self," rather than the "passive and constrained" actor model of traditional sociology.

The authors also allude to one area of the everyday life theorizing that is especially rich from the standpoint of feminist theory: a constructionist view of the emotions. The authors describe this approach in the following terms:

[This] . . . approach to the study of the emotions does not rule out a biological component but focuses instead on how these physiological processes are molded, structured and given meaning. Emotions do not exist independent of everyday life experiences, they argue; rather, these experiences call out, modulate, shape, and ultimately create feelings. These are then labeled, assessed and managed through and by interaction. Structural and cultural factors influence the feeling and interpretation of various emotions due to the way they constrain possibilities and frame situations.[29]

Although the authors are providing an overview of the area, and hence cannot fill in the blanks on a number of the questions that naturally occur to a reader, the manner in which they sketch the sociology of everyday life immediately ties into the concerns we have raised here, both in the obvious sense in which they deepen Oakley's analysis of the failure of the sociological establishment to notice, for example, housework, and in the less obvious sense in which they penetrate what Smith calls the "taken-for-grantedness" of the androcentric view in paradigmatic sociology. For the authors are alluding to a mode or method of approaching problems; one who does sociology of everyday life is doing sociology at a micro- rather than a macrolevel. And it is sociology at this level, according to Adler, Adler, and Fontana, that has been deemed unscientific and "astructural" or "trivial." The critics of this approach hold that it trivializes an object of analysis, whether it be an institution, a relationship, or an emotional construct, to inquire about it in a way that deals with its phenomenological familiarity to us rather than proposing to view it as though it were completely foreign. And it is, of course, this way of seeing, of viewing, that is inherently feminist and that subverts the androcentric view, for it is the latter that turns away from the easy modes of familiarity in examining the world and promulgates examination of the world as if one did not live in it as the ideal.

Sociology, and sociology of knowledge, provide us with fruitful ways of evaluating the construction of knowledge, and the epigram that "meanings are established in social interaction" is a valuable one for the feminist theorist. Although it may seem beyond dispute that the sociological perspective ties into CCP and its ramifications, as detailed specifically in chapters four, five, and seven, I want now to spend some time on the intersection between our naturalized epistemic model and the feminist sociology of knowledge.

## CCP AND FEMINIST SOCIOLOGICAL THOUGHT

In the previous chapter, when discussing the plurality of women's voices and our model, I focused on the nuances of interpersonal communication and even spent some time on nonverbal communication and sexuality as a mode of communication. Although it is clear that this aspect of the model is still relevant here—especially since Cook and Fonow, in particular, focus on communication as a methodological device—I want to come to terms with sociology of knowledge and CCP largely along the lines of the importance of context. For context is at the heart of sociology of knowledge: The broad point with which we are dealing, even when this area of sociology is thought of in its classic form, as constructed by Mannheim or Gurvitch, is that no set of claims or starting point for knowledge is without its bias. So sociology of knowledge commences with the assumption that, as Gurvitch has it, "[it] poses to epistemology the problem of the validity of an almost infinite number of perspectives on knowledge."[30]

Context is also at the heart of CCP, for what distinguishes most semi-naturalized epistemologies or accounts of epistemic justification from their normative, nonnaturalized counterparts, is a reliance on the interactions of the organism with the context in which the organism functions. In the earlier portions of this work, particularly chapters one and two where I tried to provide a framework for twentieth-century analytic epistemology, I emphasized the globality of traditional epistemology and its seldom articulated fear that to admit context into epistemological themes is also to admit the possibility of error. While the historical antecedents of this sort of thinking were noted, I was also at pains to establish the more contemporary normative style as related to developments in logic, which allowed theorists to hope (in the vein of the early Russell) that demarcating phenomena precisely and in a logically proper manner would preclude the possibility of error at a later point.

Sociology of knowledge may be thought of, then, as a form of naturalized epistemology. Unlike the versions of naturalized epistemology to which I have alluded here, sociology of knowledge has little interest in the perceptual apparatuses we employ to come to grips with the world, nor does it have much interest in trying to weave material from psychology—or from any mentalistic view—into its larger picture. But sociology of knowledge is epistemology naturalized insofar as that epistemology focuses on social interaction. Thus, given the nature of CCP and the importance of context and interaction within its scope, sociology of knowledge fits nicely into a gynocentric epistemics that is sensitive to context, grounding, and in-the-bodiness.

Smith lets us know that the actor normally functions "[in] the immediate local and particular place in which he is in the body. . . ."[31] This pertains to the vast majority of women almost all the time, and also pertains to many males when they are not functioning in the "governing mode." Thus the physical context of the actor's location and the network of relationships in which the actor is enmeshed at any given moment normally provide the backdrop for the actor's functioning. Because any female who later is able—for professional or other reasons—to adopt the governing mode is already fully familiar with this daily mode, the female theorist has greater access to the possibility of "chasm crossing" on a regular basis.[32] This gives the female theorist peculiar insight into the mode of functioning of others, and, more importantly, means that the female theorist is able to see the governing mode or voice for what it is—simply another mode, rather than the mode of dispassionate neutrality. In other words, when Smith is able, as a feminist sociologist, to see that her description of the Indian family watching her train is merely one among many possible descriptions, she has already been able to cross the chasm and can see the juxtaposition of the mode of everydayness alongside the male line of alleged objective inquiry.

What Smith is acknowledging, then, is that the sociological theorist always functions (insofar as justification is applicable to a set of sociological phenomena or problems) along the lines, roughly speaking, of conditions (ii) (a) (1)–(2) of CCP as formulated on pages 117–21. Here we mean, of course, to paint in very broad strokes: It is not necessary that an actual question be developed, nor that an articulable response appear, as the dialectic nature of the model would seem to demand. Rather, the point is, justification for my view in sociological terms relies on the notion that what counts as justification is based on the norms and practices of a given situation—including those very situations that would pretend not to be subject to norms and practices. If I am watching an Indian family from my train, I am aware that I, the investigator, am not Indian, that my point of view relies on my past, that there is another point of view here (namely, the Indian family watching me), and so forth. As Stehelin's work points out, and as Harms's analysis of Mannheim's work suggests, there is no "objective meaning" for social acts, that is, no account that is uninterpreted. A gynocentric epistemology understands this, and our localized gynocentric account is simply a more developed way of suggesting that the localized nature of epistemic justification is ubiquitous. The work of Smith and of Stehelin brings this focus on context, locale, and everydayness into a larger framework, so that a gynocentric sociology of knowledge results.

Our model probably meshes most intriguingly with the work done by Cook and Fonow, for they exhibit an unusual self-reflective sensitivity to the importance of context in areas where context is being investigated. It is one thing to be aware of the impact context has on allegedly scientific or objective investigations: It is still another thing to be able to theorize about this impact within the framework of one's overall view. Thus the portion of their methodology that asks the sociologist to refrain from adopting the putatively neutral stance recommended for sociological fieldwork exhibits the following self-reflective characteristics, which provide a striking exemplar of contextualization at work on a number of levels at once.

First, Cook and Fonow recommend that the feminist sociologist proceed by "allow[ing] the respondents to 'talk back' to the investigator."[33] This "talking back" will then trigger new lines of inquiry, which might not have been made available had the investigators chosen not to "talk with" the respondents. Clearly, the verbal input from the respondents yields new verbal output from the investigators, and so on, in a chain with great ramifications. These chains may then actually shift the ground of the original inquiry (at least to some extent, especially if no genuine attempt is made to retain the ground), and a new verbal context is created, itself subject to the same permutations, and so on.

Now when one takes into account Cook and Fonow's stated objective of challenging the norm of objectivity that "assumes that the subject and object of research can be separated from one another," one understands that the results of this research (already different in its methodology) will be interpreted along different lines; lines of actor-in-context rather than actor-as-objectified-individual.[34] So a double contextualization results, and the larger goal of the new methodological apparatus is at least—on a very small level, at each event—fulfilled.

This sort of inquiry does, in fact, constitute a virtual instantiation of much of CCP, for the investigators are asking, broadly, for justification. They may possibly be asking for narrowly focused epistemic justification, but even if they are not, what they are asking for is how the agent came to hold the beliefs that she is reporting. Her output, which for the moment assumes the role of justificatory set, then passes into input for the investigator (and, again, if one follows the model closely, one can think of naturalized mentalese here), which will in general start new lines of inquiry, and so forth, until the exchange is terminated. Intentionality is crucial, not only in the obvious sense that the agent must intend that the investigators recognize her response but also in the less obvious sense in which both agent and investigators must assume that the other recognizes their (mutual) desires to elicit further responses, and so on.

Thus Cook and Fonow not only construct a new sociological method that is in line with gynocentric epistemics, but, perhaps more important, they also advocate the utilization of that method for deeply feminist purposes.

Finally, both Oakley's work and the work of Adler, Adler, and Fontana exhibit strains that are in line with the naturalized model. Perhaps what is most interesting about Oakley's work, as I indicated at an earlier point, is the extent to which she is aware of the early and ubiquitous socialization for housework among females. As she says, "preparation for housewifery is intermingled with socialization for the feminine gender role in the wider sense."[35] Oakley does not explicitly discuss much of this socialization, but we know from our own experience that it consists both in extensive modeling of the practices (little girls spend hours, typically, watching their mothers wash, cook, and sew) and in verbalization of what the situation requires. The young female can not only see that older females are engaged in these tasks, but she is also frequently told that a certain method is the best, that a given way to do it is the appropriate way, and so forth. Rarely is she explicitly told that "women do housework" (it is, of course, unnecessary to say so), but she may occasionally be told that, too. Thus verbal and nonverbal patterns of communication and enactment provide the ground for the absorption of this socialization. Although I have not focused on the intersection of socialization and the more psychoanalytically oriented accounts that I have cited throughout the text, the obvious way in which one reinforces the other (also true for little boys) presents itself immediately. In the instance in which the youngster attempts to model behavior deemed appropriate to the opposite sex, he or she is often quickly dissuaded, taken to task, or pointed in another direction. Because of the importance of male rupture for the further socialization, it is probably true in most households that the little boy who shows much interest in housework receives even greater impetus to alter direction than the little girl who shows comparatively little, or who prefers outdoor or athletic activity.

Although the Adler work does not specifically allude to feminist theory, it is interesting to note that the same bifurcation between subject and object that is the topic of most of the work cited here is also crucial to their work. In other words, the sociology of everyday life requires that this bifurcation, or as they call it, the "subject–object dualism," be abandoned. One can imagine that the methodology they would advocate must in some sense be similar to Cook and Fonow's, since part of what it would mean to construct the sociology of the everyday would be to retain, as investigator, the everyday stance. They do not explicitly say this, however, in their article.

In this chapter I have attempted to provide a view of some feminist work in sociology of knowledge, as well as trends in sociology of knowledge in general, at least partly because the conventional wisdom in analytic philosophy has always tended to shove naturalizing moves in epistemology under the rubric of sociology of knowledge. What is interesting to note, however, is that there are dissimilarities between the two endeavors, and the articulation of the dissimilarities goes some distance toward helping to clarify issues that are relevant to a feminist epistemology.

## GYNOCENTRIC EPISTEMICS AND FEMINIST
## SOCIOLOGY: CONVERGENCES AND DIVERGENCES

As I have indicated in the preceding pages, sociology of knowledge will admit of no epistemic priority, and in this sense the traditional questions of epistemology—and indeed, of much of the rest of analytic philosophy insofar as it is related to epistemology—are irrelevant. They are irrelevant not simply because of their normative nature, but also because they seem to assume a view that is fundamental to and the groundwork for other views. But this tension, which I have described in various terms throughout the work (it is, to some extent, the normative/descriptive distinction itself, although it has also been referred to here, borrowing terminology, as the conflict between the view from nowhere and the view from everywhere) cannot simply be resolved, and indeed an awareness of the tension would seem to be conducive to epistemic health.

The androcentric normative project is a project among many, and it has an appeal and a history that make it, in certain circumstances, a project worth doing. The difficulty for the naturalizing epistemologist, the gynocentric epistemologist, or the epistemologist enamored of a certain psychological model of mind that would appear to be relevant to epistemological theory, has simply been that most of those who have worked on the normative project have deemed it to be the *only* project. From the standpoint of philosophy—that is, from the standpoint of epistemology *simpliciter* rather than sociology of knowledge it might be possible, were one so inclined, to utilize at least some of the material from naturalized epistemology to further the normative project. As I indicated in the second chapter, this is in fact what many theorists are currently trying to do.[36] So the gynocentric epistemics developed here has something in common with this project, insofar as it utilizes naturalized material.

That, of course, is far from being the whole story. The gynocentric view has something rather more in common with sociology of knowledge than it does with standard normative epistemology when the concept of the "view from everywhere" is taken into account. For the largest difference between the gynocentric account and the androcentric account might be thought to lie along the lines of epistemic tolerance, as it were. The goal of the gynocentric account is not to enervate the androcentric account—such an aim is itself consistent with the counterexampling, androcentric tradition. Rather the gyno-

centric account, when pressed, allows for the existence of a multiplicity of accounts, including standard normative epistemology. For when
context has great importance, it can cut through other debates. The
context for normative androcentric epistemology is, of course, professional epistemology itself, and any context-centered account would
recognize this. So part of the difference is that the gynocentric account
(more similar here to sociology of knowledge) would allow for the
existence of normative epistemology, whereas normative epistemology
does not valorize or admit the worth of naturalized accounts, gynocentric accounts, sociology of knowledge accounts, or any other accounts
that might be deviant in their structure.

The expansion of the CCP model, suggested in chapter seven by its
applicability to cross-cultural contexts and its special applicability to
cultures endowed with a strong oral tradition, as well as other areas of
behavior that are communicative but nonverbal, is fully consonant
with the framework provided by accounts drawn from sociology of
knowledge since they, too, are decided chiefly on context. The theoretic hegira provided by the move away from androcentric normative
thought leads to a multiplicity of places, rather than to just one place.
The work of the French theorists, which was examined in chapter six,
reminded us again of the strength of the psychoanalytically based
approaches to gender difference theory and underscored the development of strongly masculinist styles of thought. But even among males,
hypernormative theorizing is relevant only to certain endeavors. While
it may be true that much of the everyday thinking of males in general
retains the distancing flavor of the idealized and the normative, mundane modes of functioning (as investigated, for example, in sociology
of everyday life) do not usually readily lend themselves to intricate
theorizing. Thus CCP is applicable to all the realms of endeavor in
which the investigator—female or male, child or adult—functions
within the framework of the given and employs contextualized patterns
of awareness for knowledge acquisition.

The gynocentric view is by nature democratic in its outlook. The
hierarchical and detached nature of normative theorizing virtually
ensures the destruction of any given particular theory, since its putative universalizability can so easily be damaged by the attacks on its
consistency and coherence that it so readily spawns.

## NOTES

1. See Georges Gurvitch, *The Social Frameworks of Knowledge*, trans. Margaret A. Thompson and Kenneth A. Thompson (Oxford, U.K.: Basil Blackwell, Ltd., 1971).

2. Ibid., 19.

3. Emile Durkheim, from *Division du Travail Social*, quoted in Robert Nisbet, *The Sociology of Emile Durkheim* (Oxford, U.K.: Oxford University Press, 1974), 189.

4. Dorothy E. Smith, "Women's Perspective as a Radical Critique of Sociology," in *Sociological Inquiry* 44, no. 1 (1974):8–10.

5. Ibid., 10.

6. Ibid.

7. Ibid., 12.

8. Liliane Stehelin, "Sciences, Women and Ideology," in *The Radicalisation of Science*, ed. Hilary Rose and Stephen Rose (London: The Macmillan Press Ltd., 1976), 77.

9. Ibid., 87.

10. John Harms, "Mannheim's Sociology of Knowledge and the Interpretation of *Weltanschauungen*," *Social Science Journal* 21, no. 2 (1984):33–48.

11. Ibid., 35.

12. See, for example, Judith A. Cook, and Mary Margaret Fonow, "Knowledge and Women's Interests: Issues of Epistemology and Methodology in Feminist Research," in *Sociological Inquiry* 56, no. 1 (1986):2–29.

13. Smith, "Women's Perspective," 8.

14. Cook and Fonow, "Knowledge and Women's Interests," 5.

15. Ibid., 9.

16. Cook and Fonow are, then, advocating a view of knowledge acquisition on the part of sociologists that parallels CCP in its structure but also has the virtue of being a tool of liberation.

17. Her work is mentioned several times in Grimshaw, *Feminist Thinking*, for example. (CF. fn. 27, chap. 6.)

18. Ann Oakley, *The Sociology of Housework* (New York: Pantheon, 1974), 4.

19. Cook and Fonow, "Knowledge and Women's Interests," 24.

20. Smith, "Women's Perspective," 20.

21. Oakley, *Housework*, 4.

22. Ibid., 116.

23. Ibid., 113.

24. Emile Durkheim, from *Les Formes Elementaires de la Vie Religieuse*, trans. Anthony Giddens, and appearing in *Emile Durkheim: Selected Writings*, ed. Anthony Giddens (Cambridge, U.K.: Cambridge University Press, 1972), 265.

25. Ibid., 262.

26. Patricia A. Adler, Peter Adler, and Andrea Fontana, "Everyday Life Sociology," *Annual Review of Sociology* 13 (1987):218.

27. Ibid., 218–19.

28. Ibid.

29. Ibid., 225.

30. Gurvitch, *Social Frameworks,* 19.

31. Smith, "Women's Perspective," 8–10.

32. Ibid., 10.

33. Cook and Fonow, "Knowledge and Women's Interests," 9.

34. Ibid., 5.

35. Oakley, *Housework,* 113.

36. In chap. 2 I cited Goldman's work, in particular, along these lines.

*Part Four*

# CONCLUSION

# Chapter Nine

# The Future of the Gynocentric Model

I began this work by noting, in the Introduction, the variety of usages extant for the phrase "epistemology." I suggested that part of what was intriguing about the contemporary occurrences of the word in academic literature was the strikingly interdisciplinary quality of the citations. Just as the social sciences now employ the term "epistemology" with a great deal of frequency, the phrase "feminist epistemology" recurs throughout the sciences, and even in literary criticism. My initial suggestion was to the effect that although feminists might be inclined to want to spend theoretic time informing the epistemologists of what feminist theory could bring to bear on their efforts, a more intriguing (and rarer) employment of theoretical effort would try to show what feminist theory could learn from contemporary analytic epistemology as practiced by professional philosophers.

A great deal of effort was expended in the early chapters of this work on the point that contemporary epistemology does indeed have something to offer feminist theory, and the effort culminated in the naturalized gynocentric model of epistemic justification to be found in chapter four. The positive argument was made all the more difficult by the intrinsic conundrum that the androcentric nature of analytic epistemology, with its pretensions to universality and globality, in the style of the empiricism after which it models itself, would seem to prevent such a theory from being useful to a feminist line of thought in any discernible way.

In this concluding chapter I want to take some time to recapitulate

237

the sometimes rather intricate arguments utilized in the foregoing pages, hoping to clarify some points as I go along. More importantly, however, I want in the later sections of this chapter to spend some time on the future of feminist epistemology. In chapter two, and again in chapter five, I suggested that stronger, more empirically confirmable views were in the process of being formulated, and that the continuing intersection of epistemology and philosophy of mind (especially as formulated by those interested in the connectionist models) might in the future be the indisputable locus of more tightly constructed, naturalized epistemologies. However, as I argued in chapters six through eight, it is not enough merely to assert that a given model does a certain amount of theoretic work. Our model may at first appear to be only another of the "writ small" versions of epistemic justification so dear to contemporary epistemologists, and (one might hypothesize) useless to women's concerns and women's values. Whatever the future may hold, models employed for feminist purposes must also exhibit the "writ large" quality that, I claim, CCP does exhibit—along with focusing on epistemic justification, it is a rough-and-ready model for all the sorts of intentional interactions that, from the gynocentric point of view, form the heart of knowledge acquisition and cannot be ignored. My utilization of both object-relations theory and the socialization process as explanations for male/female differences simply reminds us of the diffuse and connecting quality of interaction seen from the gynocentric point of view. That which is a virtue—or even the defining characteristic—of standard androcentric epistemology is a defect when seen from the female point of view. Thus the challenge for a view that would attempt to construct a future for naturalized epistemics based on current work in connectionism, neural networks, and the like, is to see whether such a hypothetical advance would retain the all-encompassing quality of feminist epistemology.

## THE PRECEDING CHAPTERS: AN OVERVIEW

My argument has been a lengthy and somewhat recondite one, and I will repeat parts of it here before attempting to go on to new work. I will proceed on a chapter-by-chapter basis, and then show how tying a number of threads together from several of the more central chapters leads us in the direction of new, still more naturalized work.

In the Introduction I was concerned primarily to set the stage for the intersection of naturalized analytic epistemology and the feminist epistemology that has been manifested so far in the literature. I discussed the episodic use of the term "epistemology" in a number of disciplines, or even areas within one discipline, and I specifically cited the lack of development within philosophy itself of work that would incorporate twentieth-century analytic epistemology into feminist theory. This lacuna seems all the more regrettable, as I pointed out, because philosophy is, after all, the home or point of origin of the phrase "epistemology," and one would reason that philosophy as a discipline might have the most to contribute to the development of a feminist epistemics. I mentioned that neither feminist epistemology as currently formulated, nor the more naturalized versions of analytic epistemology, seems concerned with the traditional problems of theory of knowledge: skepticism and replies to the skeptic. One immediate area of congruence, then, for the two areas whose intersection I was hoping to construct, was shown to be their assumption that replying to skeptical views is far from paramount in importance, and that one can, at least along some lines, assume knowledge and knowers.

I then began to recapitulate, very briefly, some of the androcentric origins of contemporary epistemology as practiced by professional philosophers. Plato's concern to avoid the contamination of the bodily, and his general homoerotic stance, which implies a distanced sexuality as the analogue of his distanced epistemology, was alluded to, and I also made some mention of Descartes. I cited Keller, in particular, for her brilliant work on the relationship between Plato's view of sex and his ontological/epistemological commitments, and I also cited Bordo and Harding briefly as developing this same theme. Finally, I included a rather extensive quotation from one of the works usually presented in any contemporary graduate seminar on epistemology—Laurence BonJour's *The Structure of Empirical Knowledge*. I exhibited BonJour's work as exemplary, for he does, interestingly enough, make the distinction between epistemic justification and other "species" of justification, a distinction not frequently made by epistemologists.[1] But what I tried to show by utilizing BonJour's examples is that the most frequently employed types of justification—those that are nonepistemic—are seldom referred to in theorizing and may be more important to the development of a naturalized epistemology than has previously been thought. It is, I contended, the normative nature of virtually all standard contemporary epistemology that forces the theorist to disregard the psychologically frequent, but theoretically nonsalient, modes of justification that may very well be tied intimately to what we refer to as epistemic justification.

Finally, I referred to Gilligan's work at the close of the Introduction, and tried to make the point that the distinctions made by Gilligan in her citations of the "justice voice" and the "care voice" have their parallels in contemporary epistemic justification theory, particularly when one thinks of normative foundationalism as the analogue of the justice voice, and a more naturalized, cohering view as the analogue of the care voice. I closed the Introduction by remarking that the nature of the project was such that my focus would be on the attempt to ameliorate feminist theory with the material of naturalized analytic epistemology, rather than the converse project, which would be the attempt to explain to the analytic epistemologist what he or she could learn from feminist theory.

I opened chapter one with the note that the broad charge that twentieth-century analytic philosophy has been overwhelmingly normative, and that it leads (by however unlikely a path) to an outcome that is somewhat more naturalized and hence useful to the feminist epistemologist, is one that would have to be supported in detail. I chose to present an overview of the normative and nonnaturalized epistemology of Anglo-American analytic philosophy in chapter one, and then to move on to the more contemporary work, both naturalized and nonnaturalized, in chapter two.

I began chapter one with citations from the work of Bertrand Russell. I first noted Russell's rather well known comment that the "importance of theory of knowledge in philosophy is due to the influence of Descartes," and I then cited Russell's own philosophy of logical atomism as an exemplar of the rigidly normative and idealized character of early epistemology in this century.[2] The important philosophical points here revolve around the precision of the ontology and the alleged irrefutability of claims made in the concomitant epistemology. Russell pared down his ontology to fleeting nameables in an attempt to provide an incorrigible basis for at least some knowledge claims. I then noted that this sort of theorizing moved swiftly and inevitably to the sense-data views, where, again, the construction of a certain metaphysics seemed tied—in the right sort of way—to the construction of an epistemology that would place empirical claims on a footing analogous to the certainty of purely deductive claims.

If the sense-data views had a certain appeal because of the architectonic structure they embodied, they also made for a certain squeamishness, and I next proceeded to discuss the Austinian replies to sense-data views. The replies led, in an indirect way perhaps, to some of the work in epistemology that was eventually to become more naturalized, for Austin's focus was to a large extent on the non-naturalness of these sorts of views.

After having made note of Austin's work on "looks" locutions, I then spent quite a bit of time on that paradigm of contemporary American epistemology, the set of examples constructed by Gettier. I took the trouble to recapitulate one full-length example, for, as I remarked, these counters to the triadic thesis of justified true belief were noteworthy for their reliance on a logically formulated set of necessary and sufficient conditions. Indeed, in the example I quoted, the counter is constructed by employing the rule of the disjunction, and the sentence "Either Jones owns a Ford, or Brown is in Barcelona" is true simply by virtue of that rule, even though the two disjuncts are unrelated to each other epistemically or from the standpoint of evidence.[3]

It is the replies to the Gettier examples, as I noted at length in chapter one, that finally give rise to the developments in epistemology that are more fruitful from the point of view I have espoused here. One line of replies, somewhat parasitical on the logically structured format of the original examples, is defeasibility theory; the second, which is directly related to what later becomes naturalized epistemology, is the causal line. I provided examples from both sorts of replies but I was particularly concerned to discuss Goldman's trenchant critique of the examples, since Goldman's work led naturally into the next set of developments in epistemology. Unlike the defeasibility theorists, Goldman manifested an interest in cognitive functioning even in "A Causal Theory of Knowing," which is his response to the Gettier counters. Goldman writes of "mental states"; the defeasibility theorists are concerned only to formulate a set of noncounterable necessary and sufficient conditions for knowledge.[4]

Finally, I ended the first chapter by citing some of the moves that led to the more naturalized work of the late 1970s and early 1980s. Kornblith's assertion that "One of the legacies of positivist epistemology is a tendency to divorce epistemological questions from psychological questions" sums up much of the material in chapter one and leads into chapter two.[5]

In chapter two I tried to sketch the various relevant portions of naturalized analytic epistemology, prior to developing these, with appropriate constraints from already established feminist theory, as a feminist epistemics. I started out by citing more of Goldman's work, his book in particular, and noted the relevance of traditional psychological categories such as belief, perception, STM, and LTM to his work and to epistemology. I then spent a good deal of time on some of Hilary Kornblith's more recent work, which has an emphasis on the social features of cognition, and, indeed, on the social construction of knowledge. Traditional epistemology as worked through the analytic view has always distanced itself from the recognition of social factors—perhaps even more so than psychological factors—so I took Kornblith's work on the reliable cognition of childhood to be extremely important. Kornblith's work is also helpful simply for the very clear and precise way in which he articulates the distinction between the kinds of issues with which traditional epistemology has concerned itself and the kinds of issues that are actually germane to the topic of knowledge acquisition, and I quoted Kornblith at length on this topic.[6]

Perhaps the most exciting moves in naturalized epistemology currently stem from work in philosophy of mind, and the somewhat collectivized nature of this project becomes more evident when the layered nature of the work is made manifest. Part of what it means to naturalize either epistemology or philosophy of mind is to become cognizant, theoretically, of the importance of the computational model of mind. I cited first the work of Patricia Smith Churchland, and in passing, that of several well-known philosophers of mind and cognitive scientists. Churchland argues for the in-principle reducibility of most of the extant work in mind to the neurophysiological level, and this, of course, has immediate ramifications for the naturalizing epistemologist. As I noted while beginning the tie-in to more overtly feminist material, "The upshot of the naturalization of views of the mental . . . is that . . . [it] will almost doubtlessly reveal trends in behavior which are more consonant with several lines of endeavor suggested by feminist theorists. . . . All that we know currently . . . suggests that input conditions for cognitive functioning are affected markedly by environment. . . ."[7]

Finally, I cited the superb work of Lynne Rudder Baker in *Saving Belief*, which turns out to be highly relevant to any attempt to develop a feminist epistemics from naturalized epistemology. For Baker catalogues a number of positions in contemporary philosophy of mind that hinge on the now-crucial question of the status of folk-psychological terms. It has been suggested by those who have attempted work in feminist epistemology, or more specifically feminist philosophy of mind, that the importance of "beliefs" and contexts for beliefs cannot be overestimated. But some of the work in highly rigorous philosophy of mind has tended to suggest that folk-psychological terms are irredeemably non-nomological: One might well wonder whether there is a way out of this contretemps. Baker's work on Dennett's instrumental use of folk psychology is cited, and her arguments against some of the rampantly anti-folk material explored.[8] I ended the second chapter with some notes on the newer, connectionist material, and the warning that since naturalized material proceeds to reproduce apace, the feminist theorist who wants to remain current in this area has her work cut out for her.

In chapter three my concern was to introduce the material in feminist epistemology as it has been done up to now in a manner such that it would lend itself readily to a meshing with naturalized epistemology. Perhaps the main difficulty is one of style: The work that has been done in feminist epistemics so far, probably because it is taken to be an exemplar of the very epistemology it promulgates, has tended to be somewhat less than rigorous, relying on an intuitive comprehension of folk-psychological terminology. In addition, much of what has driven the construction of a feminist epistemology has derived from material culled from other disciplines: The object-relations theory of traditional psychoanalysis has had a major impact, and Marxist theory, contemporary Continental work, and work from such disciplines as sociology and anthropology has been given a prominent place.

In chapter three I devoted a great deal of time to an attempt to explicate the feminist epistemology of three theorists: Evelyn Fox Keller, Sandra Harding, and Susan Bordo. I praised Keller's work for its reliance on actual scientific work, and for its development of a feminist philosophy of science—part, of course, of a feminist episte mology—that ties the Western epistemological tradition to the Western sexual tradition. I quoted at length Keller's commentary on slime mold models, a beautiful example of the precision of classical philosophy of science imbued with a powerful feminism.

I next turned to what many regard as the most important work on feminist epistemology in the past decade, Harding's *The Science Question in Feminism*. It is Harding who has given us many or most of the categories in which nascent feminist epistemology is usually constructed—feminist empiricism, the feminist standpoint theories, and feminist postmodernism. Because of the importance of Harding's work, I felt constrained to spend quite some time on each of these divisions, while noting what I hoped would be an important theme for the following chapter, the somewhat truncated development of feminist empiricism.

Harding's critique of feminist empiricism I summarized as being brief and to the point. The empiricist stance in feminism amounts to a commitment to the traditional canons of scientific research, its norms and its purported objectivity, along with a concern for altering the exclusionary tactics that have kept women out of the sciences, and concern for changing the topics under consideration in the research projects of the various sciences so that projects more relevant to women are brought to the fore. Harding mentions that there is a gross inconsistency at the heart of feminist empiricism: If empiricist methods are as objective as they claim to be, what difference could it make how many women are involved? And, furthermore, according to Harding, the empiricist stance has always involved itself in the "context of justification" (that is, normative matters), when it is really the "context of discovery" that should be at the core of concerns for the amelioration of scientific practice.

The feminist standpoint epistemologies, according to Harding, have more to offer: Since they derive largely from post-Marxist theory and from insights that women's social standpoint—particularly with regard to division of labor—yields a unique epistemological perspective, they are able to offer up a critique of scientific practice that is more radical and thoroughgoing than that offered by the relatively tepid feminist empiricism. Harding cites the work of Jane Flax, Nancy Hartsock, Hilary Rose, and Dorothy Smith; I focused mainly on the work of Flax and of Hartsock. Finally, as I noted, Harding ends her work with a view of what she labels "feminist postmodernism," the somewhat deconstructive view derived from Derrida and others that allows us to claim that the voice of Western culture is so fractured (and the multiplicity of women's voices so great, even when they are in opposition to Western culture) that it does not make sense to speak of a feminist epistemology or a feminist standpoint.

My concern in presenting Harding's work was twofold: I had hoped to show the importance of the categorization created by Harding, valuable as it is for future feminist theorizing, and also to indicate that I found the dismissal of feminist empiricism too quick and somewhat too heavy-handed. Hoping to set the stage for the construction of another version of what might be thought to fall under the rubric of feminist empiricism in the following chapter, I then turned to the work of Susan Bordo, and briefly to the work of other feminist theorists, before moving on to the more original and constructive work of chapter four.

Although Bordo's work is perhaps less immediately relevant to my project than either Keller's or Harding's, the incisive relevance of her work for a feminist epistemics lies at least partly in her treatment of

Descartes and the beginnings of the Cartesian tradition from an historical–cultural perspective that helps us to understand the power of the normative tradition I had outlined in chapters one and two.

Bordo writes insightfully of Descartes's renunciation of the body (and, implicitly, of the metaphysics and epistemology that flow from it) as brought on at least partially by a shift in European culture from the organic unity of the Middle Ages to the more distanced and pretentious objectivity of the late Renaissance. Here something a bit more sophisticated and polished than a straightforward object-relations view is utilized; although that terminology is no doubt directly related, Bordo writes of the "Drama of Parturition" more with respect to European culture itself than with respect to the psychological development of any one individual within the culture.[9] In any case, Bordo sees Descartes as the victim of a cultural disruption. She notes that the beginnings of a sensibility of spatial location and one's individuation within the world can be found around the time of Descartes's writings; summing up, she notes that "It seems clear that for the medieval aesthetic imagination, absorption in the world rather than locatedness in the world was central."[10] I closed chapter three by citing, briefly, the work of others who have clarified some of what is involved in a feminist epistemology—I mentioned Ruth Hubbard, Helen Longino, Elizabeth Prior and Robert Pargetter, Lorraine Code, and Alison Wylie. Although enough has already been done along the lines of the development of feminist epistemology so that much work was cited only briefly, I presented an overview of Keller, Harding, Bordo, and the authors mentioned immediately above at the close of chapter three with the hope that this material, combined with the naturalized material from chapter two and with the recognition of the strong normative tradition in epistemology that is delineated in chapter one, would move us directly to the development of a feminist epistemics in chapter four.

I began that chapter, before the presentation of the CCP model, with the major theoretical question that I claimed was directly related to the sort of question Harding attempted to respond to in her perusal of feminist empiricism. My stated goal in the opening chapters had been to develop a feminist epistemic that at the same time utilized some of the more recent work in naturalized analytic epistemology, almost all of which was developed by males and almost all of which bore no obvious relevance to feminist concerns or even to general issues of social sensitivity and progressiveness. The question, then, was this: Is it possible to utilize the androcentric analytic epistemology of standard

Anglo-American work, however naturalized, for feminist ends? In trying to argue that such work could be so employed, I developed a two-pronged response. The main positive argument was that the epistemology to be employed is naturalized, not normative, and hence is already more responsive to the kinds of concerns (of context, groundedness, and relatedness, in particular, à la the work of the standpoint epistemologists) that have characterized feminist epistemology. The second argument, itself split into two sections, was essentially a counterargument to the implicit claim that analytic epistemology, the theory of knowledge analogue of science's empiricism, should not be used for feminist endeavors: in the first I delineated the areas of theory available for feminist epistemics and categorized all available areas as androcentric, perhaps with only a variation of degrees. Second and more importantly, I argued that the virtues of analytic precision, whether they be of androcentric origin or not, are sufficiently strong that the failure of feminist theory to use them would represent a major theoretical oversight.

My positive line cited again the work of chapter two, where concern for incorrigibility and constructing a reply to the skeptic has been replaced by concern for functioning in an epistemic context, and in my counterargument I cited the androcentricity of Lacanian and Marxist theory (possible alternatives to the utilization of analytic theory), and the virtues of analytic rigor as well as the dangers of relying completely on an aesthetically appealing and metaphorically apt but vague theoretic for the development of feminist work.

I then spent several pages developing the notions of contextualization, communication, and sensory awareness from the work of such thinkers as Flax and Hartsock (as delineated by Harding) and intersecting them with the work of Kornblith, Goldman, and others. I finally presented the CCP model (Contextualist and Communicative Principles), based on responses to a coherentist model of epistemic justification originally set out by James Cornman but developed along naturalized lines that emphasize the notion of a cohering justificatory set as determined by context and intentional communication (verbal or nonverbal) within a context. My initially stated model (in standard analytic format) relied on several conjuncts, which were then further naturalized a few pages later by amending the notions of input–output of epistemic agents with computational theory. I mentioned, in passing, that there was nothing to prevent the model being still further naturalized (in the vein of a connectionist model, for example) at a later point.

Throughout the chapter, I was at pains to note that the tradition that gave rise to Gettier-type counterexampling has already come up against hard times, hence the fact that CCP is not normative and is of no use (or, at best, little use) in responding to the traditional concerns of epistemology is as irrelevant to much of contemporary theory of knowledge as it is to feminist epistemics. In any case, I sketched one more problematic area for a feminist epistemics relying on a computational model of mind and a notion of communication that involves intentionality: the inconsistencies of intentionality/computation, according to much of the recent work in philosophy of mind. Since philosophy of mind is directly tied to naturalized epistemology, as I had shown in chapter two, I devoted the following chapter to the effort to come to grips with some of the alleged theoretical inconsistencies.

Chapter five began with allusion to the problem posed by the use of folk psychological terms (such as "belief," relevant to the coherentist notion of a belief set, and determined in CCP largely by context and communication) within the framework of a computational model. Although CCP is hardly a full-fledged model in this tradition, the importance of feminist work in epistemology and philosophy of mind demands that for the future development of such work these problems be addressed.

Just as chapters two and three had been constructed around the work of major theorists, chapter five is built along the lines of a brief look at the work of four philosophers of mind: Dennett, Fodor, Stich, and Van Gulick. (A still more cursory look is taken at relevant portions of work by Millikan, Searle, and Heil.) Although the theorists vary in their commitment to the possibility of the usage of folk-psychological terms within the framework of a computational or functionalist account of mind (with Stich being the least hopeful, in this particular group), I tried to sketch some possible views of a computational model that allows the use of mundane psychological terms—even if strictly on a non-nomological basis—since the grounded and contextualized nature of a gynocentric epistemics would seem to require this.

Dennett's work was deemed to be the most optimistic. He was cited specifically for his notation that "Folk psychology is abstract in that the beliefs and desires it attributes are not—or need not be—presumed to be intervening distinguishable states of an internal behavior-causing system. . . ."[11]

As I noted in the commentary following that passage, "Thus our CCP model is at least partially vindicated by the Dennetian argument that the intentional stance is not wholly inconsistent with the computational model. . . ."[12] I then cited work from Millikan and Searle that seemed to further this general line of argument while noting that the Dennettian-Millikanian-Searlian position is far from popular in some circles.

Fodor's view, although it seems to be open to a number of interpretations, is not as hospitable, in general, to intentionality as is Dennett's. I noted that Fodor places a great deal of importance on the syntactic relations that constitute the formal operations of the computational view, and he emphasizes, insofar as his methodological solipsism is concerned, that "mental processes that explain behavior must be considered in abstraction from the environment of the individual whose behavior is to be explained."[13] This solipsism forces a theoretical underlining of the hardware portions of the computational model, which are the portions least relevant to intentionality.

Since I was concerned to mention that Fodor's view is not readily compatible with an intentionalistic outlook—at least, not in the way that Dennett's is—I took the time at that point in the text to remind the reader of what virtues the computational model allegedly possesses that other, older models do not. Although in chapter two (and to some extent in other chapters) I reminded the reader that our model, or other models reliant on mental modeling, could eventually be fleshed out in connectionist or more purely neural terms, the computational model seems regnant, at least at this time. Connectionism is still not completely developed and the popularity of the computational model needs to be addressed. I tried to be specific about the defects of the more purely behavioristic theorizing that preceded the computational model, and then turned to an overview of the importance of intentionality for feminist theory before looking at the work of other philosophers of mind.

In a brief section on the relevance of intentionality in general for gynocentric theory, I recapitulated the importance of the notion of intersubjectivity, crucial to the development of a feminist epistemology. In addition, I noted the "world-making" powers of women, both for themselves and others. Women construct personal ontologies, I argued, on the basis of their groundedness, and women are crucial in the construction of personal ontologies for others, since almost all of us are reared during our most formative years by females and since females so commonly bear the burden of the upkeep of interpersonal communication within our society.

Finally, I closed chapter five by looking briefly at Stich's anti-folk-psychology stance, and the importance of his construction of folk-psychological terms as non-nomological. I also cited Van Gulick on the ambiguity inherent in the term "representation": in one construction a representation comes with a certain degree of intentionality attached, as it were, and in another construction it does not. From a behavioral standpoint, even animals exhibit some degree of intentionality, which is why we so frequently couch our descriptions of animals' behavior in folk-psychological terms.

From chapter five on, the flavor of the work here became somewhat less analytic and certainly somewhat less rigorously theoretical, for chapters six through eight constitute another way of viewing some of the problematic areas of gynocentric epistemology. Although I have not focused on Continental theory in this work, it cannot be ignored, simply because it has already exerted a pronounced effect on American publications and it has been one of the main avenues through which feminist theory gained popularity in the United States. (At this point the reader can probably answer her or his own question as to why feminist theory might seem more palatable to many in Continental, rather than analytic, guise.) In chapter six I undertook a brief overview of recent French work, given that the postmodernist theorizing in France has had so much influence on Anglo-American work.

I initially concentrated in chapter six on Cixous, Irigaray, and Kristeva, and then added commentary on the work of Michele Le Doeuff, Arlette Farge, and Annie Leclerc. Paring down the lines of theory that, taken in toto, form French work, the natural intersection between the work of the French thinkers and Anglo-American feminist theory—particularly any theory that is relevant to the development of a feminist epistemology—is, again, the object-relations theoretical stance. For the French thinkers seem, on the whole, more ready to assimilate the importance of such a psychoanalytically based model and to derive whatever is to be derived from it in a manner consistent with the notion that there is a specifically female voice.

In focusing initially on the work of Cixous, I chose to highlight the work of someone who exploits the dissonances between male and female modes of thought (and hence, male and female voices) to the advantage of the marginalized female voice. I cited the theoretical difficulty in Cixous's work, if one is concerned about inconsistencies between the notion of forging a female voice and obtaining a voice that does not suffer from the defects of "phallogocentrism." I cited "The Laugh of the Medusa" specifically, and also utilized some material from the work of Alice Jardine, who raises our consciousness about the appropriateness (or inappropriateness) of labeling the French theorists as "feminist." The work of Irigaray is still more to our purpose, I believe, not in the least because of the fact that Irigaray makes a strong effort to tie together the object-relations view with the dominance and distancing of the scientific, detached, normatively epistemological voice. Irigaray meshes the Freudian notion that for the developing young male the mother figure is part of a "bobbin game" that involves learning how to obtain her presence—or absence—by the use of signs and language, with the notion of symbolic distancing in general, and with the notion that there is a master or male discourse. This language and mode of signification, of course, is what underlies science and the other paradigmatically male endeavors in theory. As Irigaray wrote in "Le Sujet de la Science: Est-il Sexué?": "Does discourse remain at the level of partially theoretical exchanges between generations of men concerning mastery of the mother, of nature?"[14]

Finally, Kristeva takes up, in a manner not unlike Cixous, the notion of the female voice, with special significance attached to the notion of Otherness. I cited Kristeva on the notion that the female voice displays its own ethics or jouissance, and then spent time on Le Doeuff, Farge, and Leclerc. Le Doeuff attacks straightforwardly, in the piece cited here, the notion that the female could encounter the male discourse (specifically, the form of philosophy) in anything like the manner in which the male encounters it; Farge notes the extent to which history, in France, is still a quintessentially male discourse. Leclerc, in a piece excerpted from *Parole de femme,* attacks the nature of the dichotomizing that, while inherently male, purports to be neutral and devalues the female—as in the androcentric (and culturally hegemonous) view of housework that prevails in the Western world.[15] I ended the chapter by noting one area of divergence between the French and Anglo-American theorists: While French and/or Continental notions of the female voice remain largely metaphorical, thinkers working within the Anglo-American tradition have generally opted for a more precise and theoretically rigorous characterization of the voice, and hence of its concomitant epistemology, even if some of the models have not been as rigorous or perspicuous as they could be.

In chapter seven I chose to attempt to be more specific about one of the areas that has been a glaring lacuna in most feminist theory so far: the difficulty of writing or thinking about a feminist epistemics that would encompass anything like the fragmented variety of views constituting women's voice(s). In chapter three we saw that Harding moved toward feminist postmodernism, and somewhat away from both feminist empiricism and the standpoint epistemologies, precisely because of this problem. In Anglo-American work, the voices of Third World women have frequently been omitted, and much of the early theorizing was either blatantly heterosexist or included lesbian theorizing in only the most superficial way. Chapter seven attempted to accomplish two tasks: Since CCP, the model developed in chapter four on the basis of work in both naturalized analytic epistemology and feminist epistemology, is essentially a model that relies on verbal communication—or nonverbal communication that reduces to some form of human interaction—it seemed important to try to show how CCP could account for the variety of women's voices and hence of women's ontology construction and epistemological development. Second, the emphasis on portions of the theory on sexuality and object-relations theory virtually cried out for an analysis along the lines of sexuality as a form of nonverbal communication itself, and this was the project of the latter portion of chapter seven.

In the earlier part of the chapter I attempted to utilize material from several different viewpoints to elaborate on the notion that CCP is applicable in ways more normative models simply are not. Necessarily, only a few viewpoints could be represented—because they have been comparatively underrepresented in material developed by white middle-class feminist scholars, I chose writers and thinkers from the black, Asian American, Native American, and Latin American communities as exemplary of the multitude of women's voices simply within our national boundaries. I then applied some of the insights of these thinkers about female communication within their respective traditions to the CCP model earlier developed. One emergent note was immediately obvious: All of the traditions tend to focus more on orality than does the white middle-class Anglo tradition, and this, in a sense, makes a gynocentric epistemics like CCP more, not less, applicable to the range of female thought and communicative modes. Particularly apt was material from Paula Gunn Allen, whose development of the notions of Native American metaphysics and ontology construction is virtually completely along the lines of interaction within an oral tradition. I also briefly discussed charges of relativism that, although they belong more completely within the traditional androcentric framework, might possibly be brought to bear on our model at this point.

Insofar as sexuality is concerned, I noted the extent to which our accepted models of sexual interaction (some of which are actually the product of analytic philosophers) are, again, androcentric, and focused on the male defenses of distancing (in heterosexual intercourse) from the female body and viewing the body itself, rather than the person, as the object of desire. Since a female-centered sexuality cannot and does not construe the other in such terms, CCP is metaphorically applicable in the sense that a gynocentric sexuality is centered around a notion of communication with another, and possibly less metaphorically—and more strictly—applicable if such communication is seen as the heart of sexuality. Although the focus here is on differentiating between androcentric and gynocentric views of heterosexual intercourse, one could hypothesize that the elements of lesbian theory or lesbian thought that emphasize a transcendental heightening and consummated merging in sex are simply ramifications of the gynocentric desire to know the other and to experience joy within the body that are at the core of a feminist sexual theory.

Chapter seven, then, attempted to fill in the gaps as to how the naturalized epistemic model might be relevant to what has been termed the multiplicity of women's voices. One more major task remained, however. Throughout the work, I have focused on object-relations theory and an account of the origins of androcentric theorizing that within the recent literature has sometimes been termed "the Chodorow/Gilligan thesis."[16] I have tended not to discuss the aspects of feminist theory that emphasize socialization, partly because I feel that such aspects may well be deemed secondary, insofar as the origins of androcentric theory are concerned, and partly because much of the Anglo-American literature within philosophy itself has followed the lines of the Gilligan/Chodorow interpretation.[17] But it is clear that a model like CCP, which relies on communication, is at heart a model sensitive to social nuance, and here one may cite some of the work in sociology of knowledge and sociology itself with regard to the ramifications of full-blown feminist theory.

Hence, in chapter eight I tried to be specific about the ways in which contemporary sociology of knowledge, in particular, has developed feminist lines and has provided us with a useful analysis of the origins of androcentric theory structure. As I mentioned at the outset of the chapter, sociology of knowledge is particularly relevant to the model employed herein because it goes against the normative notion that there is any one view that is epistemically privileged. Sociology of knowledge, then, has always run contra the slant of twentieth-century analytic epistemology, and this makes it a particularly fruitful tool for our purposes.

I began by citing the work of Dorothy Smith (which was also examined extensively by Harding), and I focused especially on Smith's notion that the "governing mode" of observation and theory construction is but simply one mode among many. Smith's argument on this point is recapitulated and developed to some extent by Stehelin, and still more work has been done by Cook and Fonow. The latter flatly state that "[there is a] need to challenge the norm of objectivity that assumes that the subject and object of research can be separated from one another and that personal and/or grounded experiences are unscientific."[18] It is also with Cook and Fonow that one gets the radicalized view of sociology as a force for breaking down patriarchal structure—this activist viewpoint is one that I have not emphasized here, but it is, of course, related directly to the recognition of the function of androcentricity in theory-building and in the maintenance of everyday relations in such a mode that they can more easily be interpreted androcentrically.

Further work on patterns of female socialization followed with a look at Ann Oakley's sociological analysis of housework. The importance of a sociology of the everyday is emphasized by Adler, Adler, and Fontana in an interesting piece entitled "Everyday Life Sociology." As I mentioned in my analysis of their work, they make the comment that their "everyday" sociology has encountered trouble from the sociological establishment precisely because it rejects the "absolutist stance" that tends to characterize acceptable academic sociology—a stance that is, epistemically and otherwise, androcentric. I ended the chapter by again trying to be precise about the intersection between CCP as sketched in chapter four and sociology of knowledge. Although sociology of knowledge does not in general have any interest in the perceptual or neurological capacities that inform some portions of naturalized epistemology, the convergence from the standpoint of communication alone is quite easily derived.

My recapitulation of the work done in the preceding chapters aids, I hope, in tying together some lines of argument that might have been too intricate or too detached to follow on a chapter-to-chapter basis. But in providing a review of the previous eight chapters, I hope also to set the stage for a brief foray into new material before concluding the work.

## THE CONNECTIONIST MODEL AND THE FUTURE OF FEMINIST EPISTEMOLOGY

In chapter two (and in commentary sprinkled throughout the text) I mentioned the importance of mental models that supersede the by now somewhat outdated computational model of mind and that pave the way toward a view of mental functioning that is, in general, more consonant with what we now know about physiology. I have, at various times, referred to the connectionist material and its relationship to naturalized epistemology, and also to what Churchland and others have referred to as "neurophilosophy."[19]

Although I have made the argument that this material is relevant to feminist theory at least partly because it fills in the blanks on the descriptively accurate and contextually grounded views that have informed so much of this text, there is still another sense in which the connectionist material is relevant that has received rather less emphasis here. The connectionist and neurophysiological material is relevant not only for the aforementioned reasons, but also because it is material about the body. In chapter four I mentioned briefly that the emphasis on in-the-bodiness in feminist theory could be ameliorated at least partly by adversion to, for example, the perceptual processes under investigation by naturalized epistemology, but I did not go into this topic in any depth.

The objection that naturally occurs here is perhaps similar to one of the objections we encountered at the beginning of chapter four and to some extent in our analysis of feminist empiricism and the standpoint epistemologies in chapter three. The uses of "in-the-bodiness" in the literature tend to be either rather metaphorical, or, when they are more than metaphorical, to be uses that focus on reproduction. But I take it that part of what is implicitly meant by this awareness-of-body—even if it is not completely spelled out—is that contextualization is related to and dependent upon bodily awareness of context through the senses. And in this construction of the phrase, naturalized epistemology in the form of newer movements along the lines of connectionism and neurological functioning is particularly apt for a closing look at how the future of epistemology might be relevant to feminist theory.

If the future of the connectionist model is helpful, it will be helpful at least partly because it aids us in delineating the extent to which in-the-bodiness permeates gynocentric accounts of knowledge, and delineating this in a very specific way.

Keller, in a piece not cited heretofore in this work, has argued that the notion of gaze is an important one for the examination of androcentric points of view.[20] The masculinist gaze seeks to dominate; the female-centered gaze seeks to know or become acquainted with. This account of metaphorical (or even actual) vision is, of course, related to material we have covered here at an earlier point, and is part and parcel of the distancing that we have characterized as being central to androcentrism.

But if the gynocentric gaze is different in its aim and function from the masculine gaze, then the contextual information pickup of the female may very well be different from that of the male. When the sociolinguists remind us of the important differences between male and female speech patterns, or of the manner in which males and females utilize the social and contextual knowledge that they have accrued (and here we could use some of the work of Adler, Adler, and Fontana on the sociology of the everyday from the preceding chapter), they are also, implicitly, reminding us of differences in information pickup.[21] And it is clear that, although so far connectionist models have not become sufficiently developed to aid us in a conceptual grasp of these differences, they might be able to do so in the future, particularly if neurophysiology itself can help pinpoint some relevant male/female differences (always assuming that these differences do, in fact, show up on the neurophysiological level).

In chapter seventeen of the two-volume Rumelhart and McClelland work cited earlier ("A Distributed Model of Human Learning and Memory"),[22] the authors are at pains to point out how differences between the connectionist account of memory functioning and the accounts provided by previous models are crucial in accounting for some of the empirical findings of the experimental psychologists who have worked on memory.[23] Although the authors are not, of course, interested in conveying any differences in male/female functioning, one could easily hypothesize how the material relates to the female focus on context-at-hand and sensitivity toward visual and auditory cues (especially cues of a communicative nature) within a given context.

Rumelhart and McClelland write:

A large number of experiments, going back to the seminal findings of Posner and Kiele, indicate that we appear to extract what is common to a set of experiences. On the basis of this sort of evidence, a number of theorists have proposed that memory is largely a matter of generalized representations, either abstract representations of concepts discarding irrelevant features, or prototypes—representations of typical exemplars.[24]

The authors model the functioning of such a system by assigning numerical values to postulated units and then letting values function as activations and traces. It is here that the neurophilosopher might well want to interject the point that these hypothesized units are virtually completely unspecified neurologically, and so they are. But the virtue of the model is that it is at least somewhat more isomorphic to the actual functioning of the brain and its interconnecting synapses than the previous computational model, was. Although the connectionists can no more specify whether the "unit" in question is the neural synapse, several of them, or something larger still (the work is not advanced enough here for us to be able to say), the fact that a network of units is alluded to does, as Rumelhart and McClelland claim, "model the microstructure of cognition."[25]

The model provides a degree of specificity such that the claim is that a particular feature of a visual object, such as its color, is a pattern of activation over a group of units. Thus,

> In a distributed memory system, a mental state is a pattern of activation over the units in some subset of the modules. The patterns in the different modules capture different aspects of the content of the mental states in a kind of partially overlapping fashion. . . . our model shares a number of basic assumptions about the nature of the processing and memory system with most other distributed models. In particular, the processing system is assumed to consist of a highly interconnected network of units that take on activation values and communicate with other units by sending signals modulated by weights associated with the connections between the units, according to the principles laid out [in an earlier chapter].[26]

Now what this means is that not only the color of a visible object, but also, presumably, phonemes, noises, and other sorts of heard expressions will be remembered in the same way, with all due differences in portions of the neural network to be activated accounted for (a *ceteris paribus* clause). Thus the contextual pickup that we deem to be of such central importance for a gynocentric epistemology is modeled, at least partially, by current efforts at connectionism, and one can only hypothesize that these efforts will in the future become still more sophisticated. The modeling is of still greater importance when one remembers that the contextual pickup employed in a model like CCP would require attention to nuance while simultaneously processing phonemes, and all of this while processing extraneous environmental information. Thus a strong case can be made that whatever the path down which we are led by neural models, the end can only be greater specificity for the theorist who wishes to construct a precise and theoretically rigorous feminist epistemology.

Finally, Goldman has—again—new work that, although still in its earliest stages, sheds light on another area of importance if connectionist models are to continue to be useful to gynocentric epistemics. His piece "Epistemology and the New Connectionism" helps to fill in the blanks not only on weighted averaging between neural units, but also on the importance of the notions of certainty and doubt, or epistemic instability, for a genuinely useful epistemics.[27] I allude to these notions within the context of the work we do here specifically because a model such as CCP is constructed so that it provides for a continuous evolution of the process of knowledge acquisition: What represents agreed-upon material in one context may represent discarded material in another, and the importance of context ensures that there is comparatively little of a static nature in the justificatory network.

Goldman notes that in his view, "the inhibitory connections guarantee that each unit stops if it 'sees a higher value.' "[28] Although he admits that this view may not be "terribly realistic," he also claims that his particular version of the connectionist network (which he dubs "WTA," or "winner take all") has the virtue that it

> . . . carries with it a plausible account of its complement, *uncertainty*, which is to be viewed as a condition of continuing competition among rival alternatives whose relative attractiveness—here interpreted in terms of activation level—is still in flux. It is an *unstable* state, that has not yet converged on any one contender. This depiction of uncertainty is phenomenologically appealing. Uncertainty is irresolution or indecision, a condition in which competing ideas battle one another without one clearly besting the others.[29] [Emphasis Goldman's]

Since the notion of change—"phenomenologically appealing," as Goldman admits—seems to be important both for feminist theory and at least one brand of connectionism, Goldman's analysis of his formulation of a network approach provides still further food for thought for the feminist epistemologist.

## GYNOCENTRIC EPISTEMICS:
## SOME CLOSING COMMENTS

In this, the last chapter of the work, I have spent a great deal of time reviewing the argument provided in the previous eight chapters, and some small amount of time on the possibilities of a feminist connectionism as part of the future of gynocentric epistemology. But the development of a feminist epistemology is something more than the simple adumbration of a view, however in touch the view may be with certain contemporary work, or however stringently formulated the heart of the view. The development of a feminist epistemology requires an alteration in attitude, a willingness to see things in a new way. It may mean, as Alison Jaggar suggests in a recent piece, taking an interest in the emotions and their place in any account of mental life.[30] It may also mean a commitment to try to see the possibilities of feminist theorizing in the work of thinkers—female or male—whose written product may evince no overt concern with feminist theory.[31] I want to close with some comments on our willingness to actually search for instances of feminist theory (even when they are far from obvious), and a caveat on the necessity of continuing feminist inquiry.

If, as I have just remarked, the development of a feminist epistemology requires an alteration in attitudes and modes of seeing, this alteration will manifest itself, surely, in our attitude to the work of those who preceded us. Since contemporary work, perhaps unfortunately, seems to come prepackaged (insofar as feminist content is concerned), we may feel that it is not necessary to try to sort out gynocentric or feminist strands in pieces where, presumably, if there were such strands we would know it.

But my guess is that our attitudes toward those who preceded us can be altered, and altered illuminatingly, if we are willing to search for the hidden or less-than-overt feminist content in the work of previous philosophers. I will assume that the authors of many such pieces of work were indeed female, although it is certainly true that many nineteenth-century male thinkers (oddly enough, some of whom were more-or-less blatantly misogynistic in some aspects of their theorizing) may have employed modes of reasoning that were less than strictly androcentric.

Recent issues of *Hypatia* and *Resources for Feminist Research/ Documentation sur la Récherche Féministe* have focused on the work of women philosophers who have been left out of the canon. But as Linda Lopez McAlister remarks in her preface to the issue of *Hypatia* on the history of women in philosophy, "It is not the case that all women in the history of philosophy are feminists, nor is it the case that everyone doing the history of women in philosophy employs explicitly feminist analyses."[32] What one might hypothesize, however, is that many of the women philosophers whose work we are just now beginning to explore employed implicitly feminist analyses, if the gynocentric patterns of thinking—contextualist, intentionalist, and focused on communication and bodily awareness—that we have explored here are indeed quite frequent among female thinkers.

In the same issue of *Hypatia* that contains McAlister's insightful overview, Lois Frankel provides an exemplary commentary on the work of Damaris Cudworth Masham, a seventeenth-century theorist who was also an associate of John Locke.[33] Citing just one passage from Masham with Frankel's remarks, we note how the gynocentric viewpoint can be found if the reader with the altered or changed attitude is willing to look for it.

> The *Discourse on the Love of God,* Masham's other published book, is a response to John Norris' *Practical Discourses,* the latter based on the *Principles* of Malebranche. Masham particularly objects to Norris' claim that we ought not to love creatures at all, because doing so is incompatible with loving God. . . . Masham responds to Norris' claims. . . . :
>
> > But another reason, besides the narrowness of our capacities, Why *we cannot divide our love* between God and the creature, is, *because we cannot love either of them, but upon such a principle as must utterly exclude the love of the other;* . . .
> >
> > So that to tell us, that we must not love any thing but what is our *True [Good]*; Is as much to say, that we must not be pleased with anything but what pleases us; which it is likely we are not in danger of.
>
> Here we see Masham poking fun at Norris and objecting to his dualistic and atomistic thinking with regard to the sharing of love between God and creatures. The love of God and of creatures is not so separable as Norris had claimed; indeed, she argues, the love of God is *based* on the love of creatures. Masham's position could . . . be considered feminist because it rejects separation in favor of connection.[34]

Here Frankel does what we must do if we are to continue to explore the possibilities for feminist epistemology: She reads the text with an openness to the possibility that gynocentric thinking is implicit in the text. It might be objected that this may, in some cases, do violence to the text, and so indeed it may. But the counter to this objection is, of course, the straightforward reply that in the past, most of our readings have been informed by the opposite view. Because what we have taken to be epistemology, metaphysics, or philosophy has almost always been an androcentric theory of knowledge, a masculinist ontology, and a male-oriented and male-conceptualized worldview, the views of women—and indeed, of some males—have been misinterpreted or ignored.

The gynocentric perspective has been there all the way along. It is only now that it has been noticed, articulated, and brought to the fore in a systematic and persistent manner. The future development of feminist epistemology depends on our capacity to continue to interpret, construct, and connect points of view in such a way that what women see and know can be shared by all.

## NOTES

1. BonJour, *Empirical Knowledge,* 6–7.
2. Russell, *History,* 564.
3. Gettier, "Justified True Belief," 121–23.
4. Goldman, "A Causal Theory," reprinted in Pappas and Swain, *Essays,* 84.
5. Kornblith, *Naturalizing Epistemology,* 115–16.
6. Kornblith, "Psychological Turn," 238.
7. This text, p. 76.
8. I specifically found Baker's categorization of the various sorts of positions more than helpful. See Baker, *Saving Belief,* 13–14.
9. Bordo, *Flight,* 31. In fact, Bordo is at pains to describe even the Greek culture that spawned Plato as having more respect for the body and the passions that arise from it than did the milieu to which Descartes was subjected and which his work reflected.
10. Bordo, *Flight,* 62–63.
11. Dennett, *Stance,* 52.
12. This text, p. 180.
13. Fodor, cited in Baker, *Saving Belief,* 26.
14. Irigaray, "Le Sujet de la Science," 85, 87.
15. Leclerc, in Moi, ed., *French Feminist Thought,* 76.
16. See Lois Frankel on the work of the seventeenth century philosopher Damaris Cudworth Masham. "Damaris Cudworth Masham: A Seventeenth-Century Feminist Philosopher," *Hypatia* 4, no. 1 (1989):86.
17. Frankel cites the application of this line of thought by Nancy Holland to the work of Locke, for example, and also asserts that it "identifies criteria for identifying 'feminine', if not necessarily feminist approaches to philosophy" (p. 86).
18. Cook and Fonow, "Knowledge and Women's Interests," 5.
19. Patricia Churchland, *Neurophilosophy, passim.*
20. See Evelyn Fox Keller and Christine R. Grontkowski, "The Mind's Eye," in Sandra Harding and Merrill Hintikka, *Discovering Reality* (Dordrecht, Netherlands: Reidel, 1983).
21. Much of the work of Deborah Tannen is relevant here. See fn. 43, chap. 6.
22. See Rumelhart and McClelland, *Distributed Processing.*
23. Ibid., 171.
24. Ibid.
25. Ibid., 176, 173.
26. Ibid.
27. See Alvin Goldman in Garver and Hare, *Naturalism and Rationality.*
28. Ibid., 90.
29. Ibid.

30. Alison Jaggar, "Love and Knowledge: Emotion in Feminist Epistemology," *Inquiry* 32, no. 2 (1989):151–76.

31. Cf. fn. 16 above. It may very well be the case, particularly for women thinkers whose work is pre-twentieth century, that there are hidden strands of feminist thought that must be looked for and brought out.

32. Linda Lopez McAlister, "Some Remarks on Exploring the History of Women in Philosophy," *Hypatia* 4, no. 1 (1989):3.

33. Frankel, "Damaris Cudworth Masham," 80–90.

34. Frankel, "Damaris Cudworth Masham," 87. The material from Masham is from *A Discourse Concerning the Love of God* (London: A. and J. Churchil at the Black-Swan in Paternoster-Row, 1696), 89–90.

# Bibliography

Abel, Elizabeth, and Emily R. Abel, eds. *The Signs Reader: Women, Gender and Scholarship* Chicago: University of Chicago Press, 1984.

Adler, Patricia A.; Peter Adler, and Andrea Fontana. "Everyday Life Sociology." *Annual Review of Sociology* 13 (1987):217–35.

Allen, Paula Gunn. *The Sacred Hoop*. Boston, Mass. Beacon Press, 1986.

———. *Shadow Country*. Los Angeles, Calif. American Indian Studies Center of UCLA, 1982.

———. *Studies in American Indian Literature*. New York: The Modern Language Association, 1983.

Annis, David. "A Contextualist Theory of Epistemic Justification." *American Philosophical Quarterly* 15, no. 3 (1978):213–19.

Asch, Solomon. *Social Psychology*. Englewood Cliffs, N.J.: Prentice-Hall, 1952.

Austin, J. L. *Sense and Sensibilia*. New York: Oxford University Press, 1964.

Baier, Annette. "Cartesian Persons." In *Postures of the Mind: Essays on Mind and Morals,* edited by Annette Baier. Minneapolis: University of Minnesota Press, 1985.

Baker, Lynne Rudder. *Saving Belief*. Princeton: Princeton University Press, 1987.

Baker, Robert, and Frederick Elliston, eds. *Philosophy and Sex*. Buffalo, N.Y.: Prometheus Books, 1983.

Bataille, Gretchen. "Transformation of Tradition: Autobiographical Works by

American Indian Women." In *Studies in American Indian Literature,* edited by Paula Gunn Allen. Boston, Mass.: Beacon Press, 1986.

Baynes, Kenneth, James Bohman, and Thomas McCarthy, eds. *After Philosophy.* Cambridge, Mass. The MIT Press, 1987.

Belenky, Mary Field, Blythe McGiver Clinchy, Nancy Rule Goldberger, and Jill Mattuck Tarule. *Women's Ways of Knowing: The Development of Self, Voice and Mind.* New York: Basic Books, 1986.

Benbow, C. P., and J. C. Stanley. "Sex Differences in Mathematical Ability: Fact or Artifact?" *Science* 210 (12 December 1980):1262–64.

Bleier, Ruth. *Science and Gender.* New York: Pergamon Press, 1984.

BonJour, Laurence. *The Structure of Empirical Knowledge.* Cambridge, Mass. Harvard University Press, 1985.

Bordo, Susan. "The Cartesian Masculinization of Thought." *Signs* 11, no. 3 (1988):619–29.

———. "Feminist Skepticism and the 'Maleness' of Philosophy." *Journal of Philosophy* 85, no. 11 (1988):619–29.

———. *The Flight to Objectivity.* Albany, N.Y.: SUNY Press, 1987.

Boston Women's Healthbook Collective. *The New Our Bodies, Ourselves.* Boston, Mass.: The Collective, 1984.

Braaten, Jane. "Dizzy Dames and Loopy Ladies: Feminist Commitments in the Philosophy of Psychology." Unpublished ms., University of Montana, 1987.

Burtt, E. A. *The Metaphysical Foundations of Modern Science.* Garden City, N.Y.: Doubleday, 1941.

Chipman, Susan F., Lorelei R. Brush, and Donna M. Wilson, eds. *Women and Mathematics.* Hillsdale, N.J.: Lawrence Erlbaum and Associates, 1980.

Chodorow, Nancy. *The Reproduction of Mothering.* Berkeley, Calif. University of California Press, 1976.

Churchland, Patricia Smith. *Neurophilosophy.* Cambridge, Mass.: Bradford of MIT Press, 1986.

Cixous, Hélene. "The Laugh of the Medusa. In *The Signs Reader: Women, Gender and Scholarship,* edited by Elizabeth Abel and Emily R. Abel. Chicago: University of Chicago Press, 1984.

Code, Lorraine. *Epistemic Responsibility.* Hanover, N.H.: University Press of New England, 1987.

———. "Second Persons." *Canadian Journal of Philosophy,* Supplementary Volume, "Science, Morality and Feminist Theory." (1987).

Cook, Judith A., and Mary Margaret Fonow. "Knowledge and Women's Interests: Issues of Epistemology and Methodology in Feminist Research." *Sociological Inquiry* 56, no. 1 (1986):2–29.

Cornman, James W. "Foundational vs. Nonfoundational Theories of Empirical Justification." In *Essays on Knowledge and Justification,* edited by George S. Pappas and Marshall Swain. Ithaca: Cornell University Press, 1978.

Daly, Mary. *Gyn/Ecology: The Metaethics of Radical Feminism.* Boston, Mass.: Beacon Press, 1978.

———. *Pure Lust.* Boston, Mass.: Beacon Press, 1984.

Dennett, Daniel. *Brainstorms.* Montgomery, Vt.: Bradford Press, 1978.

———. *The Intentional Stance.* Cambridge, Mass.: Bradford of MIT Press, 1987.

———. "Intentional Systems in Cognitive Ethology: The 'Panglossian Paradigm' Defended." *Behavioral and Brain Sciences* 6, no. 3 (1983):343–90.

Dinnerstein, Dorothy. *The Mermaid and the Minotaur.* New York: Harper and Row, 1976.

Dreyfus, Hubert. *What Computers Can't Do: A Critique of Artificial Reason.* New York: Harper and Row, 1972.

Duran, Jane. "A Contextualist Modification of Cornman." *Philosophia* 16, nos. 3 and 4 (1986):377–88.

———. "Descriptive Epistemology." *Metaphilosophy* 15, nos. 3 and 4 (1984):185–95.

———. "Intentionality and Epistemology." *The Monist* 69, no. 4 (1986):620–26.

———. "Reductionism and the Naturalization of Epistemology." *Dialectica* 42, no. 4 (1988):295–306.

Durkheim, Emile. *Les Formes Elementaires de la Vie Religieuse.* In *Emile Durkheim: Selected Writings,* edited by Anthony Giddens. Cambridge, U.K.: Cambridge University Press, 1972.

Ecker, Gisela. *Feminist Aesthetics.* Boston, Mass.: Beacon Press, 1986.

Engels, Friederich. *On the Origin of Family, Private Property and the State,* notes by Eleanor Burke Leacock. New York: International Publishers, 1972.

Feldman, Richard. "Lehrer's Theory of Justification." *Australasian Journal of Philosophy* 57, no. 3 (1979):266–73.

Flanagan, Owen. *The Science of the Mind.* Cambridge, Mass.: Bradford of MIT Press, 1984.

Flax, Jane. "Political Philosophy and the Patriarchal Unconscious: A Psychoanalytic Perspective on Epistemology and Metaphysics." In *Discovering Reality,* edited by Sandra Harding and Merrill Hintikka. Dordrecht, Netherlands: Reidel, 1983.

Fodor, Jerry. *The Modularity of Mind.* Cambridge, Mass.: Bradford of MIT Press, 1983.

Frankel, Lois. "Damaris Cudworth Masham: A Seventeenth-Century Feminist Philosopher." *Hypatia* 4, no. 1 (1989):80–90.

Garver, Newton, and Peter Hare, eds. *Naturalism and Rationality.* Buffalo, N.Y.: Prometheus, 1986.

Gettier, Edmond. "Is Justified True Belief Knowledge?" *Analysis* 23, no. 7 (1963):122–23.

Giddings, Paula. *When and Where I Enter: The Impact of Black Women on Race and Sex in America.* New York: Bantam, 1985.

Gilligan, Carol. *In A Different Voice.* Cambridge, Mass.: Harvard University Press, 1982.

Goldman, Alvin I., "A Causal Theory of Knowing." In *Essays on Knowledge and Justification,* edited by George S. Pappas and Marshall Swain. Ithaca: Cornell University Press, 1978.

———. "Epistemics: The Regulative Theory of Cognition." *Journal of Philosophy* 75, no. 10 (1978):509–23.

———. "Epistemology and Problem Solving." *Synthese* 55, no. 1 (1983):21–48.

———. *Epistemology and Cognition.* (Cambridge, Mass.: Bradford of MIT Press, 1987.

———. "Epistemology and the Psychology of Belief." *The Monist* 61, no. 4 (1978):525–35.

———. "The Internalist Conception of Justification." In *Midwest Studies in Philosophy,* vol. 5, edited by Peter A. French, Theodore E. Vehling Jr., and Howard K. Wettstein. Minneapolis: University of Minnesota Press, 1980.

———. "The Relation Between Epistemology and Psychology." *Synthese* 64, no. 1 (1985):29–68.

Grahn, Judy. *The Queen of Wands.* Trumansburg, N.Y.: The Crossing Press, 1982.

Green, Robert. *The 'Sissy' Boy Syndrome and Male Homosexuality.* New Haven, Conn.: Yale University Press, 1986.

Griffin, Susan. *Pornography and Silence.* New York: Harper and Row, 1981.

Grimshaw, Jean. *Philosophy and Feminist Thinking.* Minneapolis: University of Minnesota Press, 1986.

Gumperz, John. *Discourse Strategies.* Cambridge, U.K.: Cambridge University Press, 1982.

Gurvitch, Georges. *The Social Frameworks of Knowledge.* Translated by Margaret A. Thompson and Kenneth A. Thompson. Oxford, U.K.: Basil Blackwell, Ltd., 1971.

Harding, Sandra. *The Science Question in Feminism.* Ithaca: Cornell University Press, 1986.

Harding, Sandra, and Merrill Hintikka. *Discovering Reality.* Dordrecht, Netherlands: Reidel, 1983.

Harms, John. "Mannheim's Sociology of Knowledge and the Interpretation of *Weltanschauungen.*" *Social Science Journal* 21, no. 2 (1984):33–48.

Hartsock, Nancy. "The Feminist Standpoint: Developing the Ground For a Specifically Feminist Historical Materialism." In *Discovering Reality,* edited by Sandra Harding and Merrill Hintikka. Dardrecht, Netherlands: Reidel, 1983.

Heil, John. "Does Cognitive Science Rest on a Mistake?" *Mind* 90, no. 359 (1981):321–42.

Hempel, Carl. *Aspects of Scientific Explanation and Other Essays.* New York: Free Press, 1965.

Hintikka, Jaakko. "*Cogito, Ergo Sum:* Inference or Performance?" In *Descartes: A Collection of Critical Essays,* edited by Willis Doney. Garden City, N.Y.: Anchor/Doubleday, 1967.

Hubbard, Ruth. "Science, Facts and Feminism." *Hypatia* 3, no. 1 (1988):114–44.

Hymes, Dell, ed. *Language in Culture and Society.* New York: Harper and Row, 1964.

Irigaray, Luce. "Le Sujet de la Science: Est-il Sexué?" ("Is the Subject of Science Sexed?"). Translated by Carol Mastrangelo Bové. *Hypatia* 2, no. 3 (1987):65–87.

———. "Sexual Difference." [a portion of *Ethique de la Différence Sexuelle.* Paris: Editions Minuit, 1984]. Translated by Sean Hand. In *Feminist Thought: A Reader,* edited by Toril Moi. Oxford, U.K.: Basil Blackwell, Ltd.: 1987.

———. *The Speculum of the Other Woman.* Translated by Gillian C. Gill. Ithaca: Cornell University Press, 1985.

Jaggar, Alison. "Love and Knowledge: Emotion in Feminist Epistemology." *Inquiry* 32, no. 2 (1989):151–76.

Jardine, Alice. *Gynesis.* Ithaca: Cornell University Press, 1985.

Kahneman, Daniel, Paul Slovic, and Amos Tversky. *Judgment Under Uncertainty: Heuristics and Biases.* Cambridge, U.K.: Cambridge University Press, 1982.

Keller, Evelyn Fox. *A Feeling for the Organism.* San Francisco: John Wiley and Sons, 1983.

———. "Feminism and Science." In *The Signs Reader: Women, Gender and Scholarship,* edited by Elizabeth Abel and Emily K. Abel. Chicago: University of Chicago Press, 1984.

———. *Reflections on Gender and Science.* New Haven, Conn.: Yale University Press, 1985.

Keller, Evelyn Fox, and Christine R. Grantkowski, "The Mind's Eye. "In *Discovering Reality,* edited by Sandra Harding and Merrill Hintikka. Dordrecht, Netherlands: Reidel, 1983.

Kierkegaard, Soren. *Either/Or,* vol. 1. Translated by David G. Swenson and Lillian Marvin Swenson. Princeton: Princeton University Press, 1971.

Kingston, Maxine Hong. *The Woman Warrior.* New York: Vintage Books, 1977.

Kornblith, Hilary. "Ever Since Descartes." *The Monist* 68, no. 2 (1985):264–76.

————. *Naturalizing Epistemology.* Cambridge, Mass.: Bradford of MIT Press, 1985.

————. "The Psychological Turn." *Australasian Journal of Philosophy* 60, no. 3 (1982):238–53.

————. "Some Social Features of Cognition." *Synthese* 73, no. 1 (1987):27–41.

Kristeva, Julia. "Interview with Francoise van Rossum-Guyon." In *French Feminist Thought: A Reader,* edited by Toril Moi. Oxford, U.K.: Basil Blackwell, Ltd., 1987.

Krupnick, Mark. *Displacement: Derrida and After.* Bloomington: Indiana University Press, 1983.

Kuhn, Thomas. *The Structure of Scientific Revolutions.* Chicago: University of Chicago Press, 1962.

Laudan, Larry. "Explaining the Success of Science: Beyond Epistemic Realism and Relativism." In *Science and Reality: Recent Work in the Philosophy of Science,* edited by James T. Cushing, C. F. Delaney, and Gary Gutting. Notre Dame, Ind.: University of Notre Dame Press, 1984.

Lehrer, Keith. *Knowledge.* Oxford, U.K.: Clarendon Press, 1974.

Lehrer, Keith, and Thomas Paxson. "How Reasons Give Us Knowledge, or the Case of the Gypsy Lawyer." *Journal of Philosophy* 68, no. 10 (1971):311–13.

Longino, Helen. "Can There be a Feminist Science?" *Hypatia* 2, no. 3 (1987):52–53.

————. "Science, Objectivity and Feminist Values." *Feminist Studies* 14, no. 3 (1988):92–109.

Lugones, Maria. "Playfulness, 'World'-Traveling, and Loving Perception." *Hypatia* 2, no. 2 (1987):3–19.

Marks, Elaine, and Isabelle de Courtivron, eds. *The New French Feminisms.* Amherst: University of Massachusetts Press, 1980.

McAlister, Linda Lopez. "Some Remarks on Exploring the History of Women in Philosophy." *Hypatia* 4, no. 1 (1989):1–5.

McCorduck, Pamela. *Machines Who Think.* San Francisco, Calif.: W. H. Freeman & Co., 1979.

Millikan, Ruth Garrett. "Thoughts Without Laws: Cognitive Science Without Content." *The Philosophical Review* 95, no. 1 (1986):47–80.

Moi, Toril, ed. *French Feminist Thought: A Reader.* Oxford, U.K.: Basil Blackwell, Ltd., 1987.

Moore, G. E. "Visual Sense-Data." In *Perceiving, Sensing and Knowing,* edited by Robert J. Swartz. Garden City, N.Y.: Doubleday Anchor, 1965.

Nagel, Thomas. "Sexual Perversion." In *Philosophy and Sex,* edited by Robert Baker and Frederick Elliston. Buffalo, N.Y.: Prometheus Books, 1983.

Nisbet, Robert. *The Sociology of Emile Durkheim.* Oxford, U.K.: Oxford University Press, 1974.

Oakley, Ann. *The Sociology of Housework.* New York: Pantheon, 1974.

Pappas, George S., and Marshall Swain, eds. *Essays on Knowledge and Justification.* Ithaca: Cornell University Press, 1978.

Pastin, Mark. "Modest Foundationalism and Self-Warrant." In *Essays on Knowledge and Justification,* edited by George S. Pappas and Marshall Swain. Ithaca: Cornell University Press, 1978.

Prior, Elizabeth W., and Robert Pargetter. "Against the Sexuality of Reason." *Australasian Journal of Philosophy,* Supplement to 64 (1986):107–19.

Putnam, Hilary. *Reason, Truth and History: Philosophical Papers, Vol. II.* Cambridge, Mass.: Harvard University Press, 1975.

Pylyshyn, Zenon. *Computation and Cognition.* Cambridge, Mass.: Bradford of MIT Press, 1983.

Quine, W. V. O. *From a Logical Point of View.* Cambridge, Mass.: Harvard University Press, 1953.

———. "Russell's Ontological Development." In *Essays on Bertrand Russell,* edited by E. D. Klemke. Urbana-Champaign, Ill.: University of Illinois Press, 1970.

Radnitzky, Gerard, and W. W. Bartley, III, eds. *Evolutionary Epistemology, Rationality and the Sociology of Knowledge.* La Salle, Ill.: Open Court Publishing Company, 1987.

Raymond, Janice. *A Passion for Friends.* Boston, Mass.: Beacon Press, 1986.

Rich, Adrienne. *The Dream of a Common Language.* New York: Norton, 1978.

Rumelhart, David E., and James L. McClelland, eds. *Parallel Distributed Processing: Explorations in the Microstructure of Cognition.* Cambridge, Mass.: Bradford of MIT, 1986. (vols. 1 and 2.)

Russell, Bertrand. *A History of Western Philosophy.* New York: Simon and Schuster, 1960.

———. "The Philosophy of Logical Atomism." In *Bertrand Russell: Logic and Knowledge,* edited by Robert C. Marsh. New York: G. P. Putnam & Sons, 1971.

Searle, John. "The Intentionality of Intention and Action." In *Perspectives on Cognitive Science,* edited by Donald A. Norman. Norwood, N.J.: Ablex Publishing, 1981.

Senour, Maria Nieto. "Psychology of the Chicana." In *Chicano Psychology,* edited by Joe L. Martinez. New York: Academic Press, 1977.

Smith, Dorothy E. "Women's Perspective as a Radical Critique of Sociology." *Sociological Inquiry* 44, no. 1 (1974):8–10.

Solomon, Robert. "Love and Feminism." In *Philosophy and Sex,* edited by Robert Baker and Frederick Elliston. Buffalo, N.Y.: Prometheus Books, 1983.

Stehelin, Liliane. "Sciences, Women and Ideology." In *The Radicalisation of Science,* edited by Hilary Rose and Stephen Rose. London: The Macmillan Press Ltd., 1976.

Stewart, David, and H. Gene Blocker. *Fundamentals of Philosophy.* New York: Macmillan 1987.

Stich, Stephen. *From Folk Psychology to Cognitive Science.* Cambridge, Mass.: Bradford of MIT Press, 1983.

Suppe, Frederick. *The Structure of Scientific Theories.* Urbana-Champaign: University of Illinois Press, 1977.

Tan, Amy. *The Joy Luck Club.* New York: G. P. Putnam & Sons, 1989.

Tannen, Deborah. *Conversational Style: Analyzing Talk Among Friends,* Norwood, N.J.: Ablex, 1984.

Van Gulick, Robert. "Mental Representation—A Functionalist View." *Pacific Philosophical Quarterly* 63, no. 1 (1982):3–20.

Walker, Alice. *The Temple of My Familiar.* New York: Harcourt Brace Jovanovich, 1988.

Wasserstrom, Richard. "Is Adultery Immoral?" In *Today's Moral Problems,* edited by Richard Wasserstrom. New York: Macmillan and Co. 1985.

Wittgenstein, Ludwig. *Philosophical Investigations.* 6th ed. Translated by G. E. M. Anscombe. New York: Macmillan, 1953.

*Women and The Mathematical Mystique: Proceedings of the Eighth Annual Hyman Blumberg Symposium on Research in Early Childhood Education.* Baltimore: Johns Hopkins University Press, 1980.

Wylie, Alison. "The Philosophy of Ambivalence." *Canadian Journal of Philosophy,* Supplementary Volume (1987):59–73.

# Index

Adler, Patricia A., 224–26, 229, 230, 253, 255
Adler, Peter, 224–26, 229, 230, 253, 255
*After Philosophy* (Baynes, Bohman, and McCarthy), 164
Aggression: male, 76; male child and, 75
Allen, Paula Gunn, 186, 191–93, 196, 199, 205, 251
American Indian culture, 191–93, 251
Analytic philosophy, 104; feminist empiricism and, 105–110
Androcentric epistemology. *See* Epistemology; Feminist epistemology
*An Inquiry into Meaning and Truth* (Russell), 21
Annis, David, 113, 119, 127, 134
Asch, Solomon, 113, 116
Asian-American women, 186–88, 251
Austin, J. L., 25–26, 38, 60–61, 115, 241
*Australasian Journal of Philosophy*, 94
Ayer, sense-data theories and, 25

Baker, Lynne Rudder, 66, 121, 128, 140, 143, 148, 153, 154; Fodor and,

141; theory and, 58–64, 119, 123, 124, 134–45, 242–43
Bataille, Gretchen, 192
Baynes, Kenneth, 164
Behaviorism, 52
Belief: acquisition of, 50, 60; formation of, 115; modification of, 49; occurrent, 45; salvation and, 58–64, 242
"Beyond Foundationalism and Coherence Theory" (Kornblith), 36, 38–39
Black women, 188–91, 251
Bodily awareness, 114
BonJour, Laurence, 11, 239
Bordo, Susan, 8, 44, 97, 98–99, 105, 239; Cartesian shift in epistemology and, 10, 88–91, 107–108, 185, 243, 244
Braaten, Jane, 146

*Canadian Journal of Philosophy*, 95
"A Causal Theory of Knowing" (Goldman), 30–31, 241
Child-rearing practices, 97
Chodorow, Nancy, 97, 177, 252
Churchland, Patricia Smith, 66, 124, 128, 242; *Neurophilosophy of*, 53–58, 59, 61, 254

Churchland, Paul, 59
Cixous, Hélene, 109, 163, 164–67, 169, 170, 171, 173, 174, 175, 177, 249
Code, Lorraine, 95–96, 245
Cognition, 47–51
Cognitive functioning model, 52, 54
Cognitive science, 35–36, 44, 45, 47, 61
*The Color Purple* (Walker), 190
Communicative awareness, 114, 115
Connectionism, 64–67; connectionist model and, 253–57
Contextualist and Communicative Principles (CCP) model, 238; computational, 124–26; connectionist model and, 253–57; construction of, 116–23, 246–48; criticism of, 133–36; cultural context and, 185–95, 205, 251; Dennett and, 136–40; feminist sociological thought and, 226–32; Fodor and, 140–42; intentionality and feminist theory and, 145–48; mentalistic dilemma and, 142–45; naturalized, 14–15, 127–28; philosophy of the mind and feminist epistemology, 152–55; relativism and, 195–200; sexuality and, 200–204; theoretical views and, 148–52
Contextualization, 114, 115, 116, 254
Cook, Judith, 219–20, 221, 226, 228, 229, 253
Cooper, Anna Julia, 189
Cornman, James, 116–17, 128

Deconstruction, 163, 164
Dennett, Daniel, 53, 136–40, 141, 144, 148, 152, 153, 243, 247, 248
Derrida (French feminist), 163, 164, 165, 167, 168, 169, 244
Descartes, René, 3–4, 5, 6, 10, 13, 20, 22, 50, 107, 113, 185, 239. *See also Meditations* (Descartes)
Dinnerstein, Dorothy, 97
*Displacement: Derrida and After* (Krupnick), 167
"A Disturbed Model of Human Learning and Memory" (from Ru-

melhart and McClellan), 65–66, 255
*Division du Travail Social* (Durkheim), 212
Dreyfus, Hubert, 144
Durkheim, Emile, 211, 212, 217, 222–23

Engels, F., 108–109
"Epistemic Defeasibility" (Swain), 33
Epistemology: androcentric, 5–8, 44, 95, 105, 108; feminist theory and androcentric, 8–11; history of, 3–4; naturalized and gynocentric view of, 14–15, 127–28; naturalizing of androcentric, 11–14; naturalizing feminist viewpoint and, 112–16. *See also* Feminist epistemology; Theory of knowledge
*Epistemology and Cognition* (Goldman), 46–47
"Epistemology Naturalized" (Quine), 36
"Epistemology and the New Connectionism" (Goldman), 257
"Epistemology and the Psychology of Belief" (Goldman), 45
"Ever since Descartes" (Kornblith), 49–50
"Everyday Life Sociology" (Adler, Adler, and Fontana), 224, 253

Farge, Arlette, 173–75, 249, 250
*A Feeling for the Organism* (Keller), 74
"Feminism and Science" *(Hypatia)*, 91–92
Feminist empiricism, 146; analytic philosophy and, 105–110; Harding and, 80, 81, 82–83, 103–104, 127, 133, 243–44
Feminist epistemology: androcentric epistemology and, 8–11, 109; androcentrious and Keller and, 74–79; Code and, 95–96; connectionist model and, 253–57; consolidation and, 96–99; future prospects for, 257–60; Hubbard's views on sci-

ence and, 92–93; knowledge acquisition and, 8; Longino and, 93–94; *Science Question in Feminism* (Harding) and, 79–88; standpoint epistemologies and naturalized epistemology and, 110–12; theory of knowledge and, 4, 106; Wylie and, 96. *See also* Contextualist and Communicative Principles (CCP) model; Epistemology; French feminist thought; Theory of knowledge

Feminist postmodernism, 80, 81, 87, 108, 109, 110, 162, 250

Flanagan, Owen, 53, 142, 143

Flax, Jane, 84, 85, 86, 108, 109, 111, 112, 127, 139, 162, 215, 244

*The Flight to Objectivity* (Bordo), 88

Fodor, Jerry, 60, 61, 62, 140–42, 143, 144, 148, 152, 153, 247, 248

Folk-psychological notions, 62; 119, 138, 141, 143, 146, 148–52, 154, 248–49

Fonow, Mary Margaret, 219–20, 221, 226, 228, 229, 253

Fontana, Andrea, 224–26, 229, 253, 255

*Les Formes Elementaires de la Vie Religieuse* (Durkheim), 222–23

Foundationalism, 36–40, 115

*Foundations of Empirical Knowledge* (Ayer), 25

Frankel, Lois, 259

French feminist thought, 232, 249–50; Cixous and, 164–67; Farge and, 173–75; feminist epistemics and, 177–78; Irigaray and, 167–69; Kristeva and, 169–71; Leclerc and, 175–76; Le Doeuff and, 171–73; relevance of, 162–64

Freudian theory, 162, 250

*From Folk Psychology to Cognitive Science* (Stich), 149

Gettier, Edmund, 26–28, 29, 30, 32, 33, 35, 38, 44, 66, 241

Giddings, Paula, 189–90

Gilligan, Carol, 13, 14, 15, 122, 240, 252

Goldman, Alvin, 29, 35, 57, 60, 66,

114, 121, 127, 145, 241; CCP model and, 257; epistemology and, 30–32, 118; naturalization and, 44–47

Gurvitch, Georges, 211, 226

*Gynesis* (Jardine), 166

Gynocentric model. *See* Contextualist and Communicative Principles (CCP) model

Harding, Sandra, 8, 74, 92, 93, 96, 97, 98, 105, 111, 161, 162, 215, 239, 250; androcentric epistemology and, 10, 79–88; feminist empiricism and, 80, 81, 82–83, 103–104, 127, 133, 243–44

Harms, John, 217–19, 228

Hartsock, Nancy, 84, 85–86, 108, 111, 112, 127, 139, 162, 215, 244

Hegel, G. W. F., 109, 163

Heil, John, 144, 154, 247

Hispanic culture, 193–95, 251

*A History of Western Philosophy* (Russell), 19–20

Housework, 220–24, 229–30

Hubbard, Ruth, 92–93, 139, 245

Hurston, Zora Neale, 190

*Hypatia*, 91–92, 93, 258, 259

"Individuation and Locatedness: A Cultural Drama of Parturition" (Bordo), 90

"The Intentionality of Intention and Action" (Searle), 138

*The Intentional Stance* (Dennett), 136–40

Irigaray, Luce, 167–69, 170, 177, 249, 250

James, William, 12

Jardine, Alice, 166, 167, 169, 170, 249

Kant, E., 109

Keller, Evelyn Fox, 86, 92, 93, 97–98, 169, 243; androcentric epistemology and, 8–10, 74–79, 239

Kingston, Maxine Hong, 186–88, 196, 205

Knowledge. *See* Epistemology; Sociology of knowledge; Theory of knowlege
"Knowledge and Women's Interests: Issues of Epistemology and Methodology in Feminist Research" (Cook and Fonow), 219
Kornblith, Hilary, 57, 66, 112–14, 116, 119, 121, 127, 147, 242; context and, 134; social construction and, 47–51; theory of knowledge and, 36–39
Kristeva, Julia, 169–71, 175, 177, 249, 250
Krupnick, Mark, 167

Lacanian theory, 167–69
Laudan, Larry, 197–98
"The Laugh of the Medusa" (Cixous), 165, 249
Leclerc, Annie, 175–76, 249, 250
Le Doeuff, Michele, 171–73, 175, 250
Lehrer, Keith, 12
Locke, John, 259
Longino, Helen, 93–94, 139, 146, 245
Lugones, Maria, 194–95, 205

McAlister, Linda Lopez, 258, 259
McClelland, James L., 64, 65, 66, 255–56
McClintock, Barbara, 92, 93
Male child, aggression and, 75
Mannheim, Karl, 217, 218, 226, 228
Marxist theory, 108–109, 111, 147, 162, 163, 211, 215–16
Masham, Damaris Cudworth, 259
*Meditations* (Descartes): Bordo and, 10, 88–91, 98–99, 107, 244–45; epistemology and, 3–4, 5, 6, 10, 20, 22
Memory, 46, 255
Mentalism, 52
"Mental Representation—A Functionist View" (Van Gulick), 151
*Midwest Studies in Philosophy* (Goldman), 118
Millikan, Ruth Garrett, 120, 137, 138, 139, 140, 153, 154, 247, 248
Mind: belief and models of, 58, 60, 61, 62; conceptual model of, 54–58; PDP models and, 64, 65; philosophy of, 51–53, 61, 64, 133, 146, 147, 152–55; recent theoretical work on, 52
*Modularity of Mind* (Fodor), 141
Moore, G. E., 24, 38
Moral theorizing, 95

Nagel, Thomas, 136, 148, 200, 202, 203
Neurophilosophy, 53–58, 59, 61, 254, 255
*The New Our Bodies, Ourselves* (Hubbard), 92

Oakley, Anne, 213, 220–24, 229, 253
*On Grammatology,* 164
Otherness concept, 169–71

Parallel distributed processing (PDP) models, 64, 65, 66
Pargetter, Robert, 94, 245
"The Philosophy of Ambivalence" (Wyle), 96
"The Philosophy of Logical Atomism" (Russell), 21
Philosophy of mind, 51–53, 61, 64, 133, 146, 147; feminist epistemology and, 152–55
Plato, 3, 5–6, 8, 9, 10, 89, 239
"Playfulness, 'World'-Travelling and Loving Perception" (Lugones), 194
Prior, Elizabeth, 94, 245
"The Psychological Turn" (Kornblith), 49, 50
Pylyshyn, Zenon, 55

Quine, W. V. O, 23, 36, 52

*Reflections on Gender and Science* (Keller), 74, 75, 77
Relativism, 195, 200
Reliabilist theories, 49
Representationalism, 140–42, 151
*Resources for Feminist Research/ Documention sur la Récherche Féministe,* 258

Rosc, Hilary, 84, 244
Rowbotham, Sheila, 213
Rumelhart, David E., 64, 65, 66, 255–56
Russell, Bertrand, 19–20, 21–23, 24, 32, 37–38, 240

*The Sacred Hoop* (Allen), 191, 196, 199
*Saving Belief* (Baker), 58, 242
Science: Harding and *Science Question* and, 79–88; Keller on gender and, 74–79; Longino and notion of feminist, 93–94; positivistic view of, 107; science question in, 105
"Science, Facts, and Feminism" (Hubbard), 92
*The Science of the Mind* (Flanagan), 142
*The Science Question in Feminism* (Harding), 10, 79–88, 243
Searle, John, 138–39, 140, 153, 154, 247, 248
"Second Persons" (Code), 95
Self (relationally defined), 95
Senour, Maria Nieto, 193–94
*Sense and Sensibilia* (Austin), 25–26
Sexuality, 200–204, 205–206, 251–52
"Sexual Perversion" (Nagel), 200
Shaw, Anna Howard, 192
Smith, Dorothy, 84, 213–15, 218–19, 221, 228, 244, 252
Social construction, 47–51
*The Sociology of Housework* (Oakley), 221, 223
Sociology of knowledge: Adler and Adler and, 224–26; CCP model and, 226–30; Cook and Fonow and, 219–20; Fontana and, 224–26; gynocentric epistemics and, 231–32; Harms and, 217–19; Mannheim and, 217, 218; Oakley and, 220–24; overview of, 211–13; Smith and, 213–15, 218–19; Stehelin and, 215–17
Socrates, 5, 21–22, 38
Solomon, Robert, 148
"Some Social Features of Cognition" (Kornblith), 47–48

Stehelin, Liliane, 215–17, 228, 253
Stich, Stephen, 53, 59, 143, 144, 148–50, 153, 154, 247
*The Structure of Empirical Knowledge* (BonJour), 11–12, 239
Swain, Marshall, 32–35

*The Temple of My Familiar*, 190
Terrell, Mary Church, 190
*Theaetetus* (Plato), 3, 5–6, 8
Theory of knowledge: American analytic, 26–28; Churchland and neurophilosophy and, 53–58; connectionism and naturalization and, 64–67; epistemology and, 7; Goldmanian naturalization and, 44–47; historical approaches to, 3–5; Kornblith and social construction and, 47–51; logical atomism and, 20–23; naturalized theory of, 35–40; naturalizing and philosophy of mind and, 51–53; reliabilist theories and, 49; responses to Gettier's, 28–35; Russell and Descartes and, 19–20; salvation of belief and, 58–64; sense-data views and, 21, 23–26. *See also* Epistemology; Feminist epistemology
"Three Kinds of Intentional Psychology" (Dennett), 137
Tribal societies, 117

Underhill, Ruth, 192

Van Gulick, Robert, 150–52, 247, 248–49
"View from Everywhere" (Bordo), 44

Walker, Alice, 190, 205
Wells, Ida B., 190
*What Computers Can't Do* (Dreyfus), 144
*When and Where I Enter* (Giddings), 189
Wittgenstein, Ludwig, 144
*The Woman Warrior* (Kingston), 186–88
*Writing and Difference*, 164
Wylie, Alison, 96, 98, 245

# About the Author

Jane Duran has published many articles in the areas of epistemology, philosophy of science, and feminist studies and is the author of *Epistemics* (1989). The currently teaches at the University of California, Santa Barbara, and is an active member of the Society for Women in Philosophy. Her latest area of research is at the intersection of epistemology and sociolinguistics.